Chekhov

[1860–1904]

Chekhov

1860–1904

[ ]

SOPHIE LAFFITTE

Translated by Moura Budberg
and Gordon Latta

CHARLES SCRIBNER'S SONS
NEW YORK

1 3 5 7 9 11 13 15 17 19 I/C 20 18 16 14 12 10 8 6 4 2

Printed in Great Britain

Library of Congress Catalog Card Number 74-10236
ISBN 0-684-14184-1

[Contents]

CONTENTS

IV YALTA (1898–1904)

[List of Plates]

*All the illustrations appear between
pages 152 and 153*

Taganrog at the time of Chekhov's youth

The Gymnasium at Taganrog when Chekhov was a student
there

The Chekhov family in Taganrog

Chekhov, the university student, with two friends in Moscow

Moscow University in 1880

The Chekhov family in the garden of the Moscow house

The hospital outside Moscow where Chekhov served as an
intern

Melikhovo when Chekhov lived there

The Melikhovo country house

Yalta in 1899

Chekhov in his Yalta study

The Moscow Art Theatre country outing, August, 1899

Chekhov and his wife, Olga Knipper

Introduction

> Everything in this world is beautiful except what we think and what we do once we forget life's superior aims and our human dignity.
> CHEKHOV

HAPPINESS and the joy of life do not lie in money, nor in love, but in truth," wrote Chekhov. His 'merciless talent' was devoted to the expression of this truth.

Chekhov makes no prognoses, never raises his voice, does not explain, insist and above all, does not instruct. He is satisfied, in his splendid way, with showing.

And it is because of this that he is the least Russian of the great Russian writers. There is no didactic element in his work, no over-statement, none of the violence or the bitterness with which Dostoevsky's pages are charged. What he shows us is the truth of every human being, every thing, and every destiny, subtly transposed by impeccable artistry. So lightly done, so perfectly matched to his intention that its aim seems to be to prevent the reader from becoming aware of the ethereal magic of this transposition. An art totally opposed to all extremes, all exaggeration, all pathos and all spiritual dramatization. Drawn from life itself and stripped of any extraneous intrusions, but drawn with that extraordinary ability to synthesize, from which the poetry springs.

With the serenity and objectivity of a man of science and a doctor, he shows mankind its true nature. "Man will only improve when he has been shown himself as he really is." (*Notebooks*.)

The Russia of the 19th century, which we find in Chekhov's stories, is far more tragic than that displayed in Gogol's and Dostoevsky's fantastic frescoes. For the truth is that the artifices of great art, the extravagances and the most striking originality travesty and thus diminish the tragic starkness of real tragedy.

The great artist in Chekhov recognizes this. He follows Pushkin's precept: "Tell simple things simply," and declares that he found the ideal description in a schoolboy's exercise book: "The sea was large."

In contrast to Mérimée or Maupassant, Chekhov succeeds in revealing to us the complexity, the content and the tragedy of a whole life in a single page, as, for instance, in his touching *Sadness*: a coachman has lost his son; there is no one to whom he can confide his grief, and he finally confides it to his horse. Nothing occurs, there is no action of any kind, but we are instantly made aware of a whole appalling fate. The tragic state of mankind is the province in which Chekhov exercises his infallible, observant and infinite ability to feel and understand.

It has been said very rightly that "his assumption of two roles – those of writer and playwright – is unquestionably the outstanding element" in Chekhov's literary biography. "What a pleasant and peaceful occupation it is to be a writer.[1] The process of story-telling is the legal spouse, whereas the dramatic process is a mistress out to make an effect, noisy, impudent and tiring." (To Pleshcheev, 15th January, 1889.) Nevertheless, while he swore to abandon this exacting mistress, playwriting, for ever, Chekhov continually returned to it. Why did he? No doubt because the art of the theatre has more direct and immediate impact than any other, because it is a sort of test of strength between the author and the audience, a struggle to impose *his* personality and *his* feelings, from which it is intoxicating to emerge the victor. Chekhov succumbed throughout his life to the attraction of this direct dialogue with the audience, in which, under cover of his characters, hidden behind stage scenery, he could pour out his heart freely and express his ideas without being confined within the rigid boundaries imposed on him by his own conception of the short story.

It is Chekhov's voice that is heard throughout his plays, and it is the tone of that gentle, slightly hesitating voice, full of shrewdness, subtlety and emotion, which gives them their particular charm.

In *The Seagull* (1896), Chekhov, that innately reticent man, reveals more of his inner feelings than in any other of his works.

He has freed himself at last from the out-of-date relics of the 'traditional theatre' which hampered his first attempts as playwriter.[2] Chekhov said of his first straight play, *Ivanov*, that it "was not theatrical". Yet his second long play, *The Seagull*, written nine years later, is infinitely less 'theatrical', as it contains hardly any of the traditional effects. After he had finished *Ivanov*, Chekhov wrote to his brother Alexander: "I end each act as I do my stories: I lead it gently, and quietly along, then at the end, bang! right into the audience's mug." (10th–12th October, 1887.) This is what he has to say about *The Seagull*, to his friend Suvorin, 21st November, eight years later: "Well, I've finished my play. Contrary to all the rules of dramatic art, I've started it *forte* and ended it *pianissimo*. This has resulted in it turning out like a story. I am dissatisfied with it on the whole and, upon re-reading it, I realize *once again that I am no playwright*. The acts are very short; there are four of them. It is still only a framework, a project, and will undergo a million changes before next season." (To Suvorin, 21st November, 1895.)

Between the "bang! right into the audience's mug" and the

pianissimo lies the whole revolution Chekhov effected in dramatic art.

The tragedy of Chekhov's characters becomes more and more 'interiorized'; it never resides in action but much more in the inability to act: "People dine, all they do is dine, yet during this time their happiness is established, or their whole life falls apart."

This passivity, this inaction, are constant elements in the make-up of Chekhov's characters. Did he really see life in this guise, this despairingly gloomy and static aspect; men not creating but submitting to their destiny; every attempt at revolt or protest doomed to failure; love always a ceaseless torment? It does seem as though, after *Uncle Vanya*, this really was Chekhov's *Weltanschaung*, a gravely ill man's conception of the world, knowing what lies ahead of him. Chekhov had always been a misanthropist. But his idea of what a 'decent man's' life should be, the moral and social responsibilities which lay heavily on his shoulders, the energy and need for activity that were part of him and the urge to help, advise and heal, all these reasons had driven him towards an intense form of life, very different from the stagnant existence of the characters in his plays.

But if his talent and his exceptional energy had made him lead a diverse, rich, full life, he saw, around him, an ocean of indifference, idleness, boredom, existences based on routine and ignorance, so profound and heavy that the finest people he had chanced to meet appeared to be crushed by it.

In Chekhov's plays, complex and ambiguous characters perform their evolutions in a strange, almost realistic atmosphere, but one to which a subtle transposition gives an inimitable, characteristically Chekhovian undertone. And this transposition is created principally by the extreme precision of his stage directions in regard to seasons of the year, time, weather and the alternation of silences and various 'descriptive' noises, which are all woven into the psychological web of the play and invest it with an unexpected richness. The slow, extremely slow, outer life of the characters and their complex inner life unfold on

[4]

several planes at the same time. The interior tension grows from scene to scene, invisible ties are forged between the different characters and grow stronger and stronger, until the suspense among the audience becomes intolerable.

His plays have fascinated generations of spectators by the deep, subtle, very musical truth, emanating from those slow movements and those silences. Its dramatic compositions are 'fundamentally musical'. Every moment has its own tenseness, but this tenseness does not reside in the dialogue but in the silence, in the life that is following its course. "What is the point of explaining anything to the audience? One must startle it and that is enough: then it will be interested and start pondering again." (Chekhov wrote to Suvorin, 17th December, 1891.)

This is one of the keys to his aestheticism: a resolution not to explain, as 'old-fashioned' literature and theatre did, but to be content with administering shocks to the sensibility and imagination of reader or spectator. Both must collaborate with the artist, never remain passive. That is why Chekhov merely provided posts to indicate the way, and left gaps between them. These gaps, these pauses, became more and more frequent in his plays and their role more vital. He well knew the aesthetic value of these pauses: "I don't know why, but extreme happiness and misery are most often expressed by silence: lovers understand each other best when they don't speak."

There again, as in his stories, 'without beginning or end', Chekhov triumphs over the most solidly established conventions; there again, he ignores everything but his own inner imperatives, which never inclined him towards romantic or dramatic 'developments'. He never wrote novels because it was not in his temperament to portray the evolution of characters at a particular time and in a particular setting, a complex evolution unfolding against the moving backcloth of life.

Chekhov lacked a certain form of creative imagination. He was never able to depict any action of long duration or an elaborate character, whose various facets would be displayed

[5]

in various circumstances. Chekhov's art is not that of a novelist. He is epigrammatic, percussive, allusive, and expresses himself in brief jabs with a probe, delivered with a master's hand, at those points in the nervous system where the vital decisions affecting human destinies are formed. And plays should rightly stress those turning points, those privileged moments when certain mental impulses are starkly revealed. Chekhov's art was eminently suited to a poetical, psychological 'interiorized' type of play – and that is what burst on the audience with enormous impact at the first performance of *The Seagull* in the Moscow Art Theatre on 17th October, 1898. This date symbolizes one of those providential encounters so rare in the history of the theatre: the meeting of a great writer with a great man of the theatre who was capable of grasping and extracting the maximum from a text that, at first sight, might well have been disconcerting. From this meeting between Chekhov and Stanislavski sprang what one could call the 'miracle'[3] of the Chekhovian plays.

The Seagull had already been played on the stage of the Alexandrinski Theatre in St Petersburg on 17th October, 1896, and provoked one of the greatest scandals in the history of the theatre. The play was considered 'decadent' and was mercilessly booed by an audience which had been looking forward to an amusing comedy. "The play was a resounding failure. There was a tense atmosphere in the theatre, made up of perplexity, incomprehension and embarrassment. The cast played stupidly, disgracefully." "The moral is, 'never write any more plays',"[4] Chekhov wrote to his sister, the day after this memorable 'flop'.

Yet, within two years, *The Seagull* proved a triumphant success, thanks to the great care and enthusiasm of two remarkable men: Vladimir Nemirovich-Danchenko and Konstantin Stanislavski, founders and co-directors of the recently founded Moscow Art Theatre.

"It is essentially to Nemirovich-Danchenko that credit is due for having discovered the scope of Chekhov's dramatic work."[5]

[6]

Carried away by the charm of the text, which he read and re-read, pen in hand, he wrote to Chekhov on 31st May:

"I keep on re-reading *The Seagull*, searching for those little bridges which the director must make the audience cross, without becoming mechanical. The public is not yet able (and perhaps never will be) to surrender to the mood of a play, a mood which must be conveyed with all one's skill. We'll try!"

Stanislavski was more reticent: he had no great liking for the author and considered the play 'unplayable'. He admits as much, with his usual candour, in his memoirs.

But little by little, due to the enthusiasm of Nemirovich-Danchenko, who was determined to see justice done to the play and make it succeed, Stanislavski became receptive to the poetical quality of Chekhov's text, and retired to the country to prepare his plans for directing it (August, 1898). Gradually, his admiration reached the point required to send this intuitive, dedicated man 'into a trance' and convert him into what he was at his best – a director of genius.

For his part, Nemirovich-Danchenko concerned himself with the literary side of the play, its actual text. He wrote to Chekhov on 24th August, 1898:

"If you only could witness the ever-growing, fascinated interest (of the cast), the deep absorption in your text and the general nervous tension, you would begin to be proud of yourself ... We admire you infinitely, for your talent and for the fastidiousness and sensitivity of your spirit."

All this understanding and affection could not fail to produce exceptional results and, indeed, the first night of *The Seagull* was a triumph.

"The curtain fell and what happened then was something that only happens in the theatre once in ten or twenty years: a silence, a deep silence, both in the audience and on the stage; those in the audience remained frozen in their seats, those on stage had not yet grasped what had happened ... This lasted for a long time. The cast jumped to the conclusion that the first act had flopped, flopped so badly that there was not even a single

friend who could bring himself to applaud, and they were reduced to a state of nerves bordering on hysteria. Then suddenly,
it was as though a dam had broken, as though a bomb had
burst: a deafening explosion of applause. Everybody applauded,
friends and foes alike."[6]

Gorki, Chekhov's fervent admirer, wrote to him shortly afterwards:

"Naturally, you know all about *The Seagull*'s success. Yesterday, a man of great taste and discrimination said to me with
tears in his eyes, 'I've been going to the theatre now for close on
forty years and I've seen just about everything. Well, I've
never seen such *inspired heresy* as *The Seagull*. And I'm not the
only one to say it, I can assure you.'"

Gorki, Bunin and Kuprin went with Chekhov to applaud the
newly founded theatre, so full of promise. "The Art Theatre is
as beautiful and important as the Tretiakov Gallery, the Church
of St Basil the Blessed and all that is best in Moscow. It is impossible not to like it and it would be a crime not to work for it,"
Gorki wrote to Chekhov (September, 1900).

The second important play of Chekhov's to be presented by
the Art Theatre was an enormous success. So much so that even
someone as scornful of Chekhov's plays as Tolstoy[7] wanted to
see a performance of *Uncle Vanya*. After reading *The Seagull*,
Tolstoy had declared that it was "worthless twaddle". But in-
trigued by the great success of the two Chekhov plays, Tolstoy
put in an appearance at the Art Theatre on 28th January,
1900. "We never took our eyes off him during the whole performance," Nemirovich-Danchenko records. "We were convinced that the play was interesting him and holding his attention; even moving him at times. But either we were wrong or
else he was deliberately refusing to display any simple, straight-
forward feeling about it: anyway, he had not a word of praise
for anything during the intervals. He did not criticize anything
either, and seemed to be waiting to see how it would all end up.
At the end of the last act he said: 'What more did that Dr
Astrov want? The weather was good, someone was playing the

guitar, the crickets were chirping. And, yet, first he wanted to steal another man's wife and then started dreaming about God knows what!' And Tolstoy shook his head in disapproval.''

As soon as he got home, Tolstoy noted down in his Diary: "Went to see *Uncle Vanya* and was indignant." In Tolstoy's opinion, *a dramatic work should pose a problem not yet solved by mankind* and have it solved by each of the characters in the play according to his own particular nature. They are, in short, laboratory experiments. But Chekhov does not work like that. He draws the audience's attention, for instance, to the fate of unhappy creatures such as Uncle Vanya and Dr Astrov. But he only commiserates with them because they are unhappy and fails to *show us whether they are worthy or not of our pity*. He makes them declare that they are the best people in the district, without showing *how* they are the best. "I, for my part, believe that they have always been bad and mediocre and *that is why their sufferings cannot be of any interest*."

There again, as always, Tolstoy shows himself to be moralist before human, whereas Chekhov is far more human than moralist! Human in the broadest sense of the word, human because he is tolerant, compassionate and cares about those whom the great, stern Tolstoy considers 'mediocre' and, consequently, unworthy of interest or pity.[8]

Maxim Gorki, intuitive and sensitive as he was, had caught the sense of uneasiness aroused by Chekhov's 'amoral' play and expressed it in vivid terms: "I saw *Uncle Vanya* a few days ago. I saw it and wept like a woman, I came home overwhelmed and bowled over by your play ... One cannot clearly express what it awakens in the depths of one's being, but as I watched your characters on the stage, I felt as though a blunt saw was cutting me in two ... Its teeth bite into one's heart and, under the bite, the heart contracts, groans and is rent. For me, this *Uncle Vanya* is something tremendous, it is a totally new formula in the theatre, a hammer with which you strike the empty heads of the public ... In the last act, when Dr Astrov, after a long pause, speaks about the heat in Africa, I began to tremble in ecstasy at your genius and in fear at the thought of humanity and our dull, miserable existence. How sturdily you strike at the heart and how true your aim is! You have enormous talent. But tell me, what nail do you hope to drive in with such blows? Would you resuscitate mankind if you had the power? . . . It seems to me, you know, that in this play you treat mankind with a fiendish coldness . . . You are indifferent as snow, as a blizzard. Forgive me, I may be wrong; in any case, these are only my personal impressions."

And when Chekhov continued to have doubts about his work as a playwright, Gorki wrote to him again, a few weeks later:

"You say you don't want to write for the theatre any more, which compels me to say a word about the reaction of the general public to your plays. People say, for instance, that *Uncle Vanya* and *The Seagull* are dramas of a completely new kind, in which realism is elevated to become one of those symbols that unite inspiration with depth of thought. I find this quite true. Watching your play, I thought of the life sacrificed to an idol, of the irruption of beauty into the wretched lives of mankind and of many other essential truths. Plays by other playwrights don't divert mankind from reality, don't drive it towards philosophical meditations as yours do . . . You are a mighty genius . . ."

Chekhov certainly did have doubts about the worth of his plays but his nostalgia for the theatre was to haunt him until his death. In 1900–1901, he wrote *The Three Sisters* and, in 1903–1904, his last play, *The Cherry Orchard*. The Moscow Art Theatre was a powerful magnetic pole, a buoyant, dynamic cultural centre, directed by two very different men, but both with unusual, arresting personalities. In addition, Chekhov's love for Olga Knipper provided him with a strong incentive to write for the stage. When he wrote his two last plays, Chekhov had the actors for whom he was writing them clearly in view, which partly explains why his characters are so alive. *The Three Sisters* consists of a sort of long message, a long inner dialogue between the author and the far-away Olga Knipper. It is the most 'Chekhovian', the most nostalgic, the most harmonious of his plays. The audiences proved it: the play eventually beat all previous records in the number of its performances. Yet, when it was first presented, it was far less successful than *The Seagull* and *Uncle Vanya*.

The public and the critics "had had enough of Seagulls and Uncle Vanyas".[9] The novelty of the 'atmosphere' play, introduced by Chekhov, seemed to have worn thin. The very perceptive author recognized it: "My style appears to be old-fashioned ... I think that none of my lines is worth anything, is any good at all," he grumbled to his wife, 20th September, 1903.

He tried to alter his style, to write "an amusing play" – it turned out to be *The Cherry Orchard*. It was sub-titled: 'A Comedy.' "Why do they insist on calling it a drama on the poster and in the advertisements? Nemirovich and Stanislavski must see something in it different from what I wrote: I could swear that neither of them has read it carefully. Forgive me, but I assure you it's true," Chekhov wrote to his wife, 10th April, 1904, who was playing the part of Ranevskaia. And he complained to the writer, Tikhonov, that "it is Stanislavksi who makes my plays lachrymose".

However, *The Cherry Orchard*, performed for the first time on the 17th January, 1904, the author's birthday, was a great success. "This time, the audience could shed tears without any sense of guilt: directed as it was, it rang the knell of the old world."[10]

Whether tragedy or comedy, *The Cherry Orchard*, like Chekhov's other plays, had a triumphant career, due to the miraculous encounter of a great writer, a shrewd critic and an exceptionally sensitive director. This very rare combination gave birth to the joint masterpiece of Chekhov plays acted by the Art Theatre company. A masterpiece of nuance, balance, poetry and taste, which still remains one of the brightest jewels in the contemporary theatre.

As early as 1886, Chekhov was proclaiming: "New forms are

needed and if there are none – then it is better to keep quiet."

Coming to literature at a time when Turgenev's style was the dominating one in Russia, he began to blaze the trail towards a stylistic revolution. Turgenev's detailed, precise, florid, slightly limp language had had its day, in Chekhov's opinion. Literary forms needed to be regenerated. For, though the famous descriptions of nature by the author of *A Sportsman's Sketches* were beautiful, he considered that "people had lost their taste for that type of description and something else would have to be found". Very conscious of the dead, static element in those slow and 'over-polished' narratives, Chekhov finally did effect a veritable revolution in Russian literary style. After him, it was no longer possible to write in the same way as authors had done before him.

But Chekhov's life was a very short one. He knew that he had to hurry, take the shortest route, reduce experiments to a minimum and avoid repetitiveness and the exploration of divergent avenues; that he must endeavour to discover by analysis and the ceaseless exercise of intelligence and will-power exactly what he was, what he could become and what he wanted to be. He realized that true richness, true fecundity did not lie either in the number or length of an author's works "but much more in the scope of their effect". He was aware, too, that the real compass, the real impact of literary works could only be assessed after the passage of time : but it is now incontestable that Chekhov's renown is steadily growing and that for many years now, the one-time 'revolutionary' has been regarded as a classic.

It is a rare occurrence for a critical intelligence to be allied to a poetic gift : nevertheless, this was the case with Chekhov. Baudelaire said that "chance does not enter into art any more than it does into mechanics. Any felicitous piece of work is purely the result of logical reasoning, *though the intermediate deductions may sometimes have been omitted.*" These lacunae between ideas, these sudden interruptions in the middle of a conversation or description, as important as the pauses in a piece of music, are typical of Chekhov's art. But in what way was Chekhov's art revolutionary? In what way was Chekhov an innovator?

[ ]

Tolstoy had said of him:

"One cannot compare Chekhov as an artist with any of the previous Russian writers, Turgenev, Dostoevsky or myself. Like the impressionists, Chekhov possesses his own particular style. One watches him daub on such colours as he has by him with apparent carelessness, and one imagines that all these splashes of paint have nothing in common between them. But as soon as one stands back and looks from a distance, the effect is extraordinary. Before one, there emerges a picture that is striking and irresistible."

Tolstoy here has touched on one of the main points in the Chekhovian aesthetics: the relationship between the writer and his readers. Writers like Turgenev, Goncharov and even, to a certain degree, Tolstoy, himself, addressed themselves to a passive reader. Chekhov, on the contrary, has no intention of expounding anything; he merely suggests. To put it in another way, he demands constant collaboration from the reader, with the express object of "making the reader think". "When I write" – he says – "I stake everything on the reader and count on him being able to supply for himself whatever elements may be lacking from my story . . ."

This is one of the keys to his poetical method: to avoid those sermons, which 'old-fashioned' books and plays supplied only too complacently and be content with administering a series of shocks to the feelings and imagination of reader and spectator. He wants to be understood 'without words', that is to say, by deliberately skipping those 'intermediary deductions', orchestrating allusions and silences and constructing a few bridges over the gaps. He leads the reader along this path, difficult beneath its deceptive facility, towards a dénouement, which,

nearly always, opens a casement on to something more profound, and more complex than what has been explicitly stated.
Let us take, for instance, the short story (only four pages) which
was Chekhov's favourite, *The Student* (1894). It is Good Friday.
The student, Ivan Velikopolski, comes home from hunting on
a cold, tempestuous evening, his mind filled with sad thoughts:

"He was thinking that the same icy wind had blown before
in the times of Rurik, Ivan the Terrible and Peter the Great,
and that then, too, there had been the same cruel misery, the
same hunger, the same leaking thatched roofs, ignorance, sadness, solitude, darkness and oppression – that all these abomina-
tions had existed, were existing and always would exist. And
that, even in a thousand years, life would be no better."

But suddenly, he catches sight of a fire, beside which two
widows, a mother and daughter, are sitting. He comes up to
them and warms his numbed hands over the flame:

"It was on a night like this that Saint Peter warmed himself
beside a fire. So it was just as cold then!" And he tells the two
women the story of Saint Peter's denial: the elder one begins to
cry; the student "understands that it is not because he has been
able to tell the story in a moving way", but "because Saint
Peter was close to her and she was interested with all her being
in what had gone on in the Apostle's mind. Joy began to bubble
in his heart and he stopped for a moment to catch his breath.
The past, he thought, is linked with the present by an uninter-
rupted chain of events, which flows the one from the other. And
it seemed to him that he had just seen both ends of the chain,
that he had just touched one of them and the other had immediately started to vibrate. And while he was crossing the river
in the ferry . . . he thought that the truth and beauty that govern
human life, back there, in the garden and the high-priest's
courtyard (where Saint Peter had denied Jesus and then wept
bitterly), had continued to exist without interruption right up
to the present day and apparently constituted the main point
of life and everything else on this earth. And the sensation of
being young, healthy and strong – he was only twenty-two

years old – and the unspeakably sweet anticipation of happiness, an unknown mysterious happiness, gradually stole over him and life seemed exciting, wonderful and full of profound significance."

What is the meaning of this short story, its true theme, concealed beneath the thin surface anecdote, a theme that is left to the reader to discover in Chekhov's elliptic poetry? Unquestionably, the underlying theme is the theme of youth. The state of mind of the student, the young man of twenty-two, cold and famished (it is the strict Good Friday fast-day), is one of despair at the beginning of the story. Everything seems to him dark and inescapable. But then he meets two miserable and lonely old women; warms himself; manages to touch them and move one of them to tears; and, immediately he suffers an abrupt revulsion of feeling, "joy begins to bubble in his heart", the world seems to be swept clean of its miseries and a boundless hope, an indescribable expectation of happiness buoy him up: in this rapid and complete change of feeling, *in this transition from despair to joy, in this instinctive irresistible impulse towards happiness*, Chekhov was able to make *the two poles*, which are the very essence of youth, palpable, concrete and all-powerful.

This allusive art, rich in concealed resonances, this art, consciously and profoundly developed is, at the same time, the most elliptic and the most concentrated art in Russian letters.

Chekhov wrote: "The shorter it is, the better ... the art of writing consists much less in writing well, than in striking out all that is badly written ... Briefness is the sister of talent." For him, it was a question of depicting life in all its complexity, but in the most restrained, compact manner: to present, with an extreme simplicity of method, all the multiplicity of levels, all the complex stratigraphy of human life.

Every fragment of life contains a theme worthy of a work of art, if one knows how to go into it deeply, explore it to the very end. The anecdotes which serve as a basis for Chekhov's stories often appear to be simple, commonplace and trite. But they only appear to be so to a superficial observer, unable to discern what is important and meaningful in the commonplace, in the smallest facts of everyday life.

Chekhov, in fact, achieved the *tour-de-force* of attracting and fascinating readers or spectators by stories and plays devoid of romantic atmosphere, vicissitudes or concessions of any kind towards easy understanding. "In life," he said to Kuprin, "there are no clear-cut consequences or reasons; in it, everything is mixed up together; the important and the paltry, the great and the base, the tragic and the ridiculous. One is hypnotized and enslaved by routine and cannot manage to break away from it. What are needed are new forms, new ones."

This astonishing memory for sounds, colours, smells and the smallest details, barely glanced at, forms the sieve through which emerge the impressions he will make use of later on.

[ ]

In the first place, Chekhov never obeyed anything but his own inner dictates. He often repeated: "that one should never listen to anyone's advice. One should work, and, in this work, be bold. There are big dogs and little dogs, but the little ones should not allow themselves to be intimidated by the presence of the big ones: it is the duty of them all to bark, and bark with the voice that God has given them."

He worked in solitude and, like Proust, principally from his memories. In Chekhov's eyes, there was no unchanging beauty. Anything that was beautiful at a given moment ceased to be so if it did not develop, become transformed and model itself on life, which changes all the time. He made use of the 'important' and 'characteristic' elements, deposited in the depths of his memory with singular objectivity, precision and discrimination, which he attributed to his scientific training.

It would, however, be incorrect to attribute Chekhov's aesthetic conceptions solely to his medical studies, though his scientific background had certainly enriched and disciplined a mind, already naturally inclined to objectivity and synthesis: "a writer should, above all, become a shrewd, and indefatigable observer, and should train himself in such a way that it becomes a habit, second nature with him ... A man of letters should be as objective as a chemist, he should abandon the subjectivity of everyday life." He should first and foremost be "an impartial witness".

Obviously, Chekhov was far from being solely a "witness". The personal element that enhanced the material supplied by direct observation of life was always depersonalized and sublimated until it acquired a general and superior quality. For instance, Treplev and Trigorin in *The Seagull* are both mouthpieces for the author, each incarnates one aspect of his personality; so does Dr Astrov in *Uncle Vanya*; so, to a certain extent, does Vershinin in *The Three Sisters*; so does Gurov, the hero in *The Lady with the Dog*; so, more than all the others, does Monseigneur Peter in *The Bishop*. But Chekhov always carefully disguises himself behind his characters and his poignant lyricism never contains any trace of that subjectivism, which he loathed. ("Subjectivity is a terrible thing ... One must, above all, avoid the personal element.")

Nevertheless, lyrical passages appear with increasing frequency in his later writings. The following one occurs in *In the Ravine* (1900), one of his 'blackest' stories:

"Lipa walked quickly, her shawl had slipped from her head. She looked up at the sky and wondered where her little boy's soul was now; was he following her at this particular moment or was he flying about up there, close to the stars, his mother already forgotten? Oh, how lonely you felt, out in the open country at night, amidst all this singing, when you, yourself, could not sing; amidst these ceaseless cries of joy, when you, yourself, could not be joyful; *when the moon looked down on you from high up in the sky, lonely, too, but indifferent to everything, to spring as much as winter, men's lives as much as their deaths. But, on the other hand, it seemed that, however great the sorrow, it was matched by the beauty and serenity*

[17]

of the night; that truth, equally beautiful and serene, existed and would continue to exist, in the world."

And this one in his very last story, *The Bride* (1903): "One took deep breaths and liked to believe that up there, under the vault of the sky, above the trees, far out of the town, in the fields and the forests, there was burgeoning the *special life of spring-time, a mysterious, beautiful, rich and holy life, beyond weak sinful mankind's understanding*." This is echoed in his *Notebooks*:

"What dies in man is merely what is subject to our five senses. *But everything that lies beyond those senses, and, in all probability is immense, unimaginable, and sublime, continues to exist.*"

The substance of Chekhov's lyricism is even more apparent in the famous endings to his plays: "We shall rest! We shall hear the angels, we shall see the sky covered in diamonds, we shall see all earthly ills, all our suffering drowned in the mercy that will fill the whole world. And our life will become peaceful, tender and soft as a caress. I believe . . . I believe . . . we shall rest!" (*Uncle Vanya*)

"Oh God! Time will pass and we shall leave for ever; we shall be forgotten, but our suffering will be transformed into joy for those who will live after us, happiness and peace will be established on earth, and those who replace us will speak of us with kindness and bless those who are living now." (*The Three Sisters*)

"The Cherry Orchard is sold, it no longer exists, that is true, that is true, but don't cry, Mamma, please don't cry; you still have your life in front of you, you still have your beautiful, pure soul. Come with me, come my dearest, let us go! We shall plant another orchard, far better than this one, you'll see, you'll understand! And joy, a sweet, profound joy will descend on your soul, like the sun at eventide." (*The Cherry Orchard*)

We are confronted by the very Chekhovian theme of melancholy co-existing with immense hope; of acknowledgement of the evil and suffering still reigning on earth, together with faith in the advent of something noble, beneficent and undefined of which the expectation appeases, lulls and consoles.

[ ]

This abrupt irruption of the lyrical element, with its irresistible impact on the reader, is, as everything else with Chekhov, closely thought-out and deliberate. The poetry is there to compel the reader to think, to provoke him into doing what the author regards as essential – take a serious look at himself and the emptiness of his life : and, at the same time, to waken in him a longing for a better one. These are the twin objectives that Chekhov pursues in his work, they are the basis of it and always present in the background.

As regards its *shape*, which attained an almost disconcerting perfection, this had undergone ceaseless development in the course of Chekhov's twenty years of literary life.

The young author had defined his aesthetic tenets as far back as 1886, when he was only twenty-six:

"(1) absolute objectivity; (2) truth in the description of people and things; (3) maximum brevity; (4) boldness and originality; (5) compassion." And, thirteen years later, he defined the art of writing in these terms: "When one uses the minimum of gestures to produce a particular effect it is called gracefulness ... Beauty and expressiveness are only achieved in descriptions through simplicity and the use of sentences as plain as 'The sun is setting', 'it is dark', 'it starts to rain'. " He applied this same utter simplicity, in the first place, to the *composition* of his stories. What becomes of the traditional divisions of a story – prologue, exposition or development and finally dénouement or conclusion – in Chekhov's work? The 'prologue' or introduction to the story is generally reduced to nil, or to a short sentence that immediately goes to the heart of the matter. This, for instance, is how his story *My Life* starts: "The bailiff said to me : 'I'm only keeping you on out of regard for your worthy father. Otherwise, I'd have sacked you long ago!'" This is the manner in which Chekhov cuts abruptly to the very core of his themes, and, throughout the actual development of his stories, the conciseness of the means of expression is equally striking. For instance, in *Ionich*, Chekhov is content to indicate Dr Startsev's social advancement by means of a few scattered signposts. A young doctor at the start of his career, "Startsev walked unhurriedly, (he did not yet own any horses) and sang ..." A year goes by. The author does not go into detail but slips in, apparently casually: "By now, he owned a carriage and pair and a coachman, Panteleimon, in a velvet waistcoat." Four years later: "Startsev had a large practice. Every morning, he received his patients *with all possible speed* so as to be free to attend the ones who were expecting him to visit them in town: he no longer rode in his carriage, but in a troika with bells." And a few years later still comes the ultimate stage of his success: "Startsev had put on still more weight, had difficulty in breathing and walked with his head in the air. When he passed by, corpulent and blotchy, in his troika with bells, with Panteleimon, equally corpulent and red-faced on the coachman's seat, it was a really imposing spectacle, and one felt it was not a man passing by but a pagan deity." That is all. But is not his social standing perfectly clear? As regards the third element, the dénouement or conclusion, Chekhov had always appreciated its vital role in the composition. He knew that it was in the ending that the impact produced by the whole work was concentrated, particularly when the work was as condensed and compact as a short story.

In his letters, he often comes back to this fundamental problem of the ending. He wrote to Alexis Pleshcheev in September, 1889, "My intuition tells me that it is in the conclusion of a story that I must manage, skilfully, to concentrate the impact that the whole of the story will leave on the reader and to do this, I must remind him, if only to a very small extent, of what has gone before." He once wrote to Suvorin in 1892:

"I have an interesting theme for a play, but I have not yet

devised the ending. The man who discovers new dénouements will have opened up a new era! Those cursed dénouements always escape one. The hero either has to get married or commit suicide – there seems to be no other alternative."

This kind of ending did not satisfy the Chekhov of mature years. He sought for an unexpected or striking twist, such as one finds not only in plays like *Ivanov* and *The Seagull*, but also in some of the best of his early stories, like *Vanka*[11] or *Sadness*. But the more masterly his skill became, the less he sought for facile or merely striking effects.

The Chekhov of the final years ended his stories and plays abruptly, on a sort of musical chord. There is, strictly speaking, no longer an ending at all. On the contrary, a window is opened on to a distant vista. In *The Lady with the Dog*, the two leading characters are involved in an inextricable situation. And this is how the story ends: "What can I do, what can I do? – he wondered, his head in his hands. And he felt that a solution would crop up before long and that then a new and marvellous life would begin. But both of them were clearly aware that everything was far from being settled and that the most complicated, the most difficult part was only just beginning." One stage in the lives and the fortunes of the two characters had finished, but there was another to come, one that was only just beginning. That is what Chekhov is saying in this dénouement, which, in fact, is not one at all. This same form of ending is to be found in nearly all his works after 1894. His last short story, *The Bride*, ends in this way: "She walked into Sacha's room and remained for a moment quite still, 'Adieu, cher Sacha!' she thought and a new, spacious life seemed to stretch out before her, a life that though still ill-defined and full of the unknown, attracted her and beckoned her on."

[ ]

In 1887, Chekhov wrote to his brother Alexander, in reply to a letter telling him of the enthusiasm aroused by his story

Happiness (which was deeply poetical and, in his opinion at that time, his masterpiece):

"Yes, I like it, too, because of its theme . . . It is a product of inspiration. A *quasi-symphony*. But actually, it is a farrago. It only pleases the reader owing to an optical illusion. The whole trick lies in the interpolated embellishments such as the sheep and the arrangement of certain sentences. You know, one could just as easily write about coffee-grounds and amaze the reader by means of a series of tricks!"

It was during this same period that he wrote his first great story, *The Steppe*:

"The hawk flies above the earth, harmoniously flapping its broad wings: suddenly, it stops as though it were meditating on the sadness of life, then shakes its wings and is off like an arrow over the steppe, and one does not know why he flies, nor what he seeks. Then, on the summit of a hillock, a solitary poplar appears. Is it happy, this beautiful being? In the summer the torrid heat, in winter, the cold and the blizzards, in autumn the dreadful nights, when it sees nothing but darkness and hears nothing but the angry howling of the wind. And worst of all, it *remains alone, completely alone* throughout its life."

This is what the young Chekhov called tricks: *the hawk meditating on the sadness of life*, the *solitary* poplar, are images, and anthropomorphism, used to create a dull pain and a longing in the reader, which increase his receptivity towards poetry. It is a method that is allied to music, since what is important is not so much the meaning of the words as their power to enchant and cast a spell.

Music plays an immense part in Chekhov's work. The sonorous element is one of the most important in his method. If we analyse the various manifestations of this lyrical element, we see that the most outstanding is *the musicality of his style*, his way of altering his sentences so as to render them more harmonious and the precision with which he chooses and combines his words. Chekhov attached enormous importance to the musical structure of his sentences:

[22]

"I re-read my proofs not with the idea of correcting the external substance of what I have written, but because this is usually the moment when I really complete the story and alter it from what might be called a *musical* angle."

Often, a Chekhovian sentence seems to be constructed with a view to its being sung rather than merely spoken. The usual structure of such poetic sentences consists of three clauses: "After our death, we shall speak of what we have suffered, of how much we have cried, of how bitter our life was . . ." (*Uncle Vanya*). "She seemed to be more beautiful, more youthful, more tender than she really was . . ." (*The Lady With the Dog*). "Let us talk of Cleopatra, of her little girl, of life's sadness" (*My Life*). One could quote innumerable examples of these sentences with three clauses, so plaintively musical. No doubt, they spring from recollections of his boyhood, when he sang the burial service in church, modulated in three tones, when the beauty of the orthodox chant impregnated his child's sensibility.

The musical element appears again in his work in the form of real pieces of music in prose. In *The Steppe, On the Way, The Babas, The Muzhiks* and *The Reed-pipe* a "sonorous landscape" is superimposed on the other, the natural one.

This use of a sonorous landscape can be compared to another of Chekhov's innovations: the richness, variety and freshness of his onomatopoeia. There is a conventional manner for representing the various noises in nature; the barking of a dog, the mooing of a cow, the cry of a bird. But, here again, Chekhov avoids the time-worn clichés and endeavours, in his own way, to reproduce the noise of a train, for instance, or the croaking of a frog or the cry of a night-bird. In this, he is pursuing his constant aim: to make the reader break away from what he is accustomed to, strike his imagination and capture his attention by presenting something commonplace enough in itself in an entirely new way.

An innovator in his musical method, Chekhov is equally so in his visual one. His love of nature turns him into a great landscape painter, whom his contemporaries often compared to Levitan.

[23]

The anthropomorphism, the bold painting and the colours, slightly blurred at the outset, gradually make way for a monochrome design of admirable simplicity. The original somewhat vague sentimentality becomes transformed into a virile, serene melancholy. The austerity of the style accords well with the purity of the feelings it expresses and the final effect is one of extraordinary spirituality.

But the man of science, the doctor, watches over the lyrical poet. Alongside the beautiful, poetic descriptions are to be found others, both frightening and grotesque. His painterly naturalist's eyes enable Chekhov to observe the man he is depicting, take him to pieces and reveal the deep-seated brutishness that sometimes forms a part of him.

The beautiful, wicked Aksinia of *In the Ravine* has "naïve grey eyes, a naïve smile". But, "in her yellow dress, drawn tight across her breasts and eternally smiling, she resembles a young adder, which a passer-by catches sight of in the spring, hidden in the ripening corn and gathered together to strike, with its head erect". In contrast, the gentle Lipa, whose newborn child she scalds, is described as a "sky-lark". In a fight scene between father and son in *The New Villa*, the two men are likened to two foul beasts, two spiders and two monstrous puppets. Temperate artist as he is and immensely restrained, Chekhov never over-stresses: he is satisfied to suggest ugliness by a brief, but ferocious simile.

[ ]

"I know how to speak briefly on important subjects," Chekhov wrote. "It is odd but I have contracted a sort of mania for brevity. Everything I read, whether written by myself or someone else, seems to me to be too long."

This passion for brevity, so noticeable in his descriptions, is, perhaps, even more apparent in his psychological (or physical) portraits of his characters. As, for instance, this portrait in *Ionich* of the town's most intellectual and enlightened woman, a novelist in her spare time. " 'Do you publish your works?' Dr Startsev asked Madam Turkina – 'Oh, no,' she replied – 'I never publish anything. I write, and then I put the manuscript away in my cupboard. Why should I publish? *We're well off.*' "

The same lady reads her latest novel to her guests; it is about a Countess, beautiful as the day, who founds schools, libraries and hospitals and then falls in love with an itinerant artist:

"In her book she wrote of things that were non-existent in real life, but pleasant and comforting to listen to ... An hour or two passed by. In the nearby public-gardens, a band began to play and a choir was singing. When Madam Turkina closed her manuscript, there was a few moments' silence. *Nobody spoke as they listened to the choir singing 'Luchinushka', and this song contained precisely everything that the novel lacked and did exist in real life.*"

In *The Three Sisters*, Chekhov draws the distinction between the character of the refined, well-bred Olga and that of the vulgar, superstitious Natasha in this fleeting episode: Natasha is wearing a bright pink dress with a green belt, "Olga (under her breath in horror): 'A green belt! My dear, it's all wrong!' – Natasha: 'Why? Is it bad luck?' "

One could quote endless examples of this expressive laconicism. Patiently, Chekhov had the ability to create a style that was entirely his own, penetrating, allusive and extremely economical in the methods by which he achieved it. His restraint and intensity, together with the emotional content of his plays, "without a theme" and his short stories often give "a more profound conception of the infinite" than many vast, ambitious panoramas.

[ ]

Beneath this art, so full of light and shade, lurked the tragic view of life, so characteristic of Chekhov in his maturity. This tragic view is expressed in his *Notebooks*, his letters and his best works. But there is an important distinction to be drawn here.

Actually, in Chekhov's eyes, the tragedy of life existed on two separate planes, on the higher plane it was metaphysical; on the lower, social. The former was, in its nature, eternal and irremediable. The second, temporary and susceptible to improvement. One of Chekhov's favourite themes and unquestionably the most characteristic and profound is that of solitude. A metaphysical solitude, inherent to the human condition.

This general conception is expressed in many passages from his letters and *Notebooks*, and in many of his stories, as, for example, his famous *Sadness* to which we have referred previously. Jonas, the coachman, is alone with his great grief over his son's death. His grief is of no interest to anyone, and he cannot communicate it to anyone, because deep feeling, by its nature, is incommunicable: because there is an essential core of man's being that remains tragically separated from everyone. This core is composed of a whole fascicle of feelings, sensations, emotions and memories of the past, incomprehensible for those who have never experienced them. One has only to think of Proust's famous madeleine, of which the flavour, by association and some kind of mental flash-back, evoked in him a wave of emotions and memories, so personal and individual that they were only intelligible to himself. The core that lies in the depths of man's soul cannot be communicated to other people, and Jonas, the coachman, gives striking proof of it.

But if man is irremediably alone in life, he is also so in death. From this angle the story entitled *A Sad Story* is highly significant. Professor Nicolas Stepanovich, a kind-hearted, good man and an eminent scientist, knows that he is suffering from an incurable disease. He has only a few weeks or possibly months to live. Mentally, he draws up the balance sheet of his life. And despite his celebrity, despite a normal, even happy, family life, despite the great affection shown him by his adopted daughter Katia, Nicolas Stepanovich feels himself to be irremediably alone. Faced by imminent death, he is unable to find either in his past life or in the present any element of consolation or relief. As his life comes to its close, with all its outward appearance of success, this kind and intelligent man can see nothing but solitude, lack of understanding and a remoteness from everything and everyone.

A Sad Story perfectly illustrates Chekhov's metaphysical pessimism regarding the inevitable destiny of every human being, which, in the last analysis, is to be utterly alone both in life and in the face of death.

This story of Chekhov's has often been compared to a masterpiece of Tolstoy's, *The Death of Ivan Ilyich*. The difference in the two writers' viewpoints is extremely interesting. Tolstoy's hero, the victim of an incurable disease, also investigates the balance sheet of his life, the life of a conscientious, conventional and narrow-minded civil servant. But this mediocre person finds in death exactly what Chekhov's good and high-minded professor failed to find: he sees in it not only relief and serenity, but the fulfilment and very aim of all his past life. In other words, on the brink of passing on, the mediocre Ivan Ilyich suddenly understands that the law governing mankind is the law of love, and that where there is true love, there is no longer any death. At the moment of dying, Ivan Ilyich feels nothing but compassion, love and regret, not for himself, but for his dear ones. The horror and fear of death, which tormented him previously, have disappeared: "Where is it, where is death?" Tolstoy asks. "Instead of death, there was only light and understanding. 'Death is no more,' thought Ivan Ilyich, 'it no longer exists.'" Where there is love, there is no death, because love is stronger than death.

But if all this was transparent to Tolstoy, it was far from so to Chekhov. And his Nicolas Stepanovich, who actually does not love anyone and remains impervious to the very end to the true, solicitous love of his adopted daughter Katia, does not receive Ivan Ilyich's crowning revelation. Alone in life, according to Chekhov's profoundly tragic conception, he remains alone in death, towards which he advances, serenely but in despair.

However, below this philosophical and inevitable tragedy

there lies another plane, that of the social tragedy, which, unlike the former, offers hope of a cure. Culture, education, a relative prosperity can temper the horror of certain lives and certain situations, described by Chekhov in such stories as *The Muzhiks*, *In the Ravine* and *Vanka*. Society can be made better; men can become more disciplined, more refined, happier and more civilized. They will no longer torture children, they will become less coarse, less greedy, less cruel. In Chekhov's eyes, the social tragedy appears to be capable of improvement.

Who can forget the poetical endings to his plays, *Uncle Vanya* and *The Cherry Orchard*, from which there suddenly springs hope for a better future and a happiness, not only possible but certain, even though still far away? This hope, this faith are superimposed upon the fundamental theme of Chekhov's work — the constant assertion of man's inner, spiritual, moral and sentimental solitude, face to face with his fellow-men. An eternal solitude, since it is rooted in the very foundation of human nature.

So how, then, can one reconcile the personal tragedy, the irremediable solitude (which was the lot of Chekhov, himself, and most of his heroes) with the illogical hope of a problematic, future happiness? One cannot, in fact, envisage any bridge capable of surmounting the gap between these two very contradictory conceptions. And Chekhov has not attempted to reconcile them in the abstract or in the absolute. Like a true stoic he is satisfied with confining himself to action, satisfied to struggle on, while abandoning any idea of that "personal happiness which does not exist, which should not exist".

It was with a view to this future happiness, which he was never to know, that Chekhov, in his early youth, had constructed his code of ethics, which involved the "renunciation of leisure, women, wine and pursuits".

This renunciation, coupled with incessant work, was aimed at alleviating men's lives and, perhaps, in the distant future, making them happier and better.

NOTES

1. Nina Gourfinkel: Chekhov and the Moscow Arts Theatre (in The Review of the History of the Theatre) Paris 1954, IV, pp. 258–259.

2. In 1880, at the age of twenty, he had written a black comedy which he had resolutely thrown into the wastepaper basket, but which was nevertheless published in 1923 under the title: *An Unpublished Chekhov Play* and played in Paris under the title of *That Crazy Platonov*. In 1885, he wrote *On The Highway*, a dramatic sketch in one act; in 1886, *The Swan Song*, also in one act and *The Lethal Qualities of Tobacco*, a monologue in one act; in 1888 *The Bear*, a farce in one act; in 1889 *The Proposal*, a farce in one act; in 1890 *The Actor malgré lui*, a farce in one act and *The Marriage* in one act; in 1892 *The Jubilee*, a farce in one act. Some of these sketches have been constantly performed on the Russian and other stages. In *Ivanov*, a tragedy, he tried for the first time to apply his revolutionary ideas on the theatre. In spite of the play's success, he was not satisfied with it.

3. Once the author has written his text, there is another piece of work to be done which consists of creating something out of this text. The director, the stage manager, the artistic director and the actors get together and, through their common work, achieve what I call the 'miracle' (Stanislavski).

4. After reading *The Seagull* in manuscript, the famous actor Lenski had said to Chekhov: "Stop writing plays; it's not your line."

5. Nina Gourfinkel: *op. cit.* p. 261.

6. Nemirovich-Danchenko in his Memoirs.

7. "Shakespeare's plays are bad, but yours are even worse," Tolstoy once said to Chekhov.

8. Nevertheless, the great artist was once more to take precedence over the moralist. Between 1900–1904, Tolstoy wrote a very Chekhovian play, impregnated with human understanding and pity, *The Living Corpse*, the hero of which, Fedia Protasov, a kind, weak man, is certainly not 'worthy of interest' from the point of view of Tolstoyan morality.

9. Suvorin wrote on 10th February, 1902: "Saw Chekhov's *The Three Sisters*. Dull, except for the first act ... many boring monologues, often repeated, from Vershinin and Andrei: I watched the audience: no-one even thought of crying; the three sisters wept on the stage – but not a soul in the audience! What petty characters when we wanted tragic ones!"

10. Nina Gourfinkel: *op. cit.* p. 281.

11. The shoemaker's young apprentice, who is ill treated by his master and begs his grandfather to come and fetch him. He addresses his letter: "To my grandfather, in the village."

PART ONE

Taganrog

1860 – 1879

I love life, in general, but I loathe and
utterly despise the pettiness and meanness
of Russian provincial life.
CHEKHOV

[1]

The Town

TAGANROG, a small town in the south of Russia, has a two-fold claim to fame. It was here that one of the greatest Russian writers was born; and it was here, thirty-five years earlier, that the victor over Napoleon, Tsar Alexander I, had died. The latter's death, wrapped in mystery, gave rise to a legend that has never been fully elucidated.

In September, 1825, the Tsar arrived in Taganrog with his wife, the Empress Elisabeth, whose health required her to spend some time in the south. The choice of this small, remote town seemed inexplicable. The unimposing fortress built by Peter the Great at the northern extremity of the Sea of Azov (the 'Putrid Sea', the 'Palus meotis'), in a wild and marshy countryside, was to be occupied by Alexander I and his wife for two months. Then, on 19th November, 1825, Alexander died suddenly from the after-effects of a severe attack of malaria. This death gave birth to the most extraordinary rumours and created a legend which became firmly rooted in the popular imagination. Alexander I was not dead – so the story went – but had mysteriously disappeared, with the complicity of his staff, to a Palestinian monastery or a Siberian hermitage, to expiate, far away, the abominable crime of having been a party to the assassination of his father, the Emperor Paul I. The legend gradually became crystallized around the person of a Siberian hermit, Feodor Kuzmich, an old man who died in the odour of sanctity on

20th January, 1864, in the neighbourhood of Tomsk. Pushkin refers to the enigmatic Tsar as the "sphinx who carried his secret with him, unsolved, to the *grave*", and Tolstoy started writing an account of the occurrences under the title *Posthumous Notes on the staretz Feodor Kuzmich*. Although he never completed it, the subject held a curious fascination for him, as evidenced by his letter to the Grand Duke Alexander Mikhailovich: "What does it matter," he wrote in a letter dated 2nd September, 1907, "that it has proved impossible to identify the person of Alexander with that of Fiodor Kuzmich as an historical fact? The legend continues to exist in all its beauty and all its truth. I have started to write on this subject but am very much afraid that I shall be unable to finish it, that I shall not even have the time to go on working on it ... I deeply regret this; it is an exquisite idea."

Whatever the real facts may have been, Taganrog had become part of the legend.

A sleepy little town on the shores of a bay once furrowed by the wakes of ships, but now dormant and silted up, this was the Taganrog where Chekhov was born on 17th January, 1860. Peter the Great's passion for building had been responsible for the construction of this port on the north-east side of the Sea of Azov, which discharges its waters into those of the Black Sea. The first buildings of the new maritime city had arisen in 1698. In Chekhov's time, 150 years later, it counted 55,000 inhabitants. Taganrog had rapidly become one of Russia's largest ports, a centre for the export of wheat and other agricultural produce. This trade was almost entirely concentrated in the hands of Greek merchants, who formed a kind of local aristocracy, to the considerable displeasure of the autochthons.

The author's elder brother, Alexander, tells us in his memoirs[1] that more than half the population of Taganrog in 1860 consisted of foreigners: Greeks, Italians, Germans and English, with Greek predominating. The ship-owners and wealthy merchants held the town's 'proletariat' in strict dependence: in the first place, the local inhabitants, who served as off-shore men, transporting the freight of millions of tons of wheat from the warehouses where it was stored to the ships, which were compelled to anchor some thirty miles outside the port because of the silting-up of the bay; and secondly, those of a much inferior station, the 'driagnils' (from the German, *traeger*) or dockers, who attended to the loading of the cargoes.

Taganrog's aristocrats at that time bore the names of Valiano, Scaramanga, Kondoiaki, Moussouri or Sfaello, and never Ivanov or Petrov. Alexander Chekhov refers to them with undisguised bitterness. The residential district which housed these millionaires; the Greek cemetery, rich in monuments in marble, shipped straight from Paros or Carrara : the carriages drawn by thoroughbred horses; the magnificent dresses and jewels of the Greek women; the Italian opera subsidized by their husbands and the first-class musicians in the municipal orchestra; all these were the fruit of 'Greek money'. It was the opulent Greeks who drew the most famous theatrical and opera companies to Taganrog. The great Pauline Lucca sang in the cramped little theatre in Petrovskaia Street; and, on the same stage, eminent actors like the Negro Olridge and the Italian Salvini performed Shakespeare's tragedies.

This was how things were in the middle of the last century. But a dangerous rival to Taganrog was rising up in the shape of the neighbouring town of Rostov-on-Don. Trade gravitated gradually towards Rostov : the big ships no longer called in at Taganrog bay. And Taganrog slowly began to die.

But alongside the Taganrog of the rich, there was the other, poorer Taganrog, where the Chekhov family struggled to keep body and soul together. This Taganrog was wretched and still mediaeval, its unpaved streets becoming quagmires every autumn and spring. The inhabitants sank up to their ankles in the muddy tracks which, in summer, were overgrown with weeds. The two main roads were dimly lit; the others lacked lighting of any kind, and people going out at night always carried a lantern. Carts, drawn by prisoners from the municipal gaol, passed by laden with sacks of flour and buckwheat, which constituted their staple diet. The same prisoners were responsible for the extermination of stray dogs and scoured the market place, armed with cudgels and bill-hooks with which they brutally slaughtered their victims. Water was scarce and so contaminated that infectious diseases raged every summer.

It was in the centre of this poor-man's Taganrog that Anton Chekhov was born and lived. Gnutov House in Politzeiskaia Street, his actual birth-place, still exists as No. 47 in the present Chekhov Street. It is a very modest, low house of one floor and has three windows with green shutters looking out on the front. The roof is constructed of zinc. This small house was soon exchanged for another, Moisseiv House, in Monastyrskaia Street, where the young Anton spent his childhood.

His adolescent years were passed in a house built by his father in Elisavetinskaia Street. It did not remain the property of the Chekhov family for long. On the bankruptcy of Pavel Jegorovich Chekhov, it passed into the hands of a more astute man : his former lodger, Gavril Parfentievich Selivanov.

Anton Chekhov had melancholy recollections of these successive homes: "On non-fasting days, the houses smelt of cabbage soup; on fast-days, of sturgeon fried in sunflower oil. The food was bad and the water we drank polluted. In the whole town – I did not know a single honest man."[2] And, on revisiting his native town, early in April, 1887, eight years after his move to Moscow, he wrote to his sister Maria :

I am in Taganrog . . . It gives me the same impression as Herculaneum or Pompeii. All the houses seem to be falling down; their walls have not been repaired for a long time; the roofs are unpainted, the shutters closed. I realized to what an extent Taganrog was filthy, empty, lazy, ignorant and boring. There is not a single sign-board without some mistake in spelling. The streets are empty, idleness general, as is the readiness to be content with a few kopecks and an uncertain future. What is particularly odious here are those perpetually closed shutters.

Nevertheless, the house where he was born in Politzeiskaia Street, poor and cramped though it was, possessed a certain charm. The green shutters of the three windows looked welcoming and somehow surprised. Low and squat, the little white house drowsed in the shade of enormous acacia trees, in the middle of a yard smothered in weeds. Its torpor was only interrupted by the noise of ships' sirens coming from the nearby harbour and the trickle of rainwater running down the gutters to accumulate in a barrel placed at the corner of the house, in order to catch every last drop of the precious liquid.

In his childhood, little Anton had loved his native town: "It seemed to me so beautiful and warm! I loved the greenery and the calm, sun-bathed mornings; I loved the chimes of its bells. Acacia boughs, lilac bushes, wild-cherry and apple trees crowded together above the hedges and the palings . . . The twilight in May, the young and tender greenery casting its flattering shadows, the scent of lilac, the rustling of the cockchafers, the silence and the balminess of the air."[3] All this poetry atoned, momentarily at least, for the rest: the poverty, the dirt, the surrounding coarseness and the infinite sadness of the 'deaf towns' of bygone Russia. 'Deaf towns', towns lulled to sleep in a heavy silence, born of laxity, lassitude, indolence and a total lack of any hope for a better future.

NOTES

1. *European Messenger* (St Petersburg), 1907–1908.
2. Chekhov: *My Life*, 1896.
3. Chekhov: *My Life*, 1886.

[2]

The Family

ANTON'S paternal grand-
father, Jegor Mikhailovich Chekh, was born a serf. Through his
intelligence and industriousness, he raised himself to the position
of a bailiff, saved some money and, twenty years before the
abolition of serfdom, was able to buy his freedom and that of his
three sons at a cost of seven hundred roubles a head. His master,
Count A. D. Chertkov,[1] included his daughter's freedom in the
bargain for nothing. Once free, Jegor Chekh became steward
of Countess Platov's enormous estates between Taganrog and
Rostov-on-Don, where young Anton spent a number of his
holidays.

Michael, Jegor Chekh's eldest son, became a bookbinder in
Kaluga. His other two sons, Pavel and Mitrofan, settled down in
Taganrog. Pavel, after a short spell as Clerk in the Town Hall,
opened his own grocer's shop and on 29th October, 1854,
married the young Evgenia Jacovlevna Morosova, daughter of a
draper in Morchansk, a small town in the Tambov province.
This draper, Jacov Morosov, had died of cholera during a
business trip that had taken him to Novocherkassk. At the time
of his death, his wife, Alexandra Ivanovna, and their children
had been at the other end of Russia, in the Vladimir province
staying with a relative. As soon as she heard the sad news,
Alexandra Ivanovna hired a carriage and embarked on an exhausting journey across Russia to visit her husband's grave.

This journey made a deep impression on the sensitive,

imaginative mind of Anton Chekhov's mother. Evgenia Jacovlevna and her sister were to remember all their lives this apparently endless pilgrimage through dense forests, along out-of-the-way tracks frequented by brigands and tramps, with stops for the night at sinister-looking inns with barricaded doors and closed shutters, where everyone lived in constant terror of ruffians and highwaymen. Then, at last, came the contrast of emerging into the southern steppes, where the nights were tranquil and mild. Their recent fears subsided and they slept out in the open, beneath a vast and friendly sky, with nothing to break the silence but the chirping of crickets and the occasional cry of a nocturnal bird. Wonderful nights in the south, which Anton would later conjure up in *The Steppe*, as his mother had described them in her own simple, poetic way. These memories and tales, told over and over again, beguiled the childhood of the Chekhov children and fired the imagination of the remarkable little boy that Anton was fast becoming.

Grandfather Morosov's grave was never found. His widow finally decided to settle down in Taganrog with her two daughters, and it was there that Pavel Jegorovich Chekhov made the family's acquaintance and later married the younger daughter, Evgenia Jacovlevna.

Chekhov's father was an inept businessman. Trade bored him and his shop, specializing in 'colonial products', wore him out. The journey to Kharkov, some 300 miles from Taganrog, to replenish his stocks was one of considerable danger at that time. The railway did not yet exist and the roads were far from safe, being frequented for the most part by vagrants, brigands and outlaws. There was not a single town along the whole length of the journey. One had to sleep out in the open in the vast, deserted steppe, with the wind blowing in savage gusts and one's hair standing on end at the recollection of all the legends and mysterious rumours of what went on in this 'new world', unknown and almost uninhabited. Before embarking on such a journey, one had prayers offered up and prayed a long time, oneself, from prudence, precaution and, of course, piety.

For Pavel Jegorovich was pious in his own way. What attracted him most in religion was the beauty of the ceremonial, the singing and the sound of the bells; the glitter of the icons in their gold and silver casings; the mysterious coloured gleams from the candles; the smell of incense and the majesty and splendour of the orthodox service. Yes, that was what he loved above all else, for he was an artist at heart. Trade, and the shop, represented the prose of everyday life. The Church and its rites provided the poetry. Possessing a fine voice and a good ear, having taught himself to play the violin after a fashion, and painting holy pictures unskilfully but with a very personal feeling for colours (Anton Pavlovich was to keep these pictures piously all his life), Pavel Jegorovich was a would-be artist. The Church brought him the beauty and mystery so sadly lacking in his life as an impecunious shopkeeper. With all the fervour of a bluff, simple-minded soul, he clung to the warmth and poetry that religion dispensed. Later on in life, Anton was fond of saying: "We inherit our talent from our father, our soul from our mother."

Evgenia Jacovlevna, his mother, was a gentle, passive creature, as shy, tender and retiring as her husband was self-confident, domineering and brutal. She adored her children but was unable to protect them from the despotism and tyranny of their father. Not that Pavel Jegorovich disliked his children, quite the contrary; but, brought up himself in primitive, brutal surroundings, he sought to instil in them, through rigid rules of conduct, a code of ethics that was as conventional as it was rudimentary. As Anton was to say later, "Our grandfather was beaten by his masters and the lowest official could knock him about. Our father was beaten by our grandfather, and we, by our father. What nerves, what blood have we inherited!"

He was never able to forget the whip with which his father had thrashed him so often. "I remember that my father started on my education, or, more simply, to beat me, before I was five years old. When I woke each morning, my first thought was: 'Shall I be beaten today?' "[2]

Was Pavel Jegorovich ill-natured? No, neither ill-natured, nor stupid, nor really cruel; but savage and made callous by a life in which his best instincts were curbed by the poverty, lack of understanding, drabness and apathy around him. Talented, self-willed and passionate, he soon allowed his unused energies to deteriorate into the worst kind of despotism. His formal religiousness and his hatred for the shop as a despicable means of earning a living were made to weigh heavily on his children's shoulders.

Church and shop! For the Chekhov boys, particularly the two elder ones, these took on the qualities of a nightmare.

The Chekhovs had their first son, Alexander, in 1855; two years later, their second, Nicholas. Anton was born in 1860; the next year, Ivan; then came a daughter, Maria, and, finally, a fifth boy, Michael. It was the three eldest who took it in turns to look after the shop. It was they, too, who were forced to spend long hours in church, standing or kneeling (since orthodox churches do not encourage sitting), praying and singing in the choir, organized and led by their father. What discomforts they must have suffered during the long, hard winters when an icy wind blew down from the Urals; and during the sultry summers when an indigo-blue sky loomed for weeks over the sun-baked town, where clouds of white dust eddied above the narrow lifeless streets! After they came home in the icy dawn from the interminable church services, stumbling from fatigue down the dark, empty streets, their father would say: "It's not worth going to bed. You'll have to open the shop in an hour's time!" In summer, with what envious glances they followed the fortunate children who, in the heat of the day, would be rushing towards the sea, the beach and liberty, while they were confined to the church or the counter of their father's grocery store.

Pavel Jegorovich's shop opened, summer and winter alike, at five in the morning and did not close before eleven at night. It was here that the three eldest boys spent all the time not taken up by church or school. The shop not only supplied drink, but stocked a large variety of other goods. The sign above its door announced: 'Tea, sugar, coffee and other colonial products. To take away or consume on the premises': thereby clearly proclaiming the existence of the cellar, well-known to regular customers, in which the inevitable vodka lay alongside wines from the Crimea. In the shop itself was crammed the strangest assortment of merchandise: cases of tea, jars of ointment, waistcoat buckles, scent, wicks for oil-lamps, laxatives, medicinal herbs, figs, olives, macaroni, rice, coffee, candles and devotional articles. In the evening, the ill-lit, grimy premises were transformed into a makeshift drinking club, where friends and customers lingered on into the middle of the night. The two young assistants, Andriushka and Gavriushka, would fall asleep on their feet, watched compassionately by Anton from his seat behind the till. Ill-fed, wretchedly clad and in a daze from overwork, they were made still more miserable by a succession of clouts and beatings. Pavel Jegorovich shared out these 'methods of improvement' as generously to his assistants as to his children. "Papa's coming!" one of the assistants would whisper as soon as he caught sight of Pavel Jegorovich turning the corner of the street, and Anton would sit up straighter behind the till and silence would fall as everybody waited in fear and trembling for the master's entry.

He would cast a sharp glance round before bending down to inspect Anton's ledger. And woe betide him if there was the smallest error in his additions! "Without a master, the gods weep," Pavel Jegorovich used to say. But he still preferred to spend his time in church, or the town hall or with his brother, Mitrofan. After all, weren't the boys there to help him out and take his place? Later on, Chekhov was to write:

In my childhood – I had no childhood. I was a 'proletarian', selling candles behind the counter of our shop in Taganrog. Oh, how terribly cold it was in there! The latrines were about a verst from the house on waste ground. I sometimes found myself in the dark face to face with a tramp, who was sheltering there for the night. What a fright we both got!

On days following these interminable sessions in the shop, Anton would get a nought at school for homework he had failed to prepare. And for every nought and every bad report, Anton and his brothers were mercilessly whipped.

Pavel Jegorovich's business went badly. He was an incompetent tradesman and his hardness, lack of social graces, inability to adapt himself and narrow-mindedness brought him few customers, very little profit and many troubles. There was, for instance, the affair of the exorcized oil! A rat, by some mischance, had drowned itself in a barrel of oil. Rats being impure animals, Pavel Jegorovich, as an honest tradesman and fervent Christian, hit upon the only solution that would allow him, at one and the same time, to preserve his integrity and avoid the loss of a large quantity of excellent oil. He summoned a priest and asked him to read prayers of purification over the tainted barrel. This was duly done. But the whole neighbourhood soon learnt that they were being sold impure oil, and however much it might have been exorcized and 'sanctified' the irate customers went off to buy their oil elsewhere. Pavel Jegorovich's trade could not long withstand the mixture of petty avarice, religious principles and narrow-minded obstinacy, all of which formed part of his character. He had to find more lucrative occupations for his sons. The first, most obvious step was to send them to the Greek school to learn the language of the wealthy classes and make useful contacts. So Nicholas and Anton started attending the school, presided over by a certain Nicholas Stepanovich Vuchina, a powerfully built man with a fiery-red beard, of mysterious antecedents. He himself frankly admitted that he had arrived in Taganrog without 'pants' (which he pronounced 'pantalonia').

The school, according to him, comprised five classes. But in actual fact, the one dingy, dilapidated room held five rows of desks, each row being numbered I, II, III, etc., and corresponding

[43]

to a class. The pupils in the front row spelt out aloud: alpha, beta, gamma, delta; those in the back row, strapping young men wearing striped sailors' jerseys across their broad chests, mumbled through Greek history.

The two Chekhovs were placed in the first class, that is to say, in the front row. Vuchina handed each of them a small book entitled *Neon Alphavitarion* (*New Alphabet*) saying: "Tomorrow you'll bring me 20 kopecks for each book. Now, start learning: alpha, beta, gamma . . ." He handled a ruler with the same ferocity as Pavel Jegorovich did his whip. Anton hated him on sight. When their father came to ask the director if he was satisfied with the boys' progress, Vuchina assured him they were doing very well. The two brothers both obtained 'bravions' (derived from bravo) – a kind of certificate of merit. Nicholas's bravion carried the epithet of *eskvis* (meaning pious); and Anton's *epimelis* (meaning studious).

One evening, Pavel Jegorovich invited his Greek friends around to show off his sons' newly acquired talents. Unfortunately, it soon became only too clear that neither the 'pious' one nor the 'studious' one had progressed further than alpha, beta, gamma. Pavel Jegorovich's rage was appalling to witness . . . But the upshot was that in the autumn, Anton, wearing the regulation navy-blue uniform, started attending the state school.

NOTES

1. Grandfather of Vladimir Chertkov, Tolstoy's disciple.
2. Letter to Ivan Shcheglov, 9th March, 1892.

[3]

The State School

THE Taganrog state school (gymnasium) was a large, dirty-white, ramshackle building resembling a barracks, with long, permanently dark corridors. The door of each classroom contained a spyhole, through which teachers could surreptitiously observe their pupils' behaviour.

The principal, Diakonov, nicknamed 'centipede' because of his silent tread and faculty of turning up where least expected, pestered the schoolboys with his constant moral exhortations, aimed at convincing them that their first duty lay in strict obedience to the rules.

Kramsakov, the history and geography professor, never addressed his pupils as anything but ass, imbecile or scoundrel. The Latin teacher, a Czech called Urban, spied on the pupils in the senior classes and sent in innumerable bad reports stigmatizing either their immoral conduct or their alleged revolutionary plots. Exasperated by these persecutions, the boys tried to get rid of him by depositing a charge of gunpowder at his lodgings.

The only master to stand out among these mediocre and despicable men was F. P. Pokrovsky, in charge of religious instruction, a passionate admirer of literature, and possessed of both refinement and taste. He knew how to infect his pupils with his own fiery enthusiasm for Shakespeare, Goethe and Pushkin. Pokrovsky recognized Anton's talent for humour and advised him to read Molière, Swift and Shchedrin. He also provided him with a pseudonym that was to become famous as the signature of Chekhov's early works : Chekhonté,

Pavel Jegorovich, however, nursed small hope of any practical results arising from the teaching at the school. He decided that it might well be more advantageous for Nicholas, Ivan and Anton to take courses in some kind of vocational training: that chosen for Anton was tailoring. Nicholas and Ivan were soon expelled from theirs for 'over-noisy behaviour and over-slow progress' (in the words of the official documents dismissing them). Anton, alone, was judged worthy of encouragement, and presently appeared in such tight-fitting trousers (his own handiwork) that street-urchins whistled at him and called out : "Hey, Look at the macaroni!"

[4]

Escapes

CHURCH; the shop; the Greek school; the state school; the courses in cutting and tailoring. These represented the dark side of life. But, in spite of them all, there were sunny periods, ·moments of relaxation, games, pleasure and high-spirited fun.

At the far end of Politzeiskaia Street sparkled the blue line of the sea. Near by lay the port and the pier, where Anton spent happy hours with his fishing-rod. On the outskirts of the town there was a large park, Elisabeth Park (named in honour of Alexander I's wife), where the Chekhov children went 'head-hunting' in imitation of characters from Mayne Reed and Fenimore Cooper.

Behind the Chekhovs' house stretched a broad wasteland, overrun with hemp and bramble bushes. Here, Anton lay in ambush to catch goldfinches, which he sold or bartered. It was of his own childhood that he was thinking when, in 1896, he wrote *My Life*, in which the hero sells a bird for a kopeck and observes: "All the same, I made a small profit!"

But all this was nothing in comparison with the summer holidays spent with his grandfather, the manager of Countess Platov's estates, in the village of Kniazhnaia, 60 versts from Taganrog. The journey alone was an unforgettable adventure. Sixty versts of steppe, travelling in an ox-drawn cart, a journey lasting several days, across a "fantastic country which I loved" –

Chekhov wrote later to Pleshcheev in 1888 – "where I felt at home because I knew every corner of it."

Nights spent under the dark, Ukrainian sky, in sweet-smelling hay. Wood fires lit in the steppe, picnics, games and singing, far away from strict parental supervision. Glimpses of new faces in strange, poetical surroundings. Anton, with his remarkable memory for faces, places and smells, would be able to recall them many years afterwards. He would cherish these memories for a long time, and when he finally came to make use of them in *The Steppe* (1888), they made a sensation. Everything was original and striking in this short story: the simple subject, a child's (Jegorushka-Anton's) journey across the steppe; the characters, ordinary enough, but subtly observed and brought to life with an incredible freshness; the succession of poetic descriptions presented in a way that was completely new in Russian letters; and the mixture of realistic, meticulous observation with the ability to transpose this reality into bold, imaginative pictures, sparkling with youthfulness. "Nature becomes alive if you do not scorn to compare natural phenomena with human actions," Chekhov wrote to his brother, Alexander, in 1886, two years before the publication of *The Steppe*.

The story of Jegorushka's journey is a magnificent poem in prose to the glory of the countryside, where, as a child, Chekhov had been happiest.

"I can only write from recollection and I have never described directly from nature. I need my memory to strain my theme and retain, as in the bottom of a filter, whatever is important and typical," Chekhov wrote to Suvorin (1891).

In this 'poem to the glory of the steppe', Chekhov revealed his great lyrical qualities for the first time. The man who declared that he did not like poetry ("Pushkin is the only poet I can read") nonetheless had written what amounted to a series of poems in prose, encrusted like jewels in almost every page of *The Steppe*. Poems in prose which are all variations on the same theme: the ecstasy of being alive, the joy of being young, the love of beauty – and the deep, inexpressible melancholy of

man's condition. Two separate voices seem to be speaking in
these lines:

Large shadows slip across the plain, like clouds in the sky and, in the
unknown distance, if you stare at it for any length of time, fantastic,
misty figures rise up and melt into each other. Anguish overcomes
you. But as you lift your eyes to the pale-green sky, glittering with
stars, cloudless and undefiled, you understand why nature seems to
be on the watch, afraid to stir: it is anxious and is afraid to lose a
single moment of life. Only at sea or in the steppe, on moonlit
nights, can you appreciate the immeasurable, infinite depth of the
sky. It is, at one and the same time, frightening, beautiful, and
tender: it looks down on you languidly and calls to you, and its
embrace makes your head swim ... In all that you hear, in all that
you see, you begin to perceive the triumph of beauty and youth,
the blossoming of all their powers, an intense yearning for life.
Your soul echoes back to its magnificent, austere source and you
long to fly over the steppe beside the night birds. And in this triumph
of beauty, in this very transport of happiness, you feel a tension
and nostalgia, as though the steppe were conscious of its loneliness,
conscious that its wealth and powers of inspiration may perish in
vain, unsung and of no avail to anyone.

Chekhov was only twenty-eight when he wrote these lines.
In them he conjures up memories and impressions of his adolescence. It would be impossible not to be struck by the revealing
picture, at once poetic, ardent and disillusioned which the story
paints of that 'terrible world', in the midst of which Chekhov
was to live and struggle, with a courage all the more remarkable
for seeing things exactly as they were.

"In so far as I can understand the order of things, life is
composed only of horrors, cares and pettiness, following one
after the other and overlapping each other," he wrote two years
later to M. Kiseliova, 29th September, 1886.

This is of course an outburst that should not be taken too
literally. But there is no doubt that the dualism of Chekhov's
Weltanschaung – on the one side what Tolstoy was to call the
'intoxication with life'; on the other, a realism and cruel clear-

sightedness – shows that these two opposite poles did co-exist in him and gave a unique character to all his writings.)

This same duality of outlook, a tender, lyrical quality allied to an implacable realism, is to be found again in another auto-biographical masterpiece, *The Man with the Brief-Case*, written in 1898, ten years after *The Steppe*.

While *The Steppe* was devoted to the happy hours, the holidays and the 'treasured', poetic memories deposited at 'the bottom of the filter', *The Man with the Brief-Case* stigmatized the drab life and the sad, colourless hours spent at a provincial gymnasium.)

The prototype of Belikov, the 'man with the brief-case', was the director of the Taganrog gymnasium, A. F. Diakonov. Chekhov had jotted down a few short notes for the story in his 'Diary': "The man with the brief-case, wearing galoshes, an umbrella rolled-up in its cover, a watch in its pouch, a penknife in its sheath. When lying in his coffin, he seemed to be smiling; he had realized his ideal."

Unquestionably, this story is, basically, one of the cruellest that Chekhov ever wrote. It is a dark, symbolic picture of a human being, who had become completely bereft of humanity, divorced from life and all human warmth, enclosed for ever in his 'brief-case', and anticipating the grimmest, allegorical character of Kafka. Just as *The Steppe* 'smelt of hay' and was painted in a range of pastel colours – rose, blue and green – so *The Man with the Brief-Case* is monochromatic, an etching in black and white.

The whole school, the whole town feared the small man 'with the pointed face of a ferret'. "Under the influence of men like Belikov for the last fifteen or twenty years, our town had begun to be afraid of everything. Afraid to speak above a whisper, afraid of sending letters, afraid of forming friendships, afraid of reading books, being charitable to the poor, learning to read . . . and, climax of horror, riding a bicycle. 'If a master rides a bicycle, what is there left for his pupils to do? Nothing but walk on their heads! And since the riding of bicycles has never been expressly authorized in any official memorandum, it is forbidden!' says Belikov to a colleague, whose sister he is courting. The colleague loses his temper and throws him out of the house. A month later Belikov dies.

"Now that he was lying in his coffin, the expression on his face was gentle, agreeable and almost cheerful, as though he were pleased at having been finally placed in a brief-case, which he would never have to leave. Yes, he had at last achieved his ideal!"

But though the story ends on a pessimistic note: "suffering wrongs and humiliations in silence, not daring to declare oneself openly on the side of free, honest men, lying and smiling just for the sake of a bite to eat, a warm corner and God knows what miserable little professional title, not worth a penny – no, no, one cannot go on living like that!" The poet in Chekhov could not resist inserting into this black satire a kind of musical phrase, of which the tone is wholly different:

It is already midnight. To the right one can see the village, with its main street stretching away into the distance for nearly five versts. Everything is plunged into deep, peaceful slumber. Not a movement, not a sound: it is hard to believe that nature can be so silent. When one looks at this village street on a moonlit night, this street with its izbas, its haystacks and its sleeping willows, one's soul finds peace. In these restful surroundings, protected by the shades of night from all travail, cares and afflictions, it is the picture of gentleness, sadness and beauty. And it seems as though the stars themselves are looking down on it with poignant tenderness, as though evil no longer exists in the world and all is well . . .

5

First Contacts with the Theatre

T HE great playwright of the future had his first encounter with the theatre at the age of thirteen. The play was *La Belle Hélène*. The blue backcloth representing the sky was oddly crumpled and the circular moon resembled one of the big yellow balls found in chemists' windows. But, to the young Anton, everything – sky, moon and imitation marble pillars – seemed wonderful, enchanting and imbued with poetry.

His interest in 'scalp-hunting' and catching goldfinches paled beside this new passion: he did not miss a single performance. Often he was accompanied by a schoolfriend, Vishnevski, later a celebrated member of the Moscow Art Theatre and the creator of many roles in future Chekhov plays. The two friends' devotion to the theatre waxed stronger with all the difficulties they had to overcome. Permission from the school authorities was required to attend performances and Anton frequently had to resort to disguise. He used character make-up, put on a false beard, and spectacles and, thus transformed, would strut haughtily past members of the staff sent to check on the illicit presence of any of their pupils.

To secure a good place in 'the gods', Anton would arrive two hours before the start of the performance and sit alone in the empty auditorium, lit by a single gas-mantle and looking, from his lofty position, like a black bottomless pit. Presently, the gallery would fill up with its noisy, disorderly public, chattering, laughing and crunching sunflower seeds. Anton would stare at them with immense concentration and then switch his attention to the boxes occupied by the more eminent members of the audience, for the most part wealthy Greek merchants and shipowners with their bejewelled wives. Neither the animation of the common people in 'the gods', nor the ostentatious luxury in the boxes really attracted him. What already fascinated him, and would do so all his life, was the theatre's backstage. In those dusty, tortuous passages and ill-lit dressing-rooms, mingling with the stage-hands as they busied themselves with the sets – there, amidst the noise, bustle and movement, all creative to some degree, Anton felt at home. He loved this world so far removed from the dreary philistine world of the tradespeople in the Politzeiskaia Street: this world of the theatre, which his imagination invested with all the seductive charms of poetry. The poetry of magnificent speeches splendidly delivered, the poetry of a life of liberty, the poetry of the unknown, of adventure, of the unexpected and of the nomadic existence of actors, which contrasted so radically with the static, prosaic, drowsy life of his own circle.

It was not long before Anton felt an urge to create. To be in love with the theatre was not enough: he wanted to belong to it, too. At the home of a school-fellow, Andrei Drossi, a makeshift theatre came into being. The sitting-room was divided in two by a curtain, across which parrots and a huge firebird, cut out of multicoloured materials, seemed to be flying. On one side of it was the stage – on the other, the stalls. A cupboard contained the props, the 'artistes'' costumes, wigs and make-up.

They performed Ostrovsky's *Forest*, operettas and also plays by Chekhov! Yes, it was here that the first sketches and dramatic scenes, in which young Anton caricatured his fellow citizens, were acted. These early Chekhovian essays in the theatre were written down in school exercise books and torn up and disposed of by the author at the end of each performance. Nothing remains of them, except a few distant memories.[1]

NOTE

1. Dictated by Marie Steiger, born Drossi, to A. Roskin, Moscow, 1959.

6

Anton on his Own

In 1874, the Chekhov family had moved into their own house, built by Pavel Jegorovich on a plot of land given him by his father, Jegor Mikhailovich, in Kontorskaia Street (later called Elisavetinskaia Street). All his available assets were swallowed up in the construction costs, plus five hundred roubles borrowed from the local loan society. Part of the house was let to a minor official in the commercial court, Gavriil Parfentievich Selivanov, a gambler with such extraordinary luck that, in a short time, he was able to acquire horses, a carriage and a handsome property from his winnings. His brother, Ivan Parfentievich, also a gambler, had the good fortune to marry a rich widow with estates in the Don basin. On his way back from holidays spent with Ivan Parfentievich, in June, 1875, Anton contracted his first serious illness – an acute attack of peritonitis. He stayed a night in great pain at Moissei Moisseievich's inn (so well described in *The Steppe*) and, next day, was taken home, where he lay dangerously ill for a long time. When he became a doctor, he attributed the severe haemorrhoidal troubles, from which he suffered all his life, to this first illness. Dr Strempf, the school doctor, treated him with great care and devotion, and Anton became so much attached to him that he decided to study medicine himself, if possible, as his new-found friend had done, at the Dorpat (Yuriev) University in Estonia. Then came the

ill-fated year of 1876. Anton failed to gain promotion and had
to remain on in the fifth form at the gymnasium (Russian
schools had eight forms) and Pavel Jegorovich's business affairs
went from bad to worse. Unable to repay the five hundred
roubles borrowed from the loan society, he was declared bank-
rupt. At that time, imprisonment for debt still existed. So, on
23rd April, 1876, Pavel Jegorovich secretly boarded a train for
Moscow with his two elder sons and Ivan. Three months later
his wife followed him with the two younger children, Maria
and Michael. Anton was left on his own in Taganrog. He lived
in the house which had formerly belonged to his parents but
had now passed into the hands of their lodger, Selivanov. He
was given a bed there (not a room, but a 'corner' as they called
it in Russia) and his board. In return, he had to tutor Selivanov's
nephew, Petia Kravtsov, for the entrance examination to a
military school ('the Junkers' school'). On the eve of her departure his mother had entrusted him with selling what remained of the furniture and sending the proceeds on to Moscow.
He apparently failed to attend to the matter quickly enough (he
was only sixteen) for his mother showered him with reproaches:
"We have received two letters from you," she wrote him
25th November, 1876, "full of puns and jokes, when we only
had four kopecks for food and light. We were expecting you
to send us some money, it was very disappointing, probably
you don't believe us, but Masha has no cloak and I have no
warm boots, so we just stay at home; I have no sewing-
machine to earn a little money and you have not yet said
whether you will be sending us anything soon. It is a real
calamity, write at once, for God's sake and send me some money
quickly . . . do not let me die of worry."

So the sixteen-year-old adolescent not only had to live alone,
complete his studies and earn his own living, but also to sell
such property as had been left behind in Taganrog and come
to his family's assistance. Admittedly, the singing in the church
choir, the long hours spent in the shop and the paternal chas-

tisements were over; but Anton's new life of solitude was far from easy.

He gave lessons. For a few roubles a month, he hurried to and fro through the town, from one pupil to another, his feet damp and frozen in his leaking galoshes. But he had a friend, a young Jew, Isaac Borisovich Szuliov, who was even poorer than himself. Anton became very fond of this lively, intelligent young man. He shared his earnings with him; they would go together to give lessons on the outskirts of the town beyond the level-crossing, for which they received three roubles a month, and split the princely sum between them. Later, Anton was to write that his poverty at that time afflicted him like 'a perpetual toothache'. His friend Isaac Szuliov moved to Kharkov some years later, where he attended the university, but died before graduating. Anton contrived to survive.

On Sundays and feast-days he took refuge in the municipal library, where he plunged into a medley of Beecher-Stowe, Cervantes, Goncharov, Turgenev, Belinski, Bockle, Schopenhauer, as well as comic papers: *The Alarm Clock* and *The Cricket*. He and his friend, Andrei Drossi, would spend hours in the recently opened reading-room (23rd March, 1876) forgetting all about lunch, completely absorbed in their books.

The years between 1876–1879, which he spent in solitude in Taganrog, are the least known, the most obscure in Chekhov's life. All that remains of them are a few rare documents, some scattered recollections of his friends and a number of letters to his family.

Allusions to the difficulties he was undergoing occur infrequently in these letters, which already display his talent for comedy. He writes to his cousin, Michael Chekhov, 8th February, 1877:

I am your benevolent Brüder, who possesses a single Schwester and also four real Brüder, plus two Brüder twice removed and another Schwester twice removed; who therefore possesses everything, in short, except money and commonsense.

It is, unfortunately, impossible to translate the innumerable witticisms and puns with which Anton's letters to his brothers, cousins and friends are studded. His verbal virtuosity is remarkable and, at the beginning of his career, was one of the chief factors in his success. But Chekhov's youthful letters are not merely amusing, gay and whimsical; in addition to his sense of humour, they reveal his deep seriousness, his reflective nature and his precocious sensibility. About a year after his mother's move to Moscow, knowing the financial difficulties and loneliness of spirit against which this gentle, weak and passive creature must be struggling, he wrote to his cousin Michael, 10th May, 1877:

> Be kind and go on comforting my mother, who is a physical and moral wreck. Her nature is such that any moral help she receives from an outsider has a strong and beneficial effect on her. There is no one dearer to me than my mother in this wicked world, which is why you will be doing your humble servant a great favour in comforting his mother, half-dead from grief.

He seems to have forgotten the harsh treatment he received at his father's hands and all the suffering endured throughout a childhood "which consisted of nothing but suffering", when in his anxiety over his family, vegetating in the greatest misery in Moscow, he wrote to the same Michael Chekhov on 29th July the same year:

> My father and mother are unique to me in this world and there is nothing I would not do for them. If I achieve any success it will be thanks to them, thanks to these worthy people. Their boundless love for their children is beyond all praise and wipes out all their failings which may have resulted from their exceptionally hard life.

This letter, which Chekhov wrote at the age of seventeen,

could have equally well been written by him ten or twenty years later. The feelings expressed in it remained unchanged. What is striking is the precocious wisdom, the consciousness of his responsibilities displayed by this adolescent, who was soon to take his younger brother, Michael, to task in a very 'Chekhovian' manner:

There is one thing that displeases me in your letter. Why do you call yourself 'your worthless, insignificant little brother'? Are you not aware that the only possible place in which you should be conscious of your insignificance and mediocrity is perhaps in the presence of God, in the presence of the spirit, beauty and nature, but never in the presence of your fellow men. Before your fellow men, you must always remain conscious of your own dignity. (6th or 8th April, 1879.)

Four months after writing this letter, Anton joined his family in Moscow. He had passed his examinations, obtained his diploma and managed to get a grant of twenty-five roubles a month, sufficient to allow him to continue his studies at the university. He had decided to become a doctor.

On 8th August, 1879, he arrived in Moscow with two friends, Saveliev and Zembulatov, who were to lodge with the Chekhovs.

[PART TWO]

Moscow

1879–1892

I belong to Moscow for ever.
CHEKHOV

[1]

Background

CHEKHOV spent the years of his early manhood in Moscow; difficult years to begin with, but happy and active ones, too, particularly after his graduation from the university, when he very soon became a well-known writer. Moscow and the surrounding landscape, so characteristic of Central Russia, with its insidious poetry, which does not fully reveal itself at first glance but gradually pervades and captivates, cast a strong spell on Chekhov. Like his friend, Levitan, the painter, Chekhov was to become the poet of the area around Moscow and was in love with the town itself, for which later, when ill and condemned to live in the Crimea, he would never cease to pine.

He spent thirteen years of his life in Moscow. He had seen the ancient capital of Russia for the first time at the age of seventeen. Living alone in Taganrog after his parents' departure, he had finally managed to find the money for a short holiday in the spring of 1877, and Moscow had enchanted him. He became a lifelong devotee of the Kremlin, the picturesque banks of the Moskva River, the innumerable churches with their gilded cupolas and the old streets winding their way past low wooden houses and dilapidated chapels, with hedges overtopped by huge clumps of syringa, hawthorn and lilac. The large semi-Asiatic village that Moscow then was conquered the young man's heart at first sight, and it was a love that never faded.

Now he was nineteen, adoring 'his town'. But the conditions in which he found himself at the beginning of his stay were such as inevitably brought him into contact with the seamiest side of life. When he rejoined them, his family were living in the dark basement (actually, little more than a cellar) of a house adjoining the Church of St Nicholas, in Grachevka Street. The basement was damp as well as dark : the only illumination came from small ventilators, through which one could just catch a glimpse of passing feet. Wearing an old overcoat of her husband's, Evgenia Jacovlevna attended to the hardest of the domestic chores, in a constant flood of tears and complaints. The thirteen-year-old Maria did not go to school, since there was no money to pay even the registration fee, but, like her younger brother, Michael, led the life of a servant. She did the washing, ironing, mending and shopping. The two eldest boys, Alexander and Nicholas, gave a few lessons, contributed to minor, illustrated papers and reluctantly shared their meagre earnings with their parents. Nicholas, who possessed considerable talent for both painting and music, was lazy and a drunkard. Alexander, the eldest, erudite, extremely gifted and a skilled inventor, was a man of weak, unreliable character. The fourth son, Ivan, the least talented and intelligent member of the family, was taciturn and stubborn, but a hard worker, and earned a few roubles by giving private lessons while studying to obtain his teacher's diploma.

It was a dismal household to which Anton returned after three years' separation. But he was infinitely happy to find himself back again in the midst of the family, to which he was so deeply and indissolubly attached. Wise, practical and provident, he had brought two of his friends, future medical students like himself, from Taganrog, to be boarders at Evgenia Jacovlevna's, who would help to raise the standard of living and, at the same time, provide youthful high-spirits and gaiety. The Chekhovs were soon able to leave the dank, murky basement for more comfortable lodgings, though still situated in one of the least savoury quarters of the town, close to the notorious

Sobolev cul-de-sac and its rows of brothels which were immortalized by Chekhov in his story *The Crisis* (1888), which
raised the insoluble problem of prostitution.

In contrast to the tragic fallen specimens of humanity from
the cul-de-sac, by whom the young Chekhov was surrounded,
there was the motley crowd of bird-sellers and dealers in various
breeds of animals, which thronged the nearby Trubnaia Square,
so poetically described in his story of the same name.[1] It was
in this quarter of the town, with its brothels, markets (the
Sukharevka market, one of the most picturesque and busiest in
Moscow, frequented by pedlars, hand craftsmen, tramps and
sharpers, was close by, too) and low haunts of every kind that
Chekhov was to live until 1885. The family then moved to the
peaceful, remote suburb of Zamoskvorechie (to the Klimenkov
house in Bolshaia Iakimenka Street, facing the Church of Ivan
the Warrior) and finally, on 27th August, 1886, settled down in
the now-famous house, belonging to Dr Korneev, in Sadovaia
Street, in the suburb of Kudrino.[2]

It was here that Chekhov spent what was perhaps the happiest period of his life: the four years preceding his journey to
Sakhalin in 1890. Chekhov nicknamed the house in Sadovaia-
Kudrinskaia Street the 'commode' with characteristic Chekhovian accuracy, for the small red-brick baroque building does, in
fact, closely resemble an antique chest-of-drawers. It is equally
possible that he recalled the same nickname given by Pushkin to
the Moscow house near the Povrovski Gate owned by the
Trubetskoy Princes where the poet had been a frequent guest.

Chekhov used jokingly to draw attention to the democratic
'red' colour of his new abode. This unusual colour stood out
still more against the green of the shrubs and solitary tree in the
small garden in front of the house which was surrounded by a
high wooden fence.

Alexander Chekhov had moved to St Petersburg some years
before. Nicholas trailed from one furnished room to another.
Ivan had been living on his own, and his father had settled
down close by him. So it was Anton, his mother, his sister and

his brother Michael – the rest of the family – who occupied the two-storied house. Anton Pavlovich's study and bedroom lay on the ground floor, to the left of the front door. The study, despite its two windows looking out on the yard, was dark and Chekhov often retired to work in his small bedroom with its bay-window looking out on the garden. Adjoining this bedroom was that of his brother Michael, who was reading law at the time and acting as his unpaid secretary.

On the first floor were the sitting-room, dining-room and Evgenia Jacovlevna's and Masha's bedrooms. Thus, altogether, the Chekhovs occupied seven rooms. The modest, narrow dining-room and unassuming but pleasant and light sitting-room, with its yellow covers, piano, green plants and paintings by Nicholas Chekhov on the walls, were to see many of the great names in Russian literature and art pass through them: Grigorovich, Pleshcheev, Korolenko, Tchaikovsky, Levitan . . .

NOTES

1. *In Moscow in the Trubnaia Square*, 1883.
2. Converted, in 1954, into the Chekhov Museum.

[2]

The Chekhov Children

THERE were, as we have seen, six of them: Alexander, Nicholas, Anton, Ivan, Maria and Michael.

The eldest, Alexander (1855–1913), was a man of exceptional talents. With an erudition extending to natural sciences, philosophy and literature, he was an accomplished linguist, an indefatigable inventor and jack-of-all-trades, a journalist and writer, sparkling with wit and brimful of ideas that were often ingenious but more often preposterous. But despite all his gifts, he remained a brilliant failure. An incurable alcoholic, weak, unreliable and a pathological liar, he earned a precarious livelihood by his wits and died with only one achievement to his credit: that of being the father of a famous man – the younger son of his second marriage[1] – Michael Alexandrovich Chekhov (1891–1955) a pupil of Stanislavski's, an exceptionally fine actor and mimic, and the author of an absorbing book of memoirs, *The Life of an Actor*.

Nicholas (1858–1889) was Anton's favourite brother. Of an artistic temperament and possessing a real talent for both music and painting, he was a kind, gentle and generous man, but, like his elder brother, also incurably weak, lazy and an alcoholic. In Moscow, he attended the School of Painting, Sculpture and Architecture, where he became friends with several young painters, among them the famous landscape-artist-to-be, Isaac

[67]

Levitan. Nicholas's dissipated life, his sudden disappearances, his bouts of drunkenness, his inability to make any sustained effort and his indolence and casual attitude to life, were a constant source of worry to Anton. For he had a deep and very close relationship with his brother. It was Nicholas who had brought him into the circle of young Moscow painters; Nicholas who had introduced him to Levitan, who was to become his great friend; and Nicholas who helped him to write by sitting down at the piano and playing, with great feeling and an intuitionally lyrical touch, his favourite works: Chopin's preludes and nocturnes, Beethoven's *Moonlight sonata* and Liszt's second *Hungarian* Rhapsody. But Nicholas's budding talents never came to fruition.

He did a large number of drawings (potboilers) for various humorous magazines to which Anton also contributed, and left behind a few portraits, which bear witness to his genuine ability – in particular, one of his brother Anton and one of Levitan – as well as some other canvases, most of them unfinished, displaying a sentimental, human approach to his subjects (*The Young Girl in Blue, Poverty, The Seamstress*). His disorderly mode of life rapidly aggravated the lung disease from which he suffered and, in 1889, at the age of thirty-one, he died of galloping consumption. "Everyone is sobbing. Anton is the only one not weeping; a bad sign," Alexander Chekhov wrote to his father, 19th June, 1889. Nevertheless, it was Anton who was most affected by his brother's death. The loss of his favourite brother, that weak, poetical and affectionate young man, was one of the reasons which led to his extraordinary decision to visit Sakhalin Island.

Anton's third brother, Ivan (1861–1922), just a year younger than himself, was the only one of the Chekhov children without a glimmer of talent. Taciturn, obstinate, dogged and a hard worker, Ivan was the complete antithesis of his restless, imaginative and undisciplined elder brothers. At a very early age, he earned a few roubles by giving private tuition, having already decided to lead a steady, well-ordered life. ("Do whatever Vania tells you. He is a serious boy and has character. He is one of the most respectable and reliable members of our family. One can be confident in his future. He is honest and a hard worker" – this is Anton's description of him in one of his letters.) He became a teacher and remained one all his life. Physically, in his features and his smile, he bore the closest resemblance to his famous brother.

Chekhov's only sister, Maria (or Masha, Ma-pa and Ma-fa, as Levitan called her) (1863–1957), played an important role in the writer's life. She was at one and the same time matter-of-fact, practical and drawn to the arts. This explains why as well as attending the Rajevski university for women, gaining her diploma and becoming a history and geography teacher at the Rajevski school, she also studied painting, principally as a pupil of Levitan's, and throughout her life took an interest in the theatre, literature and all the other artistic manifestations of her time. Sweet-tempered and firm, efficient, highminded and full of commonsense, she had an unbounded admiration for Anton. To him, she was a friend, a prop and an invaluable helper, and it was largely because she could not bear to be separated from him and wished to devote herself to his welfare that she gave up all idea of marriage. Anton had a deep affection for her and trusted her completely. It was she who became his executor; who edited the first volume of his letters (in 1916); and who founded the Chekhov Museum in Yalta and acted as its Keeper until her death. Her letters to her brother are curious and fascinating: full of facts, figures and practical advice, they are just as childish, matter-of-fact and disappointing as those written to Dostoevsky by his faithful and efficient wife, Anna Grigorievna. But under this superficial dryness, what a wealth of self-sacrifice and endless devotion !

The last of the Chekhov children, Michael (1865–1936), was gay, witty and occasionally frivolous, and at the same time extremely gifted. A lawyer by profession, he was an excellent black-and-white artist, a journalist and a translator, as well as a writer of some perceptive memoirs.

Being the youngest of the five brothers, he was the one to spend the most time in Anton's company. Lively, obliging, likeable and constantly joking, he distracted and amused his elder brother. He also had the advantage of being an imaginative cook, and the gourmet in Anton greatly appreciated his culinary inventions (his *zakuski*, in particular). Having acted as Anton's secretary and general factotum for a number of years, Michael subsequently became one of his best biographers. It is to his excellent memory and skilful pen that we owe many valuable books and drawings. These memoirs and sketches reconstruct many forgotten scenes and details, but, above all, recreate the atmosphere surrounding this highly unusual family, this charming 'Chekhia', as the poet Pleshcheev called them, this amazing clan, from which the writer derived one or other of his traits.

If one analyses Chekhov's character one perceives that buried and condensed in it are elements scattered among the other members of his family: Alexander's scientific propensities and literary aspirations; Nicholas's poetic feeling, artistic gifts and 'humane talent'; Ivan's tenacity and resolute determination; Masha's commonsense and efficiency; and Michael's humour, vivacity, vitality and appetite for life. All these traits, sublimated, elaborated, directed towards a high purpose and maintained by immense will-power and talent, all these traits, spread among the various members of the Chekhov tribe, become to some extent perfected in the person of Anton Pavlovich.

One of the first portraits of him shows him at the age of fourteen – in 1874 – in his school uniform, with neat, closely cropped hair. The expression on his still infantile face is strikingly tense and there is an alert, probing look about the slightly narrowed eyes. The features in the childish oval project an impression of great strength; a strength combined with a feeling of quiet determination. As a young man, particularly before Nicholas's death and the descent into hell represented by his stay on Sakhalin, Chekhov was gay, lively and sparkling with wit and humour. But if he knew how to laugh and make others laugh, he also knew how to work with immense concentration, work to become a man of all-round attainments, both an artist and of service to his fellow men. He pursued these objectives with the most praiseworthy perseverance, intelligence and unflagging zest, for he was haunted by an awareness that there was so much to be done. He reveals it in his famous letter of 7th January, 1889, to Suvorin, written with deliberate objectivity :

> What writers from the ranks of nobility receive 'gratuitously', by birthright, the commoners buy at the price of their youth. So, try to write the story of a young man, son of a serf, a one-time shop assistant, choir-boy, secondary school boy and university student; brought up to fawn on and kiss the hands of priests; having to submit to other people's whims; grateful for every crust of bread; thrashed time after time; running hither and thither, miserably shod, to give a few lessons; quarrelsome; taking pleasure in torturing animals; a hypocrite in the eyes of God and his fellow men, from no necessity but purely from the awareness of his own nonentity. Describe how this young man strives, drop by drop, to free himself from the slave within him, and how, on waking up one fine morning he realizes that it is no longer the blood of a slave that courses through his veins, but the blood of a human being.

There lies a whole curriculum vitae. Few men have followed one with such relentless determination; few men have succeeded in disciplining themselves, 'training' and recreating themselves as Chekhov did from a very early age. "To educate oneself . . . requires ceaseless, unremitting work, night and day. Every hour counts . . ." he was already writing to his idle brother Nicholas in 1886.

And, long before this, when he was only nineteen, as we have already recorded, he wrote to his brother Michael : "In front of men one should be conscious of one's dignity."

Conscious of his dignity as a man. This was his fine theme. That human dignity treated with contempt all through his unhappy childhood and the poverty-stricken, lonely years of his adolescence; that dignity debased by the example of his own family, with the narrow-minded, coarse tyrant of a father, and weak, drunken brothers; by his native town in which he did not know a single honest man; by all the primitive, disorderly, ugly life that surrounded him.

To restore man's dignity, to indicate his weaknesses and meannesses and show him that he lived badly and could and must live better – this was Chekhov's real aim. But to achieve it, what a troubled road he had to follow, a narrow road built of incessant effort, endless hard work and constant self-improvement. For he never sought to teach, moralize or preach. What he set out to do was to suggest and to demonstrate by his own personal example what a man could become by sheer determination, with no outside help from anyone, even God. An agnostic and sceptic, Chekhov did not rely on any support, supernatural or human, only on his own abilities, his intelligence and his will-power. The impact of his brother's death; a feeling of dissatisfaction despite the considerable literary success that had already come his way; the desire for self-improvement and mental discipline ("I am just a lazy southerner"); and above all, the desire to come into contact with the most wretched human conditions, to be acquainted with them in order to find a remedy for them: all this explains Chekhov's social activities and his decision, surprising at first sight even to his close friends, to visit Sakhalin Island.

NOTE

1. To the governess of his two sons, Nicholas and Anton.

[3]

Studies

As soon as he got to Moscow, Chekhov enrolled in the medical faculty. He completed his studies in June, 1884. Almost at once (in October of the same year), he embarked on a large work, *The History of Medicine in Russia*, which he intended to present as the thesis for his doctor's degree. In all, he listed, perused and annotated more than a hundred-and-twelve titles. His selection of these text-books, his approach to them and his copious, handwritten notes give evidence of his scientific, methodical turn of mind, and the breadth and depth of his outlook. But he finally flinched before the necessity of consulting archives, and all the historical re-search involved. What interested him was the present; what fascinated him were his contemporaries and the existing – not past – state of affairs in his country. This was certainly the underlying reason for his abandoning the projected historical work and replacing it with his up-to-date *The Island of Sakhalin*. In a letter to Serge Diaghilev on 20th October, 1901, Chekhov confirms the intention he formed ten years earlier to substitute this book for the other as the thesis he proposed to write at the end of his medical studies. *The Island of Sakhalin* is a very un-usual work, being a scientific study presented in an artistic form. The scientific method, dear to Chekhov, is scrupulously observed; the intimate combination of artist, psychologist and sociologist had an extraordinary outcome: seldom read and

generally underrated, *The Island of Sakhalin* is one of Chekhov's greatest claims to fame.

"My knowledge of natural sciences and scientific methods
has made me careful and I have always tried, when possible,
to take into consideration the scientific data. When it was not
possible, I preferred not to write at all," Chekhov wrote on
11th October, 1899, to one of his former fellow students, Dr
Rassolimo, a well-known neurologist, who had asked him for a
brief autobiography.

Tolstoy believed that Chekhov would have been an even
greater writer had he not been a doctor: "Medicine cramped
him." But Chekhov himself was far from sharing this opinion.
As a young man, in 1888 he had expressed his innermost feelings
to Suvorin, in a figurative manner:

Medicine is my lawful wife,
literature my mistress. When I tire of the one, I spend the
night with the other. As long as it does not become a regular habit, it is not humdrum and neither of them suffers
from my infidelity. If I did not have my medical pursuits,
I should find it difficult to devote my random thoughts and
spare time to literature.

At the time he wrote this letter, Chekhov was already a well-
known writer. It was, in fact, the year in which *The Steppe*
appeared; the year, too, in which, inspired by his medical studies
and the firsthand information gained during the period spent in
the suburbs of Trubnaia and Sretenka, he wrote and published
The Crisis: the subject of this story had been in the back of his
mind for a long time when, in 1888, the novelist Vsevolod
Garshin, a man to whom Chekhov was deeply attached, com-
mitted suicide by throwing himself down the well of a staircase.
Pleshcheev and Grigorovich undertook the completion of a
miscellany in memory of this fine, highly sensitive man, who
had died because he could not bear life in the society in which
he lived; his "soul ached too much from it".

Chekhov was asked to contribute to the book: he wrote to Pleshcheev on 15th September, 1888:

> I love men like Garshin with all my heart and consider it my duty to testify publicly to my feelings. I have a subject for a story: a man of Garshin's type, out of the ordinary, straightforward and deeply sensitive, finds himself in a brothel for the first time in his life. Since one should speak seriously of serious things, everything in this story will be called by its real name. Perhaps I shall succeed in writing it in such a way that it will produce, as I want it to do, a harrowing impression!

He set to work, drawing his inspiration from two exceptionally fine men: the dead Garshin and the novelist Gleb Uspensky. The latter, like Garshin, was extremely highminded and almost morbidly sensitive. A talented writer, he was one of the best examples of the intellectual elite of his time. But his hypersensitivity led him to experience the social injustices of Russian life so intensely, and become increasingly conscious of the depth of the abyss, growing ever deeper between the educated classes and the popular masses, that his brain was unable to withstand it: during the last ten years of his life, he became the victim of a mental illness that took the form of a split personality. All that was good in him he called by his first name, Gleb; all that was confused and melancholy, by his patronymic, Ivanovich. Like Garshin, Uspensky was too weak and vulnerable to be able to struggle and survive.

In Chekhov's story, Mayer, a medical student, Rybnikov, a student from the School of Arts, Sculpture and Architecture, and a Law student, Vassiliev (a "young man like Garshin"), visit the brothels in the Sobolev cul-de-sac. When Vassiliev left his home "it had been snowing and nature as a whole was in the grip of this fresh-fallen snow. The air smelt of snow and one could hear it crunch under one's feet. The ground, the roots, the trees and the benches on the avenue, everything was mellow, white, young; even the houses seemed different than they had been the day before; the light from the street-lamps more vivid; the air, more transparent; the noise of the carriages, muffled; and one's soul, penetrated by the light, cold air, was invaded by a feeling strongly akin to a white, fresh, filmy snow."

The students go into several of the brothels. Vassiliev is moved, embarrassed and ashamed. As he enters the various ante-rooms, where he seems to see the same drowsy porter sprawling in an armchair, he cannot help wondering: "What had this wretched, simple-minded Russian gone through and suffered before fate had landed him here? Where had he been before, what had he done? What lies ahead for him? Is he married? Where is his mother and does she know that he is a lackey here?" In every brothel, Vassiliev's attention is first caught by this porter in the ante-room. As Chekhov explains:

> There are talents such as writing, acting and painting, but Vassiliev had a special talent – *the human talent*: he possessed a magnificent, highly developed feeling in general. Just as a good actor reflects the movements and voice of others, Vassiliev can reflect in his heart the suffering of others ... It excites him, exults him and induces a state of ecstasy ... What he experienced when he felt that the problem (of prostitution) was solved was very close to inspiration. He cried, laughed and babbled ...

This passage is all-important in reaching an understanding of a certain aspect in Chekhov himself. There, as in other stories written wholly objectively, he lays bare a facet of his soul, he expresses himself under the guise of anonymity. He did it in *The Steppe* and in *The Man with the Brief-Case*, and in *The Crisis*; he was to do it the following year in *A Sad Story*, and again later in his plays and in *Ward No. 6*, *My Life*, *The Lady with the Dog* and *The Bishop*. The student in *The Crisis* is young Anton Pavlovich, with his experience as a medical student and a humble journalist at grips with the uglier sides of life; he speaks of them coldly, and impersonally in his reports and articles, but in his fiction he indulges himself in a passionate lyricism. The following Chekhovian avowal appears in *The Crisis*: "The true apostolate does not consist of sermons, but of acts." And, after describing the horrors of the Sobolev cul-de-sac, the author exclaims: "How could snow fall on this dead-end? Would that these houses were damned!"

The *leit-motiv* of snow, which runs through the black picture of the lower depths of Moscow, is a characteristic Chekhovian device. *The Crisis* is a musical composition in which the central theme is parallelled or framed by secondary, lyrical passages, which serve to underline what the author wishes to lay down, without insistence or emphasis, but persuasively, evocatively and poetically. This *leit-motiv* of white, virginal snow recurs several times, superimposed on the harsh, realistic picture of a tainted locality. Chekhov was sadly disappointed that none of the contemporary critics or men of letters noticed what Grigoro-vich was alone in perceiving: on 27th December, 1888, he wrote to Chekhov: "I was furious that no one appreciated the sentence 'How could snow fall on this dead-end?'; and I was told that there were poets present at the first reading!"

"Everybody heaped praises on my *Crisis*," Chekhov wrote bitterly to Suvorin on 23rd December, 1888, "but only Grigoro-vich noticed the description of the snow."

Earlier on 11th November, 1888, he had reproached him with: "Why does your paper never mention prostitution? It is a terrible scourge. Our Sobolev cul-de-sac is a veritable slave-market!"

[4]

Early Writings

WHILE engaged on his medi-
cal studies, Chekhov earned his living and that of his family
by writing. This is how Suvorin describes Chekhov's first literary
efforts :

"He began to write while he was still a student. His parents,
who had several sons and a daughter to support, led a very
precarious existence. Chekhov was greatly distressed at having
insufficient money to buy a cake for his mother's birthday. He
wrote a short story. It was published and the birthday was
properly celebrated with the few roubles it brought in. From
then onwards, he became the breadwinner of the family."[1]

It was in 1880, at the age of twenty, that Chekhov saw his
first work in print in a humorous magazine, *The Dragonfly*. The
piece, entitled *Letter of a Landowner in the Don District to
His Learned Neighbour*, was a very unpretentious one, which
its author did not include later in his *Complete Works*. But,
like so many that were to follow it, the story had no other aim
than to earn a few badly needed roubles. At first, Chekhov made
twenty roubles a month, then fifty, then seventy-five. His facility was remarkable. He adapted himself to all requirements
and every taste. He sold more and more of his writings as time
went on : nine stories in 1880, thirteen in 1881 and, in 1885,
achieved the figure of twenty-nine stories, articles, interviews
and various topical reports. He also wrote on the theatre, which

occupied considerable space in the critical columns of the humorous reviews to which he contributed (*The Alarm Clock, Fragments, The Spectator, The Dragonfly*). Since his adolescence, Chekhov had loved attending theatrical rehearsals and wandering about back-stage: later, on 6th March, 1900, he advised Gorki to do the same: "To write a play, you must go to the theatre, see it from close-to. By frequently attending rehearsals, you will acquire the knack more easily. Nothing enables you to understand stage conditions better than the disorder that reigns at rehearsals." Among the young Chekhov's humorous articles, written under his pseudonym of Antosha Chekhonté, was this one, devoted to Sarah Bernhardt, when she was on tour in Russia in 1881 :

"Two days ago, Moscow knew of only four elements; today she cannot stop talking of a fifth. She only knew of seven wonders of the world; now, every thirty seconds, she proclaims the existence of an eighth! The *artiste* has become our *idée fixe*. A sort of primitive folly reigns in our heads! But we, ourselves, are far from admiring Sarah Bernhardt's talent. She lacks ... the flame that alone can move us to tears. Highly intelligent, this lady possesses an extremely effective technique, she knows the human heart, she has accumulated all possible and imaginable knowledge, she turns her heroines into women as remarkable as herself. Her aim is to strike, to astonish and to dazzle."[2] Her acting is "a well-learnt lesson, but smacks less of genius than of immensely powerful hard work. Compared to her, Russian actors, 'full of soul', are lazy, scarcely work at all and lack culture." Such criticism, coming from a young man of twenty-one, shows a surprisingly precocious maturity of thought. This precocity, this independence in his opinions are strikingly evident in all that Antosha Chekhonté came to write later, be it in his articles, letters or in fiction.

The young author's first book was published in Moscow in 1884 at his own expense. It was called *Stories of Melpomena* and consisted of six short stories (*He and She; Two Scandals; The Baron; The Vengeance; Artists' Wives* and *The Tragedian*).

Only one of them, *The Tragedian*, found favour in the author's eyes and was included in later editions of his works. Chekhov had already been a regular contributor for two years to *Fragments*, a successful humorous review, published in St Petersburg. Its editor was Nicholas Leikin, a writer of no great talent, but widely read and an excellent businessman.

At a corner of a table, in the noisy dining-room where his parents and friends were eating, drinking and laughing, Anton wrote his first short stories and newspaper articles: accounts of trials, burglaries, autopsies, street accidents and various other news items. All this enriched his experience, provided plots and gave him food for thought. People, unimportant facts and happenings that others would not even have mentioned, interested and attracted Anton. Subjects for stories abounded, for he found himself able to write, regardless, on any subject. "One day," his brother Michael reported, "somebody said in front of him that it was difficult to find material for stories. 'What nonsense!' Anton exclaimed. 'I can write about anyone or anything . . .' His eyes sparkled, he glanced round for some object or other and caught sight of an ashtray: 'There, now! Look at that! Tomorrow I could write a story called *"The Ashtray"*.'"

The writer Telekhov tells how, at about this same period, he was sitting with Chekhov in a pub mainly frequented by carters and night-workers. "We sat down at a table covered with a dirty-grey damp tablecloth. We were given lemon tea and a huge kettle full of boiling water. But the slices of lemon smelt oddly of onion. 'It's splendid!' Anton Pavlovich said delightedly. 'You complain of not being able to find literary subjects. But isn't this one? It has all the material for a short story.'

"We were facing a blank, dirty wall, smeared with flaking paint. There were black stains on it and, at a certain level, large, greasy marks left by carters' and coachmen's heads, from the thick coating of oil with which they plastered down their hair at that time. It was this wall that led us into a discussion on art. 'How can you lack subjects?' Anton Pavlovich persisted.

'Everything is a subject – you can dig them up by the spadeful everywhere. Take that wall – at first sight, it seems to hold no interest whatsoever. But if you look carefully, you'll find something worth while about it – something that no one has yet noticed. Well, describe that something. I assure you, an excellent story can emerge from it . . . And isn't that a subject over there?' he asked, looking through the dirty windowpane behind which dawn was beginning to break. 'Take a look: don't you see that monk over there, who is going round begging for a new bell for his monastery? Don't you already feel an excellent subject coming to a head? There is something tragic about that black monk against the pale background of the dawn.' "[3]

But Chekhov, himself, was unimpressed by this facility of his which bordered on the miraculous. He attached no importance to what he wrote. "I shall be sending you my literary excrements on Sunday," he wrote to Leikin in 1884. He only attached real importance to his medical studies. His 'literary excrements' at that period were strictly utilitarian, designed only to enable him to feed his family.

Nevertheless, from the following year, 1885, onwards, his reputation grew steadily. On 18th July, a story of his called *The Hunter* appeared in No. 194 of the *St Petersburg Gazette*. It aroused the enthusiasm of the novelist Dmitri Vassilievich Grigorovich,[4] who drew Alexei Suvorin's[5] attention to A. Chekonté. On 27th January, 1886, *Sadness* appeared, and Suvorin published *The Sorceress* and *Agatha* in his paper on 8th and 15th March respectively.

On 25th March, Chekhov received a letter from Grigorovich, which took his breath away and was a landmark in his life.

What had he done up till then? Admittedly, he had slaved away, attending courses, working in the hospital, passing examinations, giving lessons, contributing to newspapers and taking his first steps in the literary field. But he had never *really* regarded himself as a writer; rather as an amateur, endowed with a remarkable facility and an unusually fertile imagination, who wrote little stories, which amused him and sometimes excited him, but, most important of all, enabled him to live. When he went to St Petersburg at the end of December, 1885, he met the members of the editorial staff of the *St Petersburg Gazette*. To his great astonishment, he was received "like the Shah of Persia". He was astounded by this warm welcome. "Everybody invited me and flattered me . . . I was embarrassed because so far I had written casually and negligently." (Letter to Alexander Chekhov, 4th January, 1886.)

Two days before, on 2nd January, 1886, Suvorin had asked Chekhov to contribute regularly to the *Novoye Vremia* (*New Time*), which meant that, from then on, his stories appeared in the most influential Russian daily newspaper. And then came Grigorovich's letter:

Highly esteemed Anton Pavlovich, about a year ago I happened to read a story in the *St Petersburg Gazette*: I no longer remember the title; I only remember being struck by some passages of outstanding originality and, in particular, by a remarkable accuracy, by the verisimilitude of the characters and the descriptions of nature.

From then on, I read everything that appeared under the signature of Chekhonté, though I was inwardly vexed with a man who had so little opinion of himself as to resort to the use of a pseudonym. Having once read your work I strongly advised Suvorin and Burenin[6] to follow my example. They listened to me and now have no more doubts than I have about your *very real talent*, a talent which puts you in the highest rank of today's younger writers. If I speak of your talent, I do so with deep conviction. I am sixty-five, but I still cherish so much love for literature, I follow its progress with such eagerness and I experience such pleasure when I come across something in it which is vivid and gifted that, as you can see, I could not restrain myself from stretching out both my hands to you! But I have not finished yet. What I want to add is this: due to the varied qualities of your unquestionable talent, the truth of the inner analysis, the mastery of the descriptions (the blizzard, the night, Agatha's background, etc.) and the plastic sense which sketches in a few lines a perfect picture of a cloud growing dim against the background of the sunset, "like a cinder on coals that are burning themselves up", you are destined, I am certain of it, to write some excellent, really artistic works. You will be morally very guilty if you do not fulfil these expectations. But this is particularly important: you must respect a talent which is rarely bestowed on one. Avoid all hurried work!

And Grigorovich goes on to beg Chekhov to give up his journalism; to devote himself to producing something of importance and to renounce his pseudonym and sign the next collection of his stories, *Motley Tales*, already in the press, with his own name.

It is obvious enough, even without this letter from Grigorovich, that Antosha Chekhonté would have become Anton Chekhov. But the 'awakening' effect of the letter is understandable. The year 1886 marks a dividing point in Chekhov's career. In every man's life there comes a moment when he sets about taking stock, tries to find out and understand what he really is. Particularly, when he is a man of genius. The gay, brilliant, witty Antosha Chekhonté lived in an eddy of work, worry and success. A deep interior silence fell on him after he received Grigorovich's letter. Mentally closing his eyes, he had a vision of himself as he had been, as he no longer was and as he no longer wanted to be. On the last day of March that year he replied to Grigorovich:

Your letter struck me like a thunderbolt. I nearly burst into tears, I was overwhelmed and I feel now that it has left a profound impression on my soul ... It is as if I were drunk ... I have not the strength

to judge whether this high reward is deserved or not. I
can only repeat: I am overwhelmed.

If I possess a gift which should be respected, and I
believe the sincerity of your kind thoughts, it is one I have
not respected up till now. I felt that I possessed this gift,
but had got into the habit of believing it to be mediocre . . .
During the last five years of my vagabondage from paper
to paper, I grew used to viewing my work with contempt,
and put my hand to anything that came my way! That
is the first reason for my carelessness. The second one is
that I am a doctor and immersed in medicine up to my
neck. The proverb about the two hares that one cannot
pursue simultaneously has never kept anyone from sleeping as much as it has me. Up till now, I have treated my
literary work with great levity, carelessness and lack of
thought. I cannot recollect a single one of my stories on
which I spent more than a day, and *The Hunter*, which
you liked, was written as I lay on the bench of a bathing
establishment . . . What first drove me to criticize my own
work was a very kind, and I believe sincere, letter from
Suvorin. I was preparing to write something serious, something really good, but nevertheless I still had no real faith
in my literary worth.

And then your letter dropped in on me out of the
skies . . . As a result, I felt a vital urge to hurry, to get out
of the rut in which I had become bogged down . . . All hope
lies in the future. I am only twenty-six. Perhaps I shall still
have time to achieve something, though time rushes past.

At the same time, he wrote a letter to his brother, the painter
Nicholas, which was the fruit of his meditations on the responsibilities imposed by the evidence of that divine gift, talent:

You have often complained
of being misunderstood. Not even Goethe or Newton complained about that. Only Christ did, but he was not speaking of himself, but of his teaching. You are very well

understood, and if you do not understand yourself, it is
not other people's fault ... I can assure you that, as your
brother, I understand you and sympathize with you with
all my heart. I know all your qualities. You are kind to
the point of susceptibility, generous, devoid of egotism,
sincere; you are devoid of jealousy and malice; you are
guileless and compassionate towards men and animals; you
are neither slanderous, vindictive or suspicious. You have
received a gift from Heaven that others do not possess –
talent. This talent places you above millions of human
beings, for in this world one only counts on one artist out
of two million men. But you have a flaw: your complete
lack of education ... Forgive me, but *veritas magis
amicitiae*. Talent has introduced you into an intellectual
circle, you belong to it, but the philistine core is perceptible, the one brought up by a rod in a wineshop, and it
is difficult, terribly difficult, to overcome it.

Educated men should, in my opinion, fulfil the following conditions:

1. They respect their fellow men, which is why they are
always tolerant, gentle, polite and good-natured. They do
not become angry because of the loss of a hammer or an
eraser. If they go to live with someone, they do not insist
that they are only doing it as a favour, nor, as they leave,
do they say: it is impossible to live with you! They forgive
the noise and the cold and the overcooked meat and the
jokes and the presence of strangers in the house ...

2. They are compassionate, not only towards beggars and
cats. Their hearts are also moved by what is not visible to
the naked eye.

3. They respect other people's property and, when they
leave, they pay their debts.

4. They are sincere and fear lies like the plague. They
never lie, even in small matters. Lying is offensive to the
hearer and lowers his opinion of the one who indulges in
it. They are not pretentious and behave when they go out

[85]

as they do at home; they do not try to dazzle smaller fry. They are not garrulous and do not foist their confidences on people who have not asked for them.

5. They do not belittle themselves with the object of arousing pity in others. They do not say: "I'm misunderstood!" or "I've wasted my gifts for nothing!" because this seeks to produce an effect that is cheap, vulgar, outmoded and false.

6. They are not vain, nor attracted by paste diamonds in the nature of meeting celebrities, shaking hands with some Mr X or other. When they have produced a painting only worth a penny, they do not pretend that their sketchbook contains those worth a hundred roubles, and they do not boast of having been admitted to places from which other people have been excluded. Genuine talent always remains in the shade, lost in the crowd, away from all display. Even Krilov[7] said that an empty barrel makes more noise than a full one.

7. If they have some kind of talent – they respect it. They sacrifice leisure, women, wine and futile pursuits to it. They are proud of it.

8. They cultivate an aesthetic sense in themselves. They do not allow themselves to sleep in their clothes, see a crack in the wall full of bugs, breathe polluted air, walk on a floor covered with spit, cook on an oil stove. They try to subdue as far as possible and ennoble the sensual instinct ... What they ask of women is not their bed ... In particular, those who are artists ask of them freshness, elegance, humanity and the faculty of being not a mistress but a mother. They do not quench their thirst with vodka ... they only drink occasionally, in their leisure-time, for they need a *mens sana in corpore sano*.

This is the nature of educated men. To educate oneself to avoid being inferior to the circle in which one has landed, it is not enough to have read *Pickwick* or to have learnt by heart a monologue from *Faust*. No, in addition to that it requires ceaseless work day and night, constant reading and the development of willpower. Every hour is precious ... Come, now, break your carafe of vodka, stretch out and read and read, even if it is only Turgenev, whom you have never read. I'm waiting for you! We all expect it of you.

This letter is a true profession of faith. At twenty-six, Chekhov had already elaborated a system of ethics, which one might well call stoic: that of renouncing "leisure, wine, women and futile pursuits". He would have liked to persuade his brother to follow it, knowing full well that he would never succeed. But he himself would be able to adhere to it, be able to renounce everything that did not serve his art or help to maintain his high conception of life and his duty towards his fellow men.

He cannot be said to have undergone any sudden change. Outwardly, he remained the same. But something had come to fruition within him and the tone of his letters was transformed just as, almost imperceptibly, the tone of his stories had already been transformed.

NOTES

1. *Suvorin's memoirs of Chekhov* in 'Russkoe Slovo', 1904.
2. *Sarah Bernhardt*, 1881.
3. Teleshov, *A Writer's Memoirs*, Moscow, 1943.
4. D. Grigorovich (1822–1899), author of *The Unlucky One, The Village*, etc., played an important part in the literary circles of his time. It is he who introduced Dostoevsky to Nakrassov and Belinski and 'discovered Chekhov'.
5. Editor of *New Time*.
6. Literary critic of *New Time*.
7. I. Krilov (1768–1844), the Russian La Fontaine.

[5]

An Intellectual Friendship, Alexei Suvorin

A T the same time as Grigorovich, Pleshcheev and literary circles in St Petersburg were beginning to talk seriously of the highly talented, new writer, Anton Chekhov became friends with an influential but much criticized man, Alexei Suvorin.

The friendship might well, at first sight, seem strange. Yet Chekhov's only true friend in his self-imposed seclusion was this elderly, disillusioned, cynical man. Shunning ideologies as he did ideologists, Chekhov was to find shelter in the friendship of the 'opportunist' Suvorin, editor of the *Novoye Vremia*, who had first invited him to contribute to it in 1886.

Chekhov protected his inner independence all his life. He wanted to work everything out for himself, which is why he always kept aloof from the infatuations and enthusiasms of his fellow university students, and away from all collective activities. His positive turn of mind and innate suspiciousness, inherited from his peasant ancestors, prevented him from altogether believing what he read in newspaper articles and books. They also led him to dismiss philosophy, poetry and everything that could not be clearly defined, encompassed and expressed. What attracted him were the exact sciences, disciplines based on experience and observation; natural sciences and medi-

[88]

cine. The hero of *A Sad Story*, Professor Nicholai Stepanovich, says: "With my last breath I shall continue to believe that science is the most important, the most beautiful and the most vital thing in human life; that it always has been and always will be the highest manifestation of love and that through it man will come to triumph over both nature and himself." And, later, he wrote in his *Notes*: "If you wish to understand life, stop believing in what is said and what is written, and, instead, observe for yourself and ponder."

Observe and ponder was what he had always done, as had the brilliant, self-taught, Suvorin. Like Chekhov, Suvorin, son of a private soldier who had fought at Borodino, sprang from the people. Grandson of a serf, nature had endowed him, as it had Chekhov, with a great intuitive intelligence and the most diverse talents. After teaching in a remote village in the centre of Russia, at a salary of 14 roubles 75 a month, Suvorin had come to Moscow and embarked on a career in journalism. He contributed to the important reviews of the period, *The Contemporary* and *The Annals of the Fatherland*. The eminent Alexei Pleshcheev, a well-known poet and extremely warm-hearted man, discerned Suvorin's outstanding individuality, and helped him in so far as he could. Suvorin's daring, intelligent and penetrating articles signed *The Unknown*, soon made him known. In 1876, he bought from a certain Trubnikov the daily newspaper *Novoye Vremia*, and from then on his rise was rapid. He gave his paper a definite pro-government slant and presented himself as a defender of the established order and a whole-hearted monarchist. This *volte-face* earned him the contempt and hatred of the avant-garde intelligentsia. But his future was secured. The government granted him a concession for all the newspaper kiosks on the Russian railways, which brought in enormous profits. However in his private *Diary* he revenged himself on those he defended and publicly flattered – on the Emperor, the ministers and the members of the Court. Chekhov seems to have been unaware of this duplicity. But Suvorin, the wily, far-seeing businessman, with so many irons in the fire, had a totally different side to him. A true Russian, he was neither satisfied with earning large sums of money nor, through his reactionary opportunist daily, influencing an important sector of the public opinion. He was also a writer and a dramatist, and had an immense enthusiasm for literature. Beyond anything else, he was a man of great experience and exceptional intellectual charm.

Chekhov valued him very highly. "You have excellent taste and I have as much faith in your first impression as I have in the fact that there is a sun in the sky." (Letter to Suvorin, 31st March, 1892.) "Tolstoy is very fond of you," he wrote Suvorin on 7th August, 1899, "and Shakespeare would have been fond of you, too, had he been alive."

Hearing that Suvorin was ill, Chekhov immediately left for St Petersburg. He wrote to his friend Shcheglov on 30th October, 1892: "If things are really as bad as Suvorin thinks they are, I do not know what to say to you. If he were to die, it would be such a loss to me that I believe I should immediately become ten years older."

Chekhov liked Suvorin's blunt, spontaneous judgements, his boldness, his exceptionally wide interests and his fundamental originality.

To be with Suvorin and remain silent is as easy as to sit at Palkin's (a well-known restaurant in St Petersburg) and not drink. Truly, Suvorin is sensitivity incarnate. He is a man of great scope. In the field of art he is exactly like a setter at a woodcock-shoot: he reacts with diabolical frenzy and is literally consumed with passion. He is a poor theorist: he has not studied any science, is ignorant of a lot of things, and is completely self-taught. From this springs his purity and integrity, wholly sensual; from this, too, the independence of his judgement. Being poor as a theorist, he has been compelled, by way of compensation, to develop what nature has generously showered on him and has raised what was instinctive in him to the level of great intelligence. It is always pleasant to talk to him, but when one has grasped his line of argument and felt the sincerity that is lacking in most conversationalists, it becomes a real joy. (Letter to Ivan Chekhov, 18th July, 1888.)

Suvorin, on his part, loved and admired Chekhov, "that eagle", without reservation. They got on extremely well, travelled together and had similar tastes and enthusiasms: books, the theatre, fishing and even cemeteries! They visited those in Provence and Italy together and Suvorin notes in his *Diary*: "What interested Chekhov abroad more than anything else were cemeteries and circuses."

Lastly, they both felt the same contempt for the majority of mankind, a contempt that was virulent and cynical on Suvorin's part, but tempered with indulgence on Chekhov's. Suvorin was one of the most disparaged and disliked men of his time. People could not forgive him for his cynicism, his caustic wit – and his success: nor could they forgive his political opportunism. But Chekhov, a strong believer in individual liberty, unattached to any literary group and resolutely opposed to the tyranny of the intellectuals on the left, was devoted to Suvorin and wrote him the most beautiful, imaginative and sincere letters, which are of engrossing interest. Chekhov confides his innermost thoughts in them as he has done to no one else. His trust in the man to whom he wrote with such lack of restraint must have been immense when one considers his innate modesty, secrecy and reserve.

"I write to no one and can only talk at any length with you. I only feel free with you." He wrote to him on 7th August, 1893. Only one side of this voluminous correspondence remains: the 333 letters from Chekhov to Suvorin (the first dated 21st February, 1886; the last 1st July, 1903). Suvorin's letters were returned to him by Maria Chekhov at his request after Chekhov's death and have never been published.

[6]

The Closest Friend,
Isaac Levitan

THE more carefully one examines Chekhov's life, the more clearly one realizes that love and friendship played but a small part in it, that his solitude, far more than being material, was of a metaphysical nature.

He had been the best of sons, the best of brothers and the most considerate and loyal of friends. But around him there was an invisible barrier that no one ever crossed. Within this circle he was alone with his art, which was the only thing he ever really loved, the only thing that truly mattered to him. He knew that he had been granted an exceptional talent, and he had made up his mind to sacrifice everything to it.

He had been endowed by nature with remarkable will-power and a clarity of vision which, at a very early age, had enabled him to see beneath life's surface and appreciate the true motives governing men's actions. In actual fact, he had no spontaneous affection for humanity. His fellow man, as far as he was concerned, lay primarily in an aesthetic category. He appreciated those with exceptional talents or a picturesque quality : a Tolstoy, a Suvorin, a Levitan, a Gorki or some poor peasant whose simplicity, humour, naïvety and purity of heart attracted him. But all those who did not appeal to his aesthetic sense or did not match up to his particularly demanding moral standards repelled him, exasperated him and bored him. "I do not like human beings, I have not liked anyone for a long time ... The peasants are all alike, backward and living in filth; and it is difficult to get along with intellectuals. They are tiresome ... All our good friends are petty in thought and feeling, they do not see beyond their own noses, they grumble, they are full of spite and they are pathological scandalmongers," he was to say through his mouthpiece, Dr Astrov, in *Uncle Vanya*.

Chekhov's first instinctive reaction was one of retreat and self-defence; he entrenched himself in his own private world, to which he hardly ever granted access to anyone and in which he felt irrevocably alone. His seal bore the words: "For a man alone, the whole world is a desert" ("and it was not a pose," Gorki wrote later).

Ten years earlier, his school-friend, P. A. Serghenko, was astonished to discover that the popular writer was in fact a "lone eagle"; that he had many friends "but that he, himself, was friendly with no one, was not drawn to anyone to the point of forgetting himself".

Nevertheless, Chekhov did have two friends, Alexei Suvorin and Isaac Levitan, whose friendship dated from his early days in Moscow. But the more headway Chekhov made in life, the less he felt any desire to confide in anyone or even express himself on an intellectual level. The obscure inner exertion that went on indefatigably within him absorbed him completely, to such an extent that he used to rise from the dinner-table to jot down notes in his notebook; that his eyes always seemed to be looking beyond whoever was talking to him – even while he listened with exemplary patience; that he was *elsewhere* more and more frequently, even in the midst of a friendly, animated circle. The incessant work involved in creation completely possessed him and left little room for personal desires, feelings or revelations. He became less and less his own master, for he was dimly conscious that time pressed, that death was close and there still remained so much, so very much to accomplish.

But in his youth, during the carefree period when he liked to laugh, drink and flirt with pretty girls, when life was only just beginning and he did not yet feel drawn towards the asceticism, intense concentration and sacrifice of all else to his art, which characterized his maturity, there were two human beings to whom he unburdened himself: intellectually to Suvorin, sentimentally to Isaac Levitan.

Chekhov liked friendship for friendship's sake. If love had never seemed to him a 'respectable sentiment' (Colette), friendship, on the other hand, attracted him by its frankness, virility, purity and stimulation to the spirit. "Friendship is superior to love. My friends are fond of me, I am fond of them and, through me, they are fond of one another. Love on the other hand makes enemies of those who love the same woman ... Friendship knows no such jealousy. That is why, even in marriage, friendship is preferable to love," he said to Alexei Suvorin.[1]

He was only twenty when, in 1880, he made the acquaintance of a handsome young man with curly brown hair, a friend and fellow-student of his brother Nicholas at the Moscow School of Painting, Sculpture and Architecture. Isaac Levitan[2] was one of the most brilliant pupils in the studio conducted by the famous landscape-painter, Alexei Savrassov (who died from alcoholism at the age of 67). Savrassov had been a popular artist since 1871; and the first showing of his vernal landscape *The Rooks are Here* alongside other works, considered as revolutionary by such painters as Perov, Kramskoy and Gay, created a sensation.

Directed by Perov, the Moscow Art School, the free academy of fine arts, was at this period one of the most liberal institutions in Russia. Isaac Levitan, along with the brothers Serge and Constantine Korovin, was one of its most brilliant and promising students. Born into a poor Jewish family, an orphan from an early age, Levitan had such a deplorable childhood and adolescence that he always refused to speak of it, even to his intimate friends. He met all questions with the same obstinate silence, the same weary, despairing gesture. His elder brother,

Abel, a mediocre painter, completely overshadowed by his younger brother's fame, maintained a similar silence throughout his life. Even the name of Levitan's mother remains unknown to us, as do any details of his childhood and first years in Moscow. All we do know is that at thirteen Isaac enrolled in the Moscow School of Painting, where his brother Abel was already a pupil in 1873, and that he displayed a quite extraordinary early talent. From the very beginning he had known he would become a landscape painter. At the first sign of spring, he used to snatch up a loaf of bread and head for the Moscow suburbs, Sokolniki, Ostankino or the Sparrow Hills. And there he painted. He worked with such fire, devotion and talent that he attracted the attention of that violent, intelligent and impetuous man, Alexei Savrassov.

Adored and feared by his pupils, Savrassov used to burst into the studio with all the violence of a storm. Tall and heavy, untidily dressed, bearded and unwashed, he won Levitan's heart one day when the latter was still Perov's pupil. He had stopped behind the shy youth, who was paralysed by his presence, had carefully scrutinized his canvas and then pointed an authoritative finger, stained with charcoal, towards the part of the picture that seemed to its creator the least successful, the most fuzzy and unfinished. "That's how you should have painted the whole of that canvas of yours. There's real feeling there . . . The rest is false subtlety, colourful, but without soul . . ."

Soul! That was the heart of the matter. There lay the 'revolutionary' character of a Savrassov or a Polenov landscape; the irruption of poetry into Russian academic painting towards the end of the 19th century. The poetry of humble, commonplace things like the wretched Moscow alley painted by Polenov, or the muddy road, lined with willows shaken by the wind, which is Savrassov's second masterpiece. One of the most intelligent painters of that period, Kramskoy, wrote after seeing the 1871 exhibition: "Savrassov's canvas (*The Rooks are Here*) is the best of them all. In the others, certainly, there are trees, water and sky, but it is only in *The Rooks* that one is conscious of soul." Chekhov admired the great portrait-painter and wise man that Kramskoy was. After his death he wrote to Suvorin on 3rd April, 1888: "I thank you for *Kramskoy*,[3] which I have started to read. What a brain! Had he been a writer, he would have certainly produced long, original and sincere works, and I regret that he has not written more. Our novelists and playwrights are fond of introducing painters in their works; now, as I read *Kramskoy*, I see how little they and the general public know about Russian painters!"

Savrassov had quickly appreciated the strength of Levitan's talent. He pressed him to follow the path which he, himself, had discovered and which consisted of a kind of poetical trans-position of the Russian countryside. But he warned him against developing a narrow-minded nationalism, and strongly advised him to study Corot's work, which he admired, and whose views on the art of painting he partially shared.

Serge Tretiakov, who, unlike his brother Paul, confined his collection of paintings to those from Western Europe, possessed a number of very beautiful Corots. He commissioned Levitan to copy several of them. Meticulously following the brush-work of the master, Levitan fell increasingly under the spell of his works. "The calm emotion", of which Fra Angelico spoke so highly, seemed to be the dominating force behind Corot's in-spiration and it fascinated Levitan, as did his gift of simplicity, naturalness and perfect harmony between subject and treat-ment that distinguished the work of the great Frenchman. Levitan did not yet possess this simplicity and naturalness, and was well aware of it. But he struggled to transpose his emotions into the same unspoilt, simple language. He adored Corot and even took French lessons in order to read Roger-Miles' mono-graph on him. He may, perhaps, have come across Corot's reference to Delacroix: "He is an eagle and I am only a lark: I chirrup little songs in my grey skies." In any case, he, too, never claimed to do more than sing little songs to the glory of the humblest objects, on which, like Corot, he was able to con-fer an immortal grandeur by the magic of his art.

[96]

Savrassov's shrewdness had enabled him to envisage this, and all his hopes lay in Levitan from whom he anticipated everything that, from lack of knowledge or skill, he had failed to achieve himself. And the pupil remained loyal and grateful to his teacher. A quarter of a century later, having reached the peak of his fame, Levitan wrote in an obituary article for the master, who died in September, 1897: "Savrassov was the first to display both a lyricism in the presentation of landscapes and an unbounded love for his native land. Look at his best pictures, such as *The Rooks are Here*. What is its subject? On the outskirts of a small town, an old church, a rickety fence, a field covered in half-melted snow and, in the foreground, a few birches, on the branches of which the rooks have alighted. That is all. How simple it is ... But in this simplicity there lies a whole world of wonderful poetry ..."

This simplicity, this love of humble objects, this 'world of wonderful poetry', had been brought to life again, re-created and raised to such a degree of perfection by Levitan, that Savrassov and the master who succeeded him, Polenov, had been gradually forgotten. It was Levitan alone who survived, who remained, even for the new Russia, the undisputed master of 'lyrical realism'. The most recent retrospective exhibition of his work, in 1960, attracted immense crowds to the Tretiakov Gallery in Moscow. His poems, translated to canvas, remain up-to-date, whether it be the birch-tree wood inundated by the melting snow or the road extending as far as the eye can see, the Vladimirka along which the convicts trudged in chains towards their Siberian exile, or that vast stretch of sky and water with a half-demolished chapel, trees bent by the wind and the crosses of an abandoned cemetery in the foreground – a spellbinding foreshortening of the Volga, that immense river, so essentially Russian in its very immensity, its power and its proud, austere beauty.

Paul Tretiakov, in his role of Maecenas, enjoyed discovering talent and looked beyond the paintings of already known artists when he attended exhibitions. He had taken note of Levitan ever since the first exhibition by students of the School of Painting, and had mentioned him in a letter to that sensitive critic and painter, Kramskoy. At the students' second exhibition during the Christmas of 1879, he was struck by a landscape entitled *Autumn Day at Sokolniki* and signed Levitan; a deserted lane bordered with russet, amber and golden trees, along which walked a solitary young woman dressed in black (painted by Levitan's friend, Nicholas Chekhov). Tretiakov bought the picture for a hundred roubles. Levitan was only nineteen years old at the time. It was the beginning of his fame in artistic circles, for the Tretiakov Gallery was already the finest museum of Russian art in the world.[4]

Just as he enjoyed this first success, Levitan was faced with a new ordeal.

After the unsuccessful attempt in 1879 on the life of Alexander III by Soloviev, a member of the Land and Liberty Society, Jews were forbidden to live in Moscow. Levitan, with his brother and sister Teresa, was compelled to move to Saltykovka, a village on the outskirts, whence he travelled up to Moscow and the School of Painting by train every day. His financial difficulties grew steadily worse; he was half-starved and miserably clad; but his absorption in his work only increased. Between 1880 and 1883 he lived in Ostankino, painted relentlessly and produced landscapes of outstanding brilliance. It was at this period, when Chekhov was studying medicine at Moscow University and earning a living for his family and himself by contributing to various humorous magazines, that Levitan's more frequent contacts with him began. In July, 1884, Levitan fell ill and 'Dr' Chekhov came to visit him and offer professional advice. As a token of his gratitude, Levitan gave him *The Oak and the Birch*, a drawing which always stood on the writer's desk and accompanied him to his retreat in Yalta.

In May, 1885, Chekhov took his family to Babkino, a property situated three versts from Voskresensk (now called Istra) and some eighty kilometres from Moscow. It was here that he spent three successive summers (1885–1887). Babkino was one of those old and beautiful estates which were a source of inspiration and delight to the great Russian writers of the 19th century, ranging from Pushkin to Chekhov and Alexander Blok.

It was at Babkino that Chekhov wrote *The Hunter*, *The Sorceress* and *Agatha* and assembled the second volume of his *Motley Tales*. It was here, too, that Levitan painted a keenly perceptive portrait of the young Chekhov.

"I have rented a dacha, complete with furniture, vegetables, dairy produce etc," he wrote to Nicholas Leikin on 28th April, 1885. "The property is very beautiful and situated on the steep bank of the river flowing below it. It is full of fish. Beyond the river there is a huge forest and on this side of it – another forest. What a joy it is to see the leaves opening and hear the nightingales sing."

A few days after writing this letter, Chekhov learnt that he had Levitan as a neighbour. The painter was in the grip of a nervous depression that had driven him to the brink of suicide. Chekhov went over to fetch him and installed him at Babkino: "Levitan is staying with me," he wrote to Leikin twelve days later. "That landscape-painter is a rabid sportsman! The day before yesterday he killed a hare. But the poor fellow is in a bad way and suffering from some kind of psychosis . . . He has tried to hang himself. I have brought him over here and take him about with me. I think he is already feeling better."

Levitan called all the fish 'crocodiles', went out shooting and painted and painted. He gave Chekhov a present of one of his paintings, *The River Istra*. The really close friendship between the two of them sprang up in that summer.[5]

Imagine a soft summer evening, a lovely estate perched on the steep bank of the river Istra; below, the river and on the opposite side of it, an immense, dark forest. All around – the silence of the night. Through the wide-open windows and doors pour the sounds of Beethoven's sonatas, Chopin's nocturnes. The Kiseliovs (the owners of the estate), our whole family and Levitan are listening to wonderful playing by E. Efremova, the Kiseliov children's governess.[6]

Maria Chekhova, a painter in her spare time, became close friends with Levitan.

He had a face full of expression, a large nose, dark eyes with deep shadows under them and a mass of curly hair. I can't say he was handsome, but women found him attractive and he was often in love, himself, and very exuberant in the manifestation of his feelings. In his periods of black depression, he wanted to end his life, to hang or shoot himself, but these moods did not last long.

One beautiful summer morning, Maria Chekhova met Levitan on the road leading from Babkino to the forest. They were chatting together amicably, when Levitan suddenly dropped to his knees in front of her and made a formal proposal of marriage.

I could think of nothing better to do – she wrote – than to turn round and run away. I stayed in my bedroom, terribly upset, all day and wept, my head buried in the pillow. That evening, Levitan came to dine as usual. I didn't appear. Anton asked why. Our brother Michael told him that he had seen me crying. Anton left the table and came to my room: "Why are you crying?" I explained what had happened and confessed that I didn't know what answer to give Levitan. My brother then said: "You can marry him, of course, but you must realize that what he wants is a 'Balzac type' of young woman, not a young girl like you." I was ashamed to admit to my brother that I didn't know what 'a Balzac type' of young woman was and didn't understand what he meant. But I sensed that he intended to warn me about something. I didn't give Levitan an answer of any kind and he wandered about for a further week, looking blacker than night; while I avoided leaving the house or even my bedroom ... Later on, I met him again and thus ended our 'romance'. But during the rest of his short life, we continued to be great friends. He helped me a lot with my painting. He often said to me, and did so again shortly before his death, when he was very ill and I had come to visit him: "If I'd ever married, it would only have been with you, Masha."[7]

But Levitan never married. His life was a series of passionate love-affairs, one of which led to his estrangement with Chekhov.

In the spring of 1886, the painter was staying in the Crimea and working incessantly. At first, he was enchanted by the scenery and vegetation of southern Russia. In March he wrote to Chekhov from Yalta:

How beautiful it is here! Last night I climbed a mountain and looked down from the summit to the sea below. And, you know, I began to cry, to sob. That is where eternal beauty lies and where man becomes aware of his infinite smallness. But what's the point of talking about it: you have to see it for yourself to appreciate it.

But the fascination of his surroundings, too sumptuous, too beautiful and too 'chocolate-box', soon wore thin and at the end of April he was writing:

Nature, here, is only striking at the outset: after that, one becomes appallingly bored by it and longs to be back in the North. I love the North more than I ever did before, it is only now that I have really come to understand it.

He was longing to return to the nostalgic landscapes of Central Russia, longing to return to the beauty of Babkino, where Chekhov was staying with his family. When he did get back, Chekhov was delighted by the fifty-odd canvases and sketches he brought with him from the Crimea. "Levitan is back with us. He has brought with him from the Crimea some fifty magnificent (from what the experts say) pictures. His talent grows from day to day." (Chekhov wrote to E. Sakhrova, on 28th July.)

The success of Levitan's 'southern' pictures was enormous. So enormous that Sofia Petrovna Kuvchinnikova, who held a salon in Moscow that was attended by eminent writers and painters, was eager to make his acquaintance. The outcome of their meeting was momentous. A passionate friendship sprang up between Sofia Petrovna and Levitan which lasted for nine years, from 1886 to 1895, and she played no small part in the creation of some of his finest pictures. It was this 'affaire' that led to his estrangement with Chekhov, which kept the two friends apart for nearly three years (1892–1895).

Sofia Petrovna was the wife of Dmitri Kuvchinnikov, a doctor of forensic medicine. She was dark, with exotic features, extremely graceful, attractive, ugly, eccentric and deeply artistic. In spite of her husband's modest means – he was quiet, unassuming, indulgent and devoted to his wife – Sofia Petrovna was widely known in Moscow. She had decorated her apartment in an ultra-modern way: a 'Russian-style' dining-room with heavy rustic benches and knicknacks in painted wood; a bedroom, draped in dark colours, with a Venetian lantern and innumerable rugs, on which a brightly feathered, tame stork paraded with immense dignity. This 'artistic' type of setting was unusual in Moscow and attracted the pick of the *avant-garde*. Her husband, long-suffering and silent, never attended her musical and literary evenings, but confined himself to putting in an appearance at midnight, throwing open the dining-room door and announcing: "Ladies and Gentlemen, supper is served!" It was he who had prepared the meal, which might not be luxurious but was always plentiful and well-cooked. Sofia Petrovna never failed to thank him and compliment him on it, taking care to stress that it was he and not she who was the real 'mistress of the house'.

Chekhov did not like her. He considered her frivolous and egotistical, felt sorry for her silent over-devoted husband and set little value on her talents, despite the fact that they genuinely existed. She was an excellent pianist and had a gift for painting and décor (one of her paintings hangs in the Tretiakov Gallery). Her meeting with Levitan resulted in her applying herself more seriously to her painting. In September, 1886, she left with Levitan and another painter, Stepanov, a friend of her husband's, for the Savinskaia sloboda near Zvenigorod (the Moscow Barbizon). And in the following spring, the trio were united again on the shores of the Volga.

It was Levitan's first sight of the awe-inspiring Russian river, which was to become one of his greatest subjects. At first it disappointed him and he wrote to Chekhov:

> I was expecting the Volga to have a profound, artistic effect on me, but, instead, it seemed so dismal and lifeless that my heart sank and I felt an urge to run away. Try to picture the following monotonous landscape: the steep, right bank is covered with stunted shrubs and barren gullies. On the left bank, there is nothing but flooded forests and, above all this, a strong wind and grey skies. It's deadly! I began to wonder why on earth I had ever come here and whether I should not have been far better employed working in the vicinity of Moscow instead of feeling so completely alone, confronted by that vast stretch of water, which is killing me. And, to crown it all, it's beginning to rain!

But, very soon, the grandiose beauty of the river possessed him and he discovered such variety in the superficial monotony of its silver-grey tints that it became his favourite colour-scheme, and one which is dominant in his paintings inspired by the Volga.

When next he wrote, he said:

> I have never loved nature so much, never been so sensitive to what emanates from it, never felt so vividly that divine element, prevalent everywhere though everyone is not aware of it, to which one cannot give a name, since it does not lend itself either to reason or analysis but can only be discerned by love. Without this feeling, there can be no real artist ... But this perceptiveness, where I am concerned, is a source of deep suffering. Can there be anything more tragic than to be aware of the infinite beauty of our surroundings, to catch a glimpse of the ultimate hidden mystery, and to see God in everything without being able, conscious as one is of

one's own impotence, to give expression to these profound emotions?

It is the Volga which plays the principal role in Levitan's 1894 masterpiece, *Above Eternal Rest*. The painter, himself, regarded this as his finest work, as he wrote to Paul Tretiakov on 18th May that year:

> I am so indescribably happy that my last work, *Above Eternal Rest*, should also be in your possession, that, since yesterday, I have been in a sort of ecstasy. You may find this feeling odd, since you already own a large number of my paintings. But the fact that you should have acquired this last picture touches me profoundly, because *I put everything I have into it*, my soul and all that lies in the very depth of my being. I should have been moved to tears if this picture had not been added to your great collection (great, of course, not from the point of view of numbers or the vast sums you have spent on it, but from the excellence of the selection which testifies to your deep understanding of art and the touching, unselfish love that you devote to it).

In this painting, Levitan had expressed with great, tragic impact the relationship between all-powerful nature and man's helplessness in the face of it. Confronted by the vastness of the sky, the formidable stretch of river and the tempestuous wind, driving dark masses of cloud ahead of it, the miserable chapel and the pathetic crosses in the tiny cemetery, wring one's heart by their frailty and sad neglect. Chekhov had described similar emotions in *The Steppe*: "When one gazes for a long time at the remote, impenetrable sky, one's thoughts and one's soul mingle in a feeling of solitude. One begins to feel irremediably alone and everything that, up till then, one regarded as familiar and close suddenly becomes infinitely remote and alien."

Levitan would discuss his favourite subjects with Chekhov:

in Moscow they were virtually neighbours. When Chekhov moved into the Korneev house in Sadovaia–Kudrinskaia Street, Levitan, depressed and lonely, would often come late at night and knock on the window of the ground-floor room, where his friend's lamp would still be alight, asking "Are you asleep, crocodile?" and Chekhov would let him in. Upstairs, everybody was asleep. In the small study, under the soft light cast by the lamp with its green shade, the two friends would talk for hours. What about? Among other things, about Sofia Petrovna, the mistress, friend and loyal companion of the weeks spent near Zvenigorod or on the banks of the Volga. Chekhov would speak very little, but listen and memorize.

The extent to which he had listened became apparent on the publication of his short story *The Grasshopper*, in 1892, which nearly led to a complete breach with Levitan.

The story was founded on Levitan's and Kuvchinnikova's 'affaire'. Admittedly, the dark forty-year-old Sofia Petrovna appearing in it as Olga Ivanovna is young and blonde; admittedly, the eccentric Riabovski's resemblance to Levitan is confined to his physical appearance and certain of his mannerisms; and, equally, Doctor Kuvchinnikov lacked both the personality and quiet heroism of Doctor Dymov. But the background, the relationships between the characters and the deep philosophy that emerges from the story form a very exact though sublimated transposition of the real-life situation, of which Chekhov strongly disapproved.

On a mellow July night bathed in moonlight, Olga Ivanovna, standing on deck, as the boat sailed up the Volga, alternately watched the water and the beautiful river-banks. Riabovski stood beside her. He told her that the dark shadows on the water were not shadows but a dream; that confronted by the spectacle of these magic waters with their eerie reflections, by this boundless sky and nostalgic brooding shores, which speak to us of the futility of our lives and the existence of something far finer, blissful and eternal, it would be wonderful to sink into oblivion, to die, to become nothing but a memory. The past was vulgar and insipid, the future paltry, whereas this magnificent and unique night would soon be over and part of eternity. So what was the point of living?

Olga Ivanovna, listening now to Riabovski's voice, now to the silence of the night, believed herself to be immortal, believed that she would never die ... She thought, too, that the man beside her, leaning on the ship's rail, was genuinely great, a genius, a favourite of the gods ... All that he had created so far had been beautiful, fresh and wonderful, and what he would create in the future when, with maturity, his marvellous talent was even more firmly established, would reach unbelievable heights. This could be read in his face, in his way of expressing himself, in his appreciation of nature. He spoke of shadows, of vesperal colours, of the brilliance of the moon in the characteristic manner, the special language of his own that revealed so clearly the power he possessed over nature. And he himself was so handsome, so inventive; his life so free, independent and remote from all prosaic everyday events, so like a bird's.

The atmosphere inherent in the story, and a number of pronouncements that Levitan might not have made but easily *could* have made, were conveyed so skilfully and with such psychological plausibility that the painter was furious. And Sofia Petrovna even more so. Chekhov, much too perceptive not to have foreseen the reaction his story would produce, wrote in April, 1892, to his friend, Lydia Avilova, with apparent guilelessness:

Yes, it is lovely here, in Melikhovo. Not just lovely, but astonishingly so ... The nightingales are singing and the frogs are croaking their heads off ... Yesterday, I went to Moscow. I nearly died there from boredom and innumerable annoyances. Can you imagine, a lady-friend of mine, forty-two years old, has identified herself as the heroine (aged 20) of my *Grasshopper*? Now all Moscow accuses me of having written a scurrilous pamphlet. The chief proof lies in this superficial resemblance, wholly divorced from the situations: the lady also paints, her husband is a doctor and she has a painter as a lover.

In any case, Levitan was so outraged that he did not see Chekhov for close on three years. It was one of their mutual friends, the poetess Tatiana Shchepkina-Kupernik, who finally managed to bring the painter to Melikhovo.

"When he learnt where I was going, he began, in his usual way, to sigh and go on about how much he regretted the silly estrangement. 'In that case,' I said, with all the impulsiveness and vigour of my nineteen years, 'what's keeping you away? Since you want to come, why don't you? Come down there with me right away!' – 'What! Supposing we turn up at the wrong moment? Supposing Chekhov misunderstands?' – 'I'll take full responsibility,' I assured him so confidently that he had nothing more to say.

"A few hours later we were approaching the straggling, low Melikhovo house along a snow-covered road. Levitan was extremely agitated during the whole drive, heaving deep sighs and asking me anxiously, 'Tanechka, don't you think we may be making a great mistake?' I tried to calm him, but his agitation became catching . . . At last we arrived at the house! The dogs began to bark, Maria Chekhova came out on to the porch and, behind her, all wrapped up – Chekhov. He peered in our direction to see who had come with me – there was a short silence – and then the two friends rushed towards each other, clasped hands and . . . began the most commonplace conversation about the state of the road, the weather, Moscow . . . But at dinner, seeing the moist sparkle in Levitan's beautiful eyes and the gleam of gaiety in Chekhov's, usually so pensive, I could not help feeling pleased with myself."[8]

The reconciliation between Chekhov and Levitan took place on 2nd January, 1895. Next day Levitan wrote to him:

> I am so unspeakably happy to be back here again with the Chekhovs. I have recovered what was so dear to me and never, in fact, ceased to be.

The following summer saw the break between Levitan and his faithful Muse. Another woman forced her way into his life, another heroine of the 'Balzac type', Anna Turchaninova, mother of two pretty daughters, one of whom lost no time in falling madly in love with Levitan. The rivalry between mother and daughter, and the letters from Sofia Petrovna, full of reproaches and laments, combined to drive the sensitive Levitan to the brink of suicide. Anna wrote to Chekhov and begged him to come and attend Levitan, who had tried to shoot himself and whose condition was causing her great anxiety. Chekhov spent some days with his friend at Gorka, the Turchaninov estate. Levitan's wound was only a superficial one but his morale was very low. He wrote to Chekhov on 27th July:

Again I'm in a state of depression, a depression that is immeasurable, boundless and produces a state of torpor and horror. What am I to do? With each day that passes, I have less and less willpower to fight all the darkness surrounding me. I ought to go away somewhere, but I can't make myself do it because I find it impossible to reach a decision one way or another and I dither, dither endlessly. I don't know why, but, for me, the few days you spent here were the calmest and most peaceful of this whole summer.

Up to his death, five years later, Levitan suffered more and more acute attacks of neurasthenia, which alternated with periods of exaltation and intense inspiration. Anna remained his friend to the end. But this 'affaire' was to bring him no more happiness than the others.

Levitan died alone, as he had always lived. A few months before his death, he went to see Chekhov for the last time in Yalta. This last visit has been described by Maria Chekhova:

"It was Christmas, 1899. Levitan was sitting in an armchair in front of the fire in Anton's study. Anton was pacing up and down the room. He said that he felt nostalgic for his favourite scenery in Central Russia, that nature in the South was beautiful, but cold. I was in the room, too. Suddenly Levitan turned to me: 'Masha, bring me some cardboard, please.'

"I brought him a sheet. He cut out a piece, fitted it into a recess in the fireplace, took out his paints and set to work. In about half an hour, the sketch was finished. It depicted haystacks in a field on a moonlit night, with a forest in the background. This gift from a friend has always remained framed in the recess of our fireplace. There were two more paintings by Levitan in my brother's study : *The River Istra*, painted in 1885 at Babkino, and *The Oak and the Birch*. Levitan had given them to Anton and they never left his study, whether in Melikhovo, Moscow or Yalta."

Chekhov's and Levitan's friendship and admiration for each other increased with the years. Levitan recognized in Chekhov a master.

"I have read your *Motley Stories* and *At Twilight* again with great care, and you fill me with admiration as a landscape painter. I pass over the abundance of interesting ideas to be found in them, but the landscapes – they are really the height of perfection! For instance, in your story *Happiness* the pictures of the steppes, the tumuli and the sheep, are truly astonishing[9] ... Forgive me my silence, my genius of a Chekhov[10] ... How wonderful *The Peasants* is. An overwhelming piece of work! The narration achieves an astonishing artistic profundity. I am full of enthusiasm."[11]

Chekhov, on his part, greatly admired Levitan's art. "He is a Jew who is worth five Russians," he said to a friend.[12] And he used to tell with deep feeling how Levitan, on a visit to Italy, suddenly experienced such nostalgia for the Russian countryside that he hurried back home.

"I went to see Levitan in his studio. He is far and away the best Russian landscape artist," he wrote to Suvorin (19th January, 1885). And, in 1891, he wrote to his sister Maria from Paris: "I went to the Salon ... I must say that Russian painters are much more impressive than French painters. Compared to the landscape painters I saw yesterday, Levitan is a king."

Perhaps it should be mentioned that the French 'landscape painters' at that time were Cézanne, Renoir, Monet, Pissarro,

Guillaumin and Van Gogh. But, admittedly, it was not on the intrinsic value of Levitan's canvases that Chekhov was passing judgement. (Like so many Russians, he lacked a wide artistic culture.) The truth was that the skill of his favourite painter sprang from the same inner world as his own. It was the *subjects* of Levitan's paintings that were so close to Chekhov and so much appreciated by him. Both men were passionately fond of the Central Russian countryside and the area around Moscow, with its lowly, melancholy poetry. Both men were *lyric* artists, who could see through and beyond material appearances to the supernatural, mysterious halo, giving everything that extension which is the essence of poetry.

Levitan used to tell his pupils: "Do your utmost to depict what you feel, the state of mind that gazing at this or this spectacle of nature produces on you." He, himself, depicted, with apparent simplicity, the poetic glamour of moonlight in his picture *Moonlit Night in the Village* (1897). In the following year Chekhov published *The Man with the Brief-Case*, containing the passage quoted in page 51 which seems to have been inspired by Levitan's work.

Here, Chekhov puts into words what Levitan indicates with his palette: the melancholy poetry of inanimate objects and the spirituality that lies hidden beneath the surface of the tangible world. He came to describe them better and better as he approached the end of his life: "Yalta was scarcely visible through the morning mist; white clouds rested motionless on the mountain peaks. The leaves on the trees were still, the cicadas sang and the flat, monotonous sound of the sea rose towards them, telling of the repose, the eternal sleep that awaits us all. The sound of the sea could already be heard before Yalta ever existed, it can be heard now and it will continue to be heard, just as flat and indifferent, when we are no longer here. And in this continuity, this total indifference to the life and death of each one of us, may perhaps lie the pledge of our eternal salvation, of the perpetual progress of life on this earth, of infinite perfection."

After Levitan's death, Chekhov said bitterly to the journalist, Pervukhin:[13] "Ah, if I'd only had the money, I'd have bought Levitan's *Village*, an ugly, grey, wretched, forsaken village, but from which, nonetheless, emanates such charm that you can't tear your eyes away from it: you want to look at it again and again. Nobody has ever achieved such simplicity and such purity of conception as Levitan achieved towards the end of his life, and I doubt if anyone else ever will ... How little he is appreciated! How much his work is under-rated! It's an absolute disgrace: he possessed such great, original and exceptional talent. Something so strong, fresh and spontaneous that it should have produced a real revolution. Yes, Levitan died much too soon!"

Serge Diaghilev was even harsher in the obituary notice he wrote on Levitan: "He has never really received due recognition either from us or the West. The Russian public were scarcely aware of him, apart from a handful of art-lovers, who had watched the development of his remarkable talent for a long time ... Generally speaking, there is no common denominator by which one can compare the scope and power of Russian literature and painting. But if one seeks in our painters' canvases the freshness of Turgenev's mornings, the scent of Tolstoy's hay, or the precision of Chekhov's descriptions, one is inevitably driven to the conclusion that, among all the Russian landscape painters from the time of Venezianov to the present day, Levitan is alone in occasionally rising to the level of these great poets."[14]

NOTES

1. Suvorin's *Diary*, Petrograd, 1923.
2. I. Levitan was born in August, 1860, in Bielorussia. He was seven months younger than Chekhov and died of a heart attack at the age of forty in 1900. Chekhov only survived him by four years.
3. A life of Kramskoy, including his letters and critical articles, edited by Suvorin.

MOSCOW

4. The two brothers, Paul and Serge Tretiakov, rich Moscow industrialists, were passionate lovers of art. Paul collected Russian pictures and was the founder of the gallery. His brother became mayor of Moscow and left his collection of Western paintings to his native town.

5. All Chekhov's letters to Levitan were destroyed at the latter's request by his brother, Abel Levitan. All Levitan's letters to Chekhov are still extant.

6. M. Chekhova: *Memories From a Far-Away Past*, 1960.

7. M. Chekhova: *Memories*, 1960.

8. Shchepkina-Kupernik: Moscow, 1952.

9. *Letter to Chekhov*, June, 1891.

10. *Letter to Chekhova*, December, 1891.

11. *Letter to Maria Chekhova*, 1897.

12. Lazarev-Grusinski: *Chekhov by his Contemporaries*, Moscow, 1960.

13. M. Pervukhin: *Chekhov in Yalta*, 9th May, 1904.

14. Diaghilev: *To the Memory of Levitan*, 1900.

[7]

Sakhalin

(21st April–8th December, 1890)

In these morbid times, when European societies are
overcome by idleness, boredom with life and lack of
faith, when there reigns everywhere an alarming combination of distaste for life and fear of death, when even
the best of men sit with their arms folded and justify
their indolence and depravity by the absence of any
definite aim, heroes and ascetics are as vital as the sun.
It is they who constitute the most poetical and the
most happy-to-be-alive element in society; they are its
stimulus, its consolation and its nobility. In themselves
they are living documents, showing society that alongside those who argue about pessimism and optimism,
produce mediocre novels, useless schemes and commonplace theses from sheer boredom, succumb to de-
bauchery out of nihilism and earn their daily bread by
lying, that alongside those sceptics, Jesuits, mystics
and neuropaths, those philosophers, liberals and con-
servatives, there also exist men of a wholly different
kind, heroic men, full of faith, heading towards a
clearly determined goal ... Men like Przewalski[1] are
particularly valuable because the meaning of their
lives, their exploits, their aims and their moral personality are within the grasp of even an infant. And
this has always been the case: the closer a man gets to
the truth, the simpler and easier it is to understand him.

CHEKHOV : *N. Przewalski*, 1888

Iɴ 1890, Chekhov was thirty. His literary fame was steadily growing. In 1888, the Academy of Sciences had awarded him the Pushkin Prize for his collection of stories, *At Twilight*. He was living in his comfortable 'commode' in Sadovaia-Kudrinskaia, surrounded by attention, affection and friendship. His life had never been as rich or as happy, except where his health was concerned: the haemorrhages had been more frequent since 1884. He suffered, too, from haemorrhoids and violent headaches.

The balance-sheet, after weighing up the good and the bad, scarcely recommended undertaking a long, arduous journey, for which the underlying motives eluded even his closest friends. To them, the idea of going to Sakhalin seemed a foolish whim. Chekhov's best friend, Suvorin, said as much in a letter. Chekhov's reply of the 9th March was as follows:

You say that no one wants Sakhalin and that the island is of no interest to anyone. But is this true? Sakhalin might have been unnecessary and of no interest to a society which did not deport thousands of people there and spend millions of roubles on it . . . Sakhalin is a place of intolerable suffering . . . I regret not being sentimental; otherwise I would tell you that we ought to make pilgrimages to places like Sakhalin, as the Turks make pilgrimages to Mecca . . . From all the books I have read and am reading at the moment, it appears that we have made millions of people rot in prison, rot needlessly, for no good reason and in a barbaric manner. We have forced men in chains to cross thousands of versts in the cold. We have turned them into syphilitics, depraved them, begotten criminals and shelved the responsibility for all this on to the prison warders with their red, drunkards' noses. Now, all enlightened Europe knows that it is not the warders who are guilty, but all those of us who show no interest or concern ... No, I assure you that Sakhalin is of vital interest, and one can only regret that it is I who am going there and not someone capable of arousing public opinion.

Chekhov adds: "This journey will involve six months of hard work, physical and intellectual: therefore it is essential that I undertake it: I'm a southerner and beginning to grow lazy. One must discipline oneself!"

But these personal reasons, expressed in the half-serious, half-joking vein characteristic of Chekhov whenever he begins to speak of himself, and which serves to conceal the shyness that assails him as soon as he comes close to revealing his deep feelings, these reasons are entirely superficial. It is not a matter of self-discipline or his alleged laziness, but something quite different: in Chekhov's view, a man of letters is someone endowed with a particularly exacting conscience, someone, too, whose mission is to awaken the conscience of his contemporaries. Evidence of this is to be found in his wonderful story, *Gooseberries*, in which he puts so-called *happiness* on trial, the happiness that, to him, is nothing but moral blindness and a form of selfish satisfaction:

We neither see nor hear those who are suffering and all that is appalling in life takes place somewhere off-stage. Everything is calm and peaceful and only mute statistics prove the opposite: so many people driven insane, so many buckets of vodka drunk, so many children dead from hunger. And this state of affairs is apparently necessary. Apparently, the happy man only remains so because the unhappy ones bear their burden in silence, and, without that silence, happiness would be impossible. It amounts to mass hypnosis. Behind the door of every contented, happy human being, there should be someone armed with a small hammer, the blows of which would constantly remind him that unhappy people do exist and that however contented he may be, life will sooner or later show him its claws; misfortune, illness and poverty will eventually strike him down and, when they do, no one will see or hear him, just as now, he, himself, neither sees nor hears anyone. But the man with the hammer does not exist, the happy man goes on living, small everyday cares touch him lightly, much as the wind gently stirs the leaves of the aspens, and everything continues as before ... In actual fact, there is no happiness and there should be none, but if our life has any meaning or aim, that meaning and aim are in no way concerned with our personal happiness but with something far wiser and more important.

Chekhov wrote these words in 1898, long after his return from Sakhalin. But it would be wrong to assume that it was the sight of the prison and the appalling misery of the convicts that had inspired his ideas. No, long before his visit to the doom-laden island, he had expressed the same thoughts (for instance, in *The Enemies* in 1886 and *The Princess* in 1888). Unquestionably, it was not the prison that aroused Chekhov's conscience; on the contrary, it was his infinitely exacting and scrupulous conscience that drove him to undertake the journey to Sakhalin so that he might observe for himself human conditions at their worst.

As early as the 10th December, 1884, Chekhov had written to Nicholas Leikin, editor of the review *Oskolki* ('Fragments'): "For three days now, God knows why, blood has been pouring from my throat. This haemorrhage stops me writing and will stop me from going to Petersburg. For three days, I haven't seen a single *white* sputum ..." And, on 14th October, 1888, he mentioned it explicitly in a letter to Suvorin:

I had my first haemorrhage three years ago (in fact it was four) ... It lasted for three or four days and put my mind in a whirl. The blood flowed from my right lung. Since then, I have had at least two haemorrhages every year. I had another one the day before yesterday, and yesterday, too. It has stopped today. Every winter, autumn and spring, and on every damp day in

summer, as well, I cough. But it only alarms me when I
see blood: there is something menacing in that blood pouring from my mouth, as there is in flames from a fire.

In 1889, his condition grew worse. In December of that year,
he refused an invitation from Suvorin to come to St Petersburg;
he had a bad cough and was afraid that the jolting of the
train might bring on another haemorrhage.

Between 1884 and the end of 1889, he had had eleven haemorrhages; the attacks occurred two or three times a year and
were increasingly severe. Nevertheless, four months after writing to Suvorin of his fear of being jolted in the train, he embarked on a long, dangerous journey; in fact, it was to take
him fifty days to reach Sakhalin. His itinerary was as follows:
from Moscow to Jaroslavl by train; from Jaroslavl to Perm by
boat down the Volga and the Kama; from Perm to Tiumen by
train; from Tiumen to Lake Baikal by *tarantass*, an open carriage
without springs; across Lake Baikal by boat and another long
drive to Sretensk; from Sretensk all the way down the Amur
to Nikolaevsk; and finally across the Strait of Tartary to the
northernmost point of Sakhalin. In all, it meant that Chekhov
had to cover some 4,000 versts (about 2,700 miles) by carriage.

He left Moscow on 21st April, 1890. Six days earlier he had
written to Suvorin: "I have bought myself a sheepskin jacket,
a military, leather raincoat, a pair of Wellington-boots and a
large knife to cut sausages and keep the tigers at bay! I have
fitted myself out from head to foot." He wrote to his sister
from Ekaterinburg on 1st May: "I have spent two or three days
here, restoring my coughing, haemorrhaging self." And two
weeks later he wrote: "I desperately need warmth and a comfortable bed. You cannot imagine how lonely one feels surrounded by a howling, savage horde, in the open fields, before
dawn, with fires near and far, eating up the grass without warm-
ing the cold night air to the smallest degree! Oh, how low my
spirits are! We are just off. The insides of my felt boots are as
wet as a W.C."

[117]

On 20th May, Chekhov had a haemorrhage brought on by the jolting of the cart, tiredness, the severe cold, perpetually damp feet and, more than anything, hunger that tormented him all through the journey across Siberia. Three weeks after his departure he wrote to Suvorin from Tomsk: "The whole way, I was as ravenous as a dog; I stuffed my belly with bread so as to prevent myself from dreaming of turbot, asparagus and so on. I dreamt of buckwheat gruel. I dreamt of it for hours on end."

A fortnight later, he wrote to his brother Alexander from Irkutsk: "The most irritating thing is that in all these main little district towns *there is nothing to eat*. As you approach the town, you dream of swallowing a mountain; then you arrive – and what do you find? No sausage, no cheese, no meat, not even herrings; nothing but the same insipid eggs and milk as you get in the villages!"

And a week after that, on the shores of Lake Baikal he wrote to Feodor Schekhtel: "It is raining, the lake is enveloped in fog and *there is nothing to eat*; on the other hand, there are any amount of bugs and cockroaches. In short, it is not life, but a real operetta! Depressing and absurd!"

He was able to eat his fill for the first time aboard the *Yermak*, in which he crossed the lake: "For heaven's sake – soup! Half my kingdom for a plate of soup! Grigori Ivanovich, the cook, rose to the occasion and gave us a wonderful meal," he was able to write to his mother the next week. "The weather was calm and sunny. The Baikal waters are turquoise blue and more transparent than those of the Black Sea ... What a skunk Levitan was in refusing to come with me. On my right, I can see a forest growing up the mountain-side. On the left – another one running down to the lake. What precipices, what rocks! The colour of the lake is warm, tender."

In spite of the cold, exhaustion and the thousand and one discomforts and dangers encountered on the journey, in spite of the hunger and cough that tormented him, Chekhov was enchanted by everything he came across in these vast, still virginal, expanses, inhabited by a rough, strong, abstemious race of people, with a primitive integrity of their own. After reaching Tomsk, he wrote to his sister on 14th–17th May, 1890 :

> The people here are kind, good and true to fine traditions; the rooms are simply furnished but clean and even have some claims to luxury; the beds are soft, with eiderdowns and large pillows; the floors are painted or covered with carpets of hand-woven cloth. All this is clearly due to a certain affluence, to the fact that a family here owns a plot of sixteen dessiatines (about 43 acres) of good land, which produces excellent grain. But affluence and plenty is not responsible for everything; one must do justice to their way of life. When you come into a room late at night, you are not choked by Russian affluvia and smells. Admittedly, an old woman wiped a teaspoon on her behind before giving it to me. But tea is never served to you here without a cloth on the table and people do not search their hair for lice or belch in your presence; when they hand you a glass of water or milk, they do not dip their fingers in it; the crockery is clean and the kvass as transparent as beer – generally speaking, the cleanliness here is such as our Little-Russians could only dream of and, mark you, our Little-Russians are so much cleaner than our Great-Russians!
>
> The bread here is delicious! I stuffed myself with it for the first days. Very good, too, are the pies and pancakes and various cakes. But, on the other hand, none of the rest suits a European stomach. For instance, everywhere I went I was given a soup made from wild duck. It is disgusting stuff, a turbid liquid with small pieces of duck and badly cooked onion floating about in it. The ducks' stomachs are badly cleaned and when you eat them you begin to think that the mouth and rectum have changed places.

From Irkutsk, on Lake Baikal, he gave further details of his journey to Alexis Pleshcheev :

I divide everything that I have experienced in Siberia into three periods: (1) from Tiumen to Tomsk, a distance of fifteen hundred versts: terribly cold day and night, sheepskin coat, felt boots, icy rain, wind and a struggle for life against the rivers in spate; meadows and roads were under water and I constantly had to exchange my vehicle for a boat and proceed like a Venetian in his gondola; waiting for the boats and the crossing itself took up so much time, that I could only cover 70 versts instead of 400 or 500 during the two last days before reaching Tomsk; (2) from Tomsk to Krasnojarsk, a distance of five hundred versts in deep mud; my vehicle and I sank into this mud like a fly into thick jam. How often my vehicle was damaged! How many versts I had to cover on foot! How often my face and clothes were spattered! I floundered along through the mud. And how often I argued and quarrelled! My brain could no longer think, only argue. I was completely exhausted and greatly relieved when I reached Krasnojarsk. (3) From Krasnojarsk to Irkutsk, a distance of fifteen hundred and seventy versts; heat, smoke from forest-fires, dust; dust in one's mouth, one's nose and pockets; when I saw myself in the mirror, I thought I must be wearing make-up ... When I get back I shall tell you about the Yenissey and the taiga[2]; it is very interesting, unusual and full of novelty to a European, whereas the rest is banal and monotonous. On the whole, nature in Siberia differs little, superficially, from that in Russia.

Nevertheless, the wild beauty of eastern Siberia captivated him to the extent of making him forget his ailments and discomforts:

Travelling from Russia to Siberia you are bored after leaving the Urals till you reach the shores of the Yenissey ... Unusual, grandiose and beautiful nature only begins with the Yenissey ...

Never in my life have I seen a more gorgeous river. If the Volga is a beautiful maiden, adorned, modest and melancholy, the Yenissey is a valiant knight, powerful and violent, uncertain how to employ his strength and his youth. Soon after one has crossed the Yenissey, the famous taiga begins. So much has been said and written about it that one expects more from it than it can give. There are neither the trees with enormously thick trunks rising to dizzy heights, nor the utter silence I had heard about: I had been told that the taiga was silent and that its vegetation had no smell, and that was what I was expecting. But, during the whole time I went through it the birds sang at the top of their voices and the insects hummed; the pine trees, warmed by the sun, gave off a heavy smell of resin; the clearings and the borders of the forest all along the way were covered in pale blue, pink and yellow flowers, which did more than just delight the eye. Obviously, those who have described the taiga have never seen it in spring, but only in summer, a time of year when, in Russia too, the forests are silent and produce no scent.

The strength and the fascination of the taiga does not lie in its giant trees or its silence, but in the fact that possibly only the migratory birds know just how far it extends. On the first day, you are not aware of it; on the second and third, you begin to marvel; and on the fourth and fifth, you feel you will never get away from this earthly monster . . . You know that ahead lie Angara and Irkutsk, but what lies behind these forests, that stretch to the north and south on either side of the road, and how many hundreds of versts they continue, is hidden even from coachmen and peasants born in the area. When questioned, they reply: "It is endless." Suddenly, an escaped prisoner emerges from the pine trees, a sack and saucepan on his back. How small and paltry his crimes, his sufferings and he himself seem, compared with the vast taiga! The

saying that "man is nature's king" can nowhere appear so
faint-hearted and false as it does here . . .³

The further Chekhov advanced into this wild, free country,
the more he appreciated its grandiose poetic qualities:

> I am still under the influence
> of the *Transbaikalia*, which I have crossed: it is magnifi-
> cent country. One might say that the poetry of Siberia
> begins at Baikal; before Baikal, it was its prose. (Letter to
> A. Plescheev, 20th June, 1890.) I am in love with the Amur;
> I would gladly have spent two years there. It is beautiful,
> vast, free and warm. Neither France nor Switzerland has
> ever known such liberty. The lowliest of the deportees
> breathes more freely here than the greatest of the generals
> in Russia. (Letter to Suvorin, 27th June, 1890.)

This feeling of liberty and strangeness grew stronger as
Chekhov drew closer to the frontiers of the Russian empire.
Nature, men and the way of life were all new, unusual and
unfamiliar the whole way down the vast river, from which
"one sees Russia on one side and China on the other".

> On 5th July, 1890, my boat
> reached Nikolaevsk, one of the most far-eastern towns in
> Russia. The Amur, here, is very wide; the sea is only
> twenty-seven versts away. It is a majestic, beautiful spot,
> but memeories of the past, tales about the cruel winter and
> no less cruel local customs, the proximity of the deporta-
> tion area and the very sight of the neglected, dying city
> take away all desire to admire the landscape. Nikolaevsk
> was founded not so long ago, in 1850, by G. Nevelsky. Be-
> tween 1850 and 1860, when culture was being established
> along the Amur, sparing neither soldiers, prisoners nor
> emigrants, Nikolaevsk was mainly populated by officials;
> many Russian and foreign adventurers made their way
> here and the town, apparently, was brimming with curi-

osity, so that there was even an occasion when a visiting
man of science found it necessary and possible to deliver
a lecture in the local club. Now the inhabitants lead a
drowsy, drunken life and live from hand to mouth. The
town has no hotel; I was allowed to rest after dinner in
a low-ceilinged hall in the club, where, so they told me,
dances are held in the winter. To my enquiries as to where
I could spend the night, people merely shrugged their
shoulders. I had, willy-nilly, to spend two nights aboard
the boat, and when it returned to Khabarovsk I found myself like a lobster on the sand. Where, oh, where, was I to
go? My luggage was at the harbour. I paced up and down
the shore, wondering what I should do. Some two or three
versts off-shore lay the *Baikal*, the ship in which I was to
cross the Tartar Straits, but it was not sailing for four or
five days. Should I make my way there now? It might be
embarrassing, I could be told that I had come too early . . .
The wind rose. The Amur frowned, becoming as restless as
the sea. I was bored and went to the club where I had a
lengthy dinner, listening to people at the next table talking
about gold, a conjurer, and a Japanese dentist, who drew
teeth not with pincers but with his bare fingers. If you
listen and look around, heavens, how far removed from
Russia and how alien life here is.[4]

From the Siberian smoked salmon, keta, which is served
here with the vodka, to the conversations I overhear,
everything seems odd and not at all Russian. All the time I
sailed down the Amur, I had the feeling I was not in
Russia, but somewhere in Patagonia or in Texas. Leaving
aside the wholly unfamiliar landscape, it seemed to me
that our Russian way of life is quite unknown to the inhabitants of the Amur, that Pushkin and Gogol are incomprehensible here and, therefore, pointless, that our history
bores them and that we who come from Russia are regarded
as foreigners. I found complete indifference to anything
pertaining to religion or politics. The priests I came across

here eat the same food as on any other day during Lent, and I was told of one of them, who wore a white silk cassock, that he prospects for gold in competition with his flock. If you want to bore an inhabitant of these regions and make him yawn, start talking to him about Russian politics, the Russian government, Russian art, etc. And their morals, too, are very strange, far removed from ours. A chivalrous attitude towards women is a sort of cult but, at the same time, it is not considered reprehensible to lend your wife to a friend in exchange for money. Or, as a better example: on the one hand there is a lack of class prejudice – a deportee is treated here as an equal; on the other hand, it is not considered a crime to shoot a Chinese vagabond, found wandering in the woods, like a dog, or to go hunting hunchbacks.[5]

From Nikolaevsk, Chekhov crossed the Strait of Tartary and disembarked, on the North of Sakhalin Island, on the 10th July.[6] Next day, he reached Alexandrovsk, the administrative capital of the Island.

He spent three months on the island and studied it in all its aspects:

I have seen everything [he wrote Suvorin on 11th September]. So, now the question is to weigh up, not what I have seen, but the light in which I saw it. There is not a single convict or deportee in Sakhalin to whom I have not spoken. I managed to carry out a census of the children very successfully, and am pinning my hopes to it. I witnessed a man being flogged, after which I dreamt for three or four nights of the executioners and the horrible frame to which the man was tied. I spoke to men chained to their barrows ... The result is that I have wrecked my nervous system and sworn to myself that I will never return to Sakhalin.

The day after my arrival, I went to pay my respects to the Governor of the Island, V. O. Kononovich. In spite of his weariness and lack of time, the General received me very amiably and spoke to me for about an hour. He is an educated and cultivated man, with great practical experience; before being appointed to Sakhalin, he was in charge of the Kara prisons for eighteen years. He talks well, writes well, and gives the impression of being a good-hearted man embued with humanitarian propensities ... George Kennan[6] speaks of him warmly in his well-known book.[7]

The supreme commander of the whole Amur region, Governor-General Korff, made the same humane and liberal impression on Chekhov :

On 22nd July, after Mass and the military parade, a superintendent rushed up to tell me that the Governor-General wanted to see me. Baron Korff received me in a very friendly manner and spoke to me for half an hour. General Kononovich was present during our conversation. "I give you permission to go wherever you wish," the Baron said to me. "We have nothing to hide. You will be able to see everything here, you will be supplied with a pass to all the prisons and the penal colonies. All the documents you require for your work will be made available to you; in short, all doors will be open to you. The only permission I cannot give you is to visit the political prisoners, because that is something I am not entitled to do." That same evening, I attended a big dinner given by the Governor of the island. There was music and a few speeches. Baron Korff replied briefly to a toast proposed in his honour. I remember these words of his addressed to the officials present : "I have been able to state that the life of the 'wretches'[8] on Sakhalin is less arduous than in Russia and even in Europe. Nevertheless, it is your duty to devote your energies towards making it even more so, since the road to perfection is a long one." He had been in Sakhalin five years earlier and now found that considerable progress had been made, far surpassing all his expectations. His praise was scarcely compatible with such phenomena as hunger, widespread prostitution among the convicts and the cruelty of the corporal punishment, but his audience was justified in believing him : the present, compared with the state of affairs five years before, might well have appeared to be the dawn of a genuine golden age. Next day, I called on the Governor and he gave me his views on the prisons and deportations to Sakhalin. He suggested that I title the fruit of my observations: *Description of the Life of the Wretches*.

Our conversation left me with the conviction that the Baron was a magnanimous and high-minded man, but that he did not know as much about the 'life of the wretches' as he thought he did. Here are a few lines from his *Description* : "Nobody is deprived of the hope of being reinstated in all his rights. There are no life sentences. Life imprisonment is reduced to twenty years. Hard labour is not really hard. There are no chains, no guards, no shaven heads."

How close did these optimistic statements and fine words come to the actual facts ? No doubt, Governor Korff and General Kononovich, commander of the island, were upright, sincere, humane men. But they very rarely visited the convicts in their charge and the black reality, the arbitrariness and the cruel, sordid details of the prisoners' lives were unknown to them. Their fault lay in having remained blind to what was going on "within two or three hundred metres of their quarters". An administration depends less on its chiefs-of-staff than on the underlings, those subordinates who are in close contact with the day-to-day events and who distort and dishonour the generous intentions of their remote superiors, by their application of them.[9]

Chekhov soon realized this. He methodically visited everything that could be visited in Sakhalin, starting with the prisons.

I visited the Alexandrovsk prison shortly after my arrival. It is a large square yard, surrounded by six barrack-type wooden huts, enclosed by a wooden fence. The main gate always stays open and a sentry paces up and down in front of it. The yard is very cleanly swept and this exemplary cleanliness makes a favourable impression.

We enter the barrack room. It is large, well-lit and the windows are open. The walls are not painted; they are of unpolished wood and the cracks between the blackened beams are filled in with oakum; only the Dutch stoves are white. The floor is wooden, unpainted, very dry. A single bench runs the length of the room, on which the convicts sleep in two rows, head to head. The places are not numbered or separated in any way. There is no bedding. They sleep on the planks, spreading out old torn sacks, their clothes or any kind of rags beneath them – far from appetizing. On the planks one comes across caps, shoes, pieces of bread and empty milk-bottles, stoppered with paper or a rag; under the bench lie tin boxes, dirty sacks, bundles of clothes, tools and various scraps of material. A well-fed cat is strolling along the bench. Clothes, pans and tools hang on the walls; the shelves hold teapots, bread and tins.

Free men do not take off their hats in Sakhalin, when they enter their quarters. This courtesy is only obligatory on the convicts. So we walked down the barrack room with our hats on, while the prisoners stand to attention and watch us in silence. We, too, remain silent and it is as though we had come there to buy them. We pass on, enter other barrack rooms and find everywhere the same appalling misery which can no more be concealed under the rags than a fly under a magnifying glass; the same stable-type of life and nihilist in the fullest sense of the word, since it is devoid of possessions, solitude, comfort, rest and sleep . . .

[127]

Chekhov wanted to see *everything*. He believed that the only way to approach *every* deportee was to enter his home, see him and talk to him. Therefore, he decided to embark on an extremely illuminating piece of work, never yet carried out: a census of the Sakhalin population.[10] He undertook and achieved this work entirely on his own. He had forms printed, consisting of thirteen questions. Forms in hand, he visited every hut, every barrack, every mine and every deportation area. He saw every one of the island's 10,000 inhabitants and filled in 10,000 forms in his own hand. The conclusions to which he came after this immense undertaking, that took him from five o'clock every morning to late at night, were appalling.

Children on Sakhalin die, Chekhov declared. They are underfed, pale and unhappy. The state of their morals is dreadful. He was haunted for a long time by the memory of a small child who had accompanied her father to prison and clung all day on to the chain which attached him to his barrow. At night, she slept, rolled up as a ball, inside the barrow. Haunted, too, by the memory of this small boy:

When I was visiting the huts in upper Armudan, I came across one in which there was no adult person: only a small boy ten or so, fair-haired, stooping and barefoot. His pale face was freckled and resembled marble:

– What's your father's surname? I asked.
– I don't know.
– How can that be? You live with your father and don't know his name? Shame on you!
– He isn't my real father.
– How do you mean, he isn't your real father?
– He's my mother's lover.
– Is your mother married or a widow?
– A widow. She came here because of her husband.
– What does that mean, she came here because of her husband?

- She killed him.
- Do you remember your father?
- No, I'm a bastard. My mother gave birth to me in the Kara prison.[11]

. . . The Sakhalin children [Chekhov goes on] are pale, thin, apathetic, clad in rags and always hungry. They die almost exclusively from intestinal complaints. They are invariably underfed; most of them eat nothing but turnips for months on end, the richer ones – salt fish; the prevailing temperature is low; cold, damp and hunger combine to undermine the children's constitutions, slowly and exhaustingly, by producing a degeneration of all the tissues.

The children are miserable partly due to the inhumane conditions in which their mothers live.

On 1st January, 1890, *women* criminals constituted 11·5% of the total number of convicts. Fifteen or twenty years ago, women convicts who came to Sakhalin were immediately sent to brothels. Now they are taken to prison straight from the port and locked up for the night in a dormitory, prepared beforehand. The newly arrived women are then distributed between the three Sakhalin districts. As it is the Alexandrovsk officials who perform the distribution, their district gets the lion's share. The youngest and prettiest women remain there, as at the bottom of a filter. Only the old ones and those who "are not worthy of masculine attentions" remain for the remote southern district. Among the women selected for the Alexandrovsk district, some stay as servants to the officials, others enter the harems of the clerks and warders, and the third and most numerous section go to the izbas of the richest or more influential deportees. Even a convict can obtain a woman if he has any money and exercises some authority in his little concentration camp world.

Some deportees are only too happy if their concubine devotes herself to prostitution; he regards her as a useful domestic animal and respects her up to a point, that is to say ... he puts the samovar on to boil and holds his peace when she curses him.

The sole preoccupation of the free woman (one who has come to join her husband) is to keep alive and contrive to give her children enough to eat. There is no way of earning a living by working, nowhere to beg; she has to exist, she and her children, on her husband's prison ration which is barely sufficient for one adult. Little by little, she becomes embittered, wastes away, decides that delicate feelings are out of place on Sakhalin, and begins to sell her body for the sake of 5 or 10 kopecks. The husband is equally callous and attaches little importance to chastity. Young girls have scarcely reached the age of fourteen or fifteen before they are sold; the mothers sell them at home, or hand them over as concubines to rich deportees or warders. And this happens all the more readily because a free woman here spends her time in complete idleness ... The woman's dependent condition, her poverty and degradation en-courage the development of prostitution. Because of the enormous demand, neither old age, ugliness nor even syphilis in its most advanced stages present any obstacle to the practice of prostitution. Nor does extreme youth. I ran across a young girl of sixteen on the streets of Alex-androvsk, who, as they told me, had begun her career of prostitution at the age of nine. This girl has a mother, but even family ties do not always save young girls in Sakhalin. There is a free woman in the suburbs of Alexandrovsk who runs an "establishment", where the "workers" consist solely of her own daughters.

Chekhov carried on his census throughout the island. He went down the coal mines, worked by haggard, hungry, ragged specimens of humanity, whose moral condition struck him as even more appalling than their physical disintegration :

What renders work in the mines exceptionally hard is not the fact that it takes place underground in dark, damp tunnels, sometimes stretched out on one's stomach, sometimes bent double; work on construction sites and navvying in wind and rain make even greater physical demands on the workman. No, the exceptional hardship of this work does not lie in the work itself, but in what encompasses it, the stupidity and dishonesty of the petty officials, whose insolence, injustice and arbitrariness the convict must bear with all the time. Yet the convict, however deeply corrupt and unjust he may be himself, loves justice above everything, and if he does not find it among the men placed over him, he grows more and more embittered and loses faith in everyone.

When Chekhov came up from the mine "the morning was damp, dark and cold; the sea rough and surging. I remember that we stopped for a moment on the road linking the old mine to the new one, beside an old Caucasian lying on the sand in a deep faint. Two of his compatriots were holding his hands and looking round them helplessly and despairingly. The old man was pale, his hands cold, his pulse very weak. We stayed beside him for a moment or two and then went on our way without giving him any medical assistance. When I remarked to the doctor accompanying me that we should at least have given the old man a few Valerian drops, he replied that the hospital attendant at the Voievodskaia prison had no medicine of any kind at his disposal."

Doctor Chekhov was struck by the same scarcity and lack of proper attention at the Alexandrovsk hospital where he had wanted to treat some of the patients:

They brought me a small boy with a boil on his neck. It needed lancing and I asked for a lancet. The male nurse and two muzhiks who were present rose precipitately and rushed off somewhere; a few moments later, they came back, bringing me a lancet. The instrument would not cut; they told me this was impossible as it had just been sharpened. The nurse and the two muzhiks dashed off again and two or three minutes later brought me another lancet. I began to make the incision: this instrument was blunt, too. I asked for a phenol solution and they produced it but only after a long wait – it was obvious that this liquid was not often used. There was no bowl, no cottonwool, no probe, no proper scissors and not even enough water.

What could the moral state of this oppressed and despairing population be?

Lies, cunning, cowardice, poltroonery, informing, theft and all sorts of hidden vices – these are the weapons with which this humiliated population, or at least the greater part of it, arm themselves in their struggle against the senior officers and warders, whom they fear, have no respect for, and regard as enemies. To avoid hard work or corporal punishment or to obtain a scrap of bread or a pinch of tea, salt or tobacco, the deportee resorts to deception, since experience has taught him that in the struggle for survival, a lie produces the surest and most direct results. Stealing goes on continually and comes close to being a positive industry . . . the one, solitary mental enjoyment here lies in gambling; cards can only be played at night by candlelight, or out-of-doors in the taiga. Every secret pleasure, constantly repeated, develops little by little into a passion. Cards have already spread through all the prisons like an epidemic; prisons have become gambling-houses, and the settlements and army-posts – their provincial branches.

These degraded and sick specimens of humanity did not even have the consolation of religion. " 'Can a shaven-headed convict, in irons or chained to a barrow, enter a church, if he so wishes?' A priest to whom I put this question, replied: 'I don't know.' " Nor was the consolation and mental support of culture open to them: Chekhov had found 71 per cent of the men and 90 per cent of the women totally illiterate.

This Dante-like humanity lived in harsh, wild, but strangely beautiful surroundings: "The taiga remains imposing and beautiful. One comes across birch trees, aspens, poplars, willows, ash trees, elders, wild cherry trees, spiraea and hawthorn in the midst of grass as tall or even taller than a man; giant ferns and burdock, with leaves three-quarters of a metre in diameter, mingle with shrubs and trees in dense, impenetrable thickets, harbouring bears, sables and stags. I have never seen such enormous burdocks anywhere else in Russia, and it is they, in particular, that give Sakhalin's forests, clearings and meadows their novel aspect. At night, by moonlight, they appear quite eerie."

The fauna on the island was 'sumptuous', but down-trodden men make poor hunters:

From a hunter's point of view, the fauna of vertebrate animals in Sakhalin is sumptuous. Among the most valuable animals, one finds sable, fox and bear in particularly large quantities. Sable is abundant throughout the island. One also finds deer, otter, lynx, wolverine; wolves, occasionally, and more rarely, stoats and tigers. But there are very few hunters among the deportees. One may reasonably assume that hunting will never become a real profession among the settler-deportees for the very reason that they are deportees. To be a professional hunter, one needs to be free, courageous and strong, whereas deportees, for the most part are indecisive, weak and neurasthenics. The apathy, indifference and degradation are such that even the island's greatest asset – its fish – is wasted:

Sakhalin's greatest asset and, possibly, its happy, enviable future does not lie in furs or coal, as is generally supposed, but in its wealth of fish. Keta or kita, a fish of the salmon species which has the same size, colour and taste of our salmon, inhabits the northern section of the Pacific Ocean; at a certain period in its life, it fights its way into the rivers of North America and Siberia and, with irresistible strength, in innumerable quantities ascends the rivers against the current until it reaches their original source in the mountain regions. In Sakhalin, this occurs at the end of July and beginning of August. During this period, the mass of fish is so enormous and its onrush so irresistible that anyone who has not witnessed the remarkable phenomenon with his own eyes can never form a proper picture of it.

On his return from the 'hell' of Sakhalin, in the winter of 1890 Chekhov sent Suvorin this brief report :

> In regard to our coastal region and, generally speaking, our whole eastern seaboard, with its flotillas, problems and far-eastern dreams, I can only say one thing : What flagrant misery ! Misery, ignorance and incompetence that can drive you to despair. One honest man for every ninety-nine thieves who dishonour the name of Russia . . .

He remained shattered for a long time, haunted by the utter degradation of man, which he had witnessed throughout his wanderings on the island. This degradation, debasement, humiliation and contempt for human dignity, he describes in *The Island of Sakhalin*[12] with the dryness – overwhelming in its impact – of a formal report. But one discovers in this literary work traces of anger, grief, indignation and humane tenderness that are direct reactions from his journey. In his stories such as *Murder In Exile, Goussev, The Babas* and many others, Chekhov raises his voice against the degradation of man and against a society that permits and encourages such degradation, just as Dostoevsky had done in the *Memories from the House of the Dead* and Tolstoy was to do in *Resurrection*.

After his return from Sakhalin, in a long story called *The*

Story of an Unknown Man (1893), Chekhov made the following important profession of faith: "I have now firmly grasped with my mind and with my soul that had suffered so much, that man's destiny either does not exist at all, or exists in one thing only: in a love, full of self-sacrifice for one's neighbour."

This theme thenceforward was to serve as the ulterior basis of all Chekhov's works. It was to emerge, delicate as filigree, from his stories and plays. But never explicitly expressed, merely suggested without any pathos, or stress, though remaining a constant reminder of all 'that took place off-stage' which a man worthy of that name should never allow himself to forget.

But while the Sakhalin expedition further stimulated Chekhov's humane and social susceptibilities, it had had another effect as well: that of awakening another side of this complex man, his poetic, rebellious and dreamy facet, curious about life and avid for it in all its aspects. Tired, morally and physically, he passionately longed for something other than the spectacle of disintegration, misery and ugliness: "What I want now are carpets, a hearth, bronzes and intelligent discussions! Where women are concerned, I put beauty before anything else, and in the history of humanity, a culture that finds expression in carpets, vehicles with springs and mental acumen," he wrote to Suvorin, 30th August, 1891.

Three months after his return from Sakhalin on 8th December, 1890, he escaped from Moscow, his writing desk and his memories and, in March, 1891, set off with Suvorin on his first trip to Europe.

NOTES

1. A celebrated Russian explorer.
2. The Russian word for the swampy, coniferous Siberian forests which separate the tundra from the steppes – translator's note.
3. Chekhov: *Notes on Siberia*, 1890.
4. Chekhov: *The Island of Sakhalin*.

5. Chekhov: *The Island of Sakhalin*. The Japanese had explored Sakhalin as early as 1613; the Russian, Krachennikov, in 1752. In June, 1787, the Comte de la Pérouse set foot on the western side of Sakhalin, which he took to be a peninsula. The Englishman W. A. Broughton made the same mistake in 1796, as did the Russian admiral Krusenstern in 1805. It was only in 1849 that the explorer G. Nevelski realized that Sakhalin was an island.

6. George Kennan (1845–1924) had visited the Siberian prisons in 1885–1886 and had contributed a series of articles to the American Review, the *Century Illustrated Monthly Magazine* (1887). These articles, in book form, were translated into Russian but, banned originally in Russia, were published first in Paris and London and only appeared in Russia in 1906. Tolstoy greatly admired Kennan's work and corresponded with him in the early 'nineties.

7. Chekhov: *The Island of Sakhalin*.

8. That was Baron Korff's name for the convicts.

9. The whip, of all the punishments inflicted in Sakhalin, was the most revolting, from its cruelty and the ceremony surrounding it, and the judges in European Russia who condemned vagabonds and recidivists to it would have long since given up the practice had it been carried out in their presence. They were however saved from this shameful spectacle, intolerable to a sensitive person, by article 478 of the Criminal Code which laid down that the sentences of Russian and Siberian Tribunals should be carried out at the deportation centre. One day, when I was sitting with General Kononovich, a resolute opponent of corporal punishment, in his salon, he said to me in the presence of a number of officials and a mining-engineer passing through Sakhalin, "Here, in Sakhalin, we rarely resort to corporal punishment, almost never." He did not know that men were flogged every day within 200 or 300 metres of him.

10. It is worth noting that this census was the first one carried out in Russia on a scientific basis. Up till then there had only been incomplete 'revisions' in Russia since the time of Peter the Great.

11. Chekhov: *The Island of Sakhalin*.

12. Chekhov wrote *The Island of Sakhalin* between 1891–1893. This great work was first published in a review, *Russian Thought*, between October, 1893–July, 1894 (nineteen instalments). The full text of twenty-three chapters only appeared in book form in 1895.

[8]

Chekhov and the West

 I T was in 1891 that Chekhov saw Western Europe for the first time. And for the last time – in 1904. He, who loved his country so much, was fated to die in a German spa, Badenweiler, in the Black Forest.

He made five journeys in all to Italy, France, Germany and Austria. And, like all intellectual Russians, he was faced with the eternal problem of East–West relations.

The problem of the relationship between Russian culture and Western civilization has played an important role in the history of Russian thought. Was Russia a continent apart, a 'Eurasian' world, which should jealously preserve its own customs, traditions and evolution? Or, on the contrary, was it part of Europe, with a duty to do everything in its power to become integrated in the Western bloc, absorb as much as possible of its culture and share its moral, philosophical and artistic conceptions? The two trends were in conflict throughout the 19th century, represented by two groups, the 'Slavophils' and the 'Westerners'. These two streams of thought, of which it is actually very difficult to establish and define the precise divergences, are reflected in the works of all great writers, whether Pushkin, Aksakov, Turgenev, Tiutchev, Dostoevsky or Tolstoy, but it would be an elementary error to try to place them definitely in one or other of the categories. It is, however, a fact that both these ideological trends can be found in different measures and aspects in the work of each of them. It is, in fact, impossible to be Russian and not be torn between what Dostoevsky, an ardent nationalist, had, nonetheless, defined as his 'two father-lands'. (Every Russian has two fatherlands, Russia and Europe.)

How, then, did Chekhov resolve this problem, which inevit-ably faced every thinking Russian? It seems clear that his point of view came closest to that of Turgenev. Turgenev had been classified as a Westerner, because he knew and greatly admired European literature, had studied philosophy in Germany, loved Pauline Viardot and spent a great part of his life in Paris and Baden-Baden. Also because he had written *Smoke*, in which he caricatured the narrow nationalism of certain Slavophils. But due attention was not paid to the counterpart of this 'western-ism' (which had been the cause of Dostoevsky's dislike for him), a counterpart which carried considerable weight as evidence since those of his works which will survive for ever belong to it: *A Sportsman's Sketches*, a poetical and deeply perceptive pic-ture of the Russian peasant; *A Nest of Noblemen*; *Fathers and Sons*, or any other of his best novels in which he depicts Russian society, idealizes the Russian woman and sings the praises of Russian nature, that same modest, monotonous, poor country-side of Central Russia, which Anton Chekhov was to depict, romanticize and love beyond anything.

European in his culture, his respect for science and his liking for the comforts and refinement of life, Turgenev had re-mained fundamentally Russian in his tastes, sympathies and essential propensities. Chekhov was the same, save on this point: he was far more interested in his fellow men and in the improvement of their condition. (Turgenev would never have gone to Sakhalin.) Unlike Turgenev, he was not of aristocratic origin, did not belong to the enlightened and Francophil nobil-ity that gave birth to Russian culture and letters, had not been born on an estate equipped with a library filled with the work of great European writers, had not attended philosophy lectures in Berlin and had not frequented the intellectual élite of several European capitals. But, springing from the people, he appreciated quite as well as Turgenev (and much better than Dostoevsky or Tolstoy) the need to spread Western civilization in Russia, adopt Western working methods and overcome the Slavonic inertia, procrastination and idleness. His great affection for his country, instead of blinding him to its faults and plunging him into an excessive romantic nationalism, wholly incompatible with his lucid mind, led him to clear-sighted understanding of the positive and negative sides of the national life and character. He wrote in his *Notebooks*, "Our pride and presumption are European; our degree of development and our actions are Asiatic."

The same thought turns up again in a letter written after his return from Sakhalin, describing a brief stop in Hong Kong:

A magnificent bay ... very good roads, omnibuses, a rack-and-pinion railway, museums, botanical gardens; everywhere you look you see evidence of the tender solicitude of the English for those whom they administrate; there is even a club for sailors. I had a ride in a rickshaw, a vehicle drawn by a man, and listened with indignation to my Russian companions accusing the English of exploiting the natives. I thought to myself: yes, the English exploit the Chinese, the Sepoys and the Hindus, but in return they bring them roads, aqueducts, museums and Christianity. Whereas you, you are exploiters too, but what do you give in exchange? God's world is beautiful. The only thing that is not is – ourselves. How little justice and humility there is in us, how badly we understand the notion of patriotism! The newspapers say that we love our great country, but how do we manifest that love? Instead of knowledge, we display an arrogance and presumption beyond all bounds; instead of work, laziness and filth; the conception of honour goes on further than respect for uniforms ... It is vital that we learn and work, and all the rest can go to the devil! (To Suvorin, 9th December, 1890.)

[139]

Indefatigably, he denounced the cause of all Russian ills, which in his eyes was *ignorance*, the ignorance that made the people "hate and despise everything that is new and useful; they hated and killed doctors during the cholera epidemic, but, on the other hand, they love vodka! According to the degree of people's love or hate one can assess the value of what they love and hate ... And what about the aristocrats? The same physical ugliness, the same uncleanliness, the same expectorations, the same toothless old age and the same loathsome death as those of the lower middle classes." (*Notebooks*.) These dreadful small minded bourgeois who inhabited the Taganrog of his childhood, who inhabited other Russian towns and who needed to be guided and educated. "In what way are these stupid, cruel, lazy, dishonest men any better than drunken, superstitious peasants, or animals, which panic, too, whenever anything happens to break the monotony of their lives, restricted by their instincts? I can remember dogs, tortured to death and driven mad, sparrows plucked alive by urchins and then thrown into the water, and a long, long list of slow, dumb suffering which I have been able to observe since my childhood." (*My Life*, 1896.)

Struggling to dispel this darkness and improve these men by showing them to themselves as they were, Chekhov hoped to achieve his ends by education and the propagation of scientific knowledge that has no country. "There is no national science just as there is no national multiplication table; for what is national is no longer science." (*Notebooks*.)

But while deeply sensitive to all that was lacking in Russian life and to its backwardness and wretchedness – particularly depressing for someone who acknowledges loving nothing but beauty, intelligence, talent, inspiration and liberty in its most absolute form; for someone who desires above everything to free himself from "brute force and all falsehood, however it may express itself" (to Pleshcheev, 4th October, 1888); for someone who "hates red tape and despotism" – Chekhov nonetheless remained attached to his native land by every fibre of his being. He was always bored abroad. A period of rapturous enthusiasm was invariably followed soon after by boredom and disenchantment. Far from home, far from Moscow and the Moscovite countryside, he felt unable to work, and consequently, to live. The most beautiful panoramas in France or Italy did not inspire him at all. One finds very little reference to them in his works, despite the five visits, some of them of considerable length, that he paid to Western Europe. The first trip was in March, 1891. Chekhov was spurred on to undertake it both by the need to forget the Dante-like visions of the island prisons and the desire, which never left him, to get to know new places and new people. He went with Suvorin on a tour of Austria, Italy and France.

His first reaction to European life was enthusiastic: on 19th March he arrived in Vienna and, next day, wrote to his family:

Ah, my friends, the Tunghuzes, if you only knew how beautiful Vienna is! One cannot compare it with any of the other towns I have seen in my life. The streets are wide and elegantly paved; there are masses of boulevards and squares, all the houses are six or seven storeys high; as for the shops – they are not shops, but a dream, something to make your head spin! Take ties alone, there are billions of them! And such marvellous objects in bronze, porcelain and leather! The churches are immense, but do not crush you by their size; they delight the eye because they seem to be a web of lace ... Everything is magnificent and it is only yesterday and today that I have realized that architecture is truly an art. And this art is not only to be seen in small fragments as at home, but extends over a stretch of several versts. Lots of monuments. And in every small street, without fail, a bookshop! *What seems strange here is that you can read everything and speak quite freely.*

All the women are "beautiful and elegant", and dress with taste. The restaurants are excellent. the food delicious.

[141]

Chekhov's artistic and sensual sides were very susceptible to this. (Did he not write to Gorki a few years later: "I am bored. Not in the sense of *weltschmerz*, nor in the sense of hankering after life, but just that I am bored without intelligent people, without the music I like and without women, who do not exist in Yalta. I'm bored without caviar and sauerkraut.") (Letter of 15th February, 1900.)

For this wise, profound man was very fond, and always would be, of the small, transitory pleasures of life – a gold watch, a cloak, a carpet, a delicately wrought *objet-d'art*, a delicious dish, a bottle of good wine.

He bought innumerable presents in Vienna and, a few days later, fell under the spell of Venice:

> In my whole life I have not seen a more remarkable town than Venice. [He wrote to his brother Ivan.] It is constantly dazzling, enchanting, and exhilarating. I spend the whole day in a gondola ... or stroll on the Piazza San Marco. That is where St Mark's Cathedral stands, a marvel impossible to describe, and the Doges' Palace and monuments that make my heart sing, as would a piece of music. I am touched by this astonishing beauty and delighted by it. Merezhkovski,[1] whom I met here, is wild with enthusiasm. *Russians, wretched and humiliated as they are, can easily go crazy in this world of beauty, wealth and liberty*. One would like to stay here for ever.

But this is how Merezhkovski described the same meeting:

> I spoke enthusiastically about Italy. Chekhov walked by my side, tall, stooping a little as usual, with a gentle smile on his face. He, too, was in Italy for the first time. For him, too, Venice was the first Italian town he had seen, but I noticed no enthusiasm about him. It even shocked me a little. His attention was taken up with minor unexpected details, which struck me as

completely devoid of interest: the guide and his uncommonly bald head, the voice of the violet-seller on the Piazza San Marco, the ceaseless ringing of bells in Italian stations.

Merezhkovski, with his abstracted, methodical mind, had little psychological intuition. It was precisely Chekhov's own particular genius that led him to notice typical details, outside his companion's range of vision, blend these details in a subtle, unexpected way and thus achieve an alloy that was original and rich in its infinite applications. But Chekhov was in no way a 'naturalist', a photographer. He did not search for documentation as did, for instance, Zola. External facts and their logical sequences interested him very little. Much more than a sociologist, he was an anthropologist, a psychologist and, first and foremost, a poet. What really moved him was the hidden meaning of things, the subterranean streams in which the roots of human feelings and actions are steeped. And in his poetic world, it is probable that the violet-seller in the Piazza San Marco and the strident bell-ringing in Italian stations had more importance, more direct interest than monuments, described a thousand times before, in which he, personally, as an artist and creator had no concern.

His discerning friend, Suvorin, saw him as he was:

> He loved everything living, emotionally moving or moved, everything that was colourful, gay or poetic whether in nature or in life . . . We went abroad together twice. Both times we visited Italy. Art, statues, paintings, churches – held little interest for him. As soon as we arrived in Rome, he wanted to lie down on the grass and rest. Venice enchanted him by its originality, but much more by the life in general and the serenades than by the Doges' Palace.[2]

The greater the artist, the more personal and strict is the *choice* he makes instinctively from the diverse material offered him by life. And it was natural that Chekhov should have sought both from life and the arts only that which would serve to enrich his own particular art.

Nevertheless, it would be wrong to reproach Chekhov for his lack of enthusiasm for Italy and its manifold beauties. He has, himself, testified to the spell it cast on him:

> Italy is an adorable country. Had I been an artist, free from family ties and rich, I should spend my winters here. In addition to its climate and warmth, Italy is the only country in which one is conscious that art is really sovereign, and this conviction gives one courage. (To his sister, 1st April, 1891.)

When Suvorin went to Italy without him in March, 1895, Chekhov asked him to give his greetings to that country 'which he loved so warmly'. "Lombardy made such an impression on me that I believe I remember every tree; and I only have to shut my eyes to see Venice again."

Three-and-a-half years before his death, he saw Italy for the last time. He wrote to Olga Knipper from Florence: "Everything is wonderful here. Anyone who has not seen Italy has not lived." (29th January, 1901.)

In France, he knew Paris, Biarritz and Nice. In 1891, he spent a few days in Paris (from 18th to 27th April) after having been in Monte Carlo and Nice. He lost five hundred francs at roulette, and was delighted; he was now in a position to tell his grandchildren that he had gambled and experienced all the emotions of a gambler! The restaurants astonished him:

> Alongside the Casino and the roulette – there is another kind of roulette: the restaurants. They fleece you, but the food is magnificent. Every dish is a real artistic composition, before which one should kneel in veneration, but, in any case, eat it. Every piece is richly embellished with artichokes, truffles and every kind of nightingales' tongues ... But, oh, my God, how contemptible and disgusting this life is, with its artichokes,

palm-trees and scent of orange-blossom! I love luxury and riches, but this roulette-luxury gives me the impression of a sumptuous water-closet. There is something in the air, here, that offends one's sense of respectability and vulgarizes nature, the noise of the sea, the moon. (He writes in his *Notebooks*: Monte Carlo – full of cocottes, an environment of cocottes; one feels that the palm-trees and chicken at dinner are cocottes too.) Up till now, of all the places I have visited, Venice is the one that has left the most luminous impression on me. Rome, when all is said and done, resembles Kharkov and Naples is dirty. (To his brother Michael, 15th April, 1891.)

The comparison of Rome to Kharkov may come as a surprise, but we must remember, here, Suvorin's summing up: artistic monuments left Chekhov cold, and history bored him. It cannot be sufficiently stressed that, being essentially an anthropologist, Chekhov was interested in his fellow creatures, in the men of his time, whose feelings he noted, understood, recorded and analysed with incomparable subtlety. The relics of the past and the poetic quality of Rome had impressed him as little as, thirty years earlier, they had impressed another great Russian, Tolstoy: "I must admit that ancient art did not make the same extraordinary impression on me as it did on my companions. In my opinion, the art of Antiquity, in general, is over-rated. And, generally speaking, it is man alone who really interests me."[3] And Tolstoy wrote to a friend: "You may not believe me, but, really, I should prefer to live in any little hole in the provinces than in Venice, Rome or Naples. Something so solemn, and an elegance so uniformly similar, conventional and, in my opinion, vulgar, hangs over these towns and on the life led in them, that it disgusts me even to think of it." (To P. Golokvastov, 17th–20th March, 1876.)

Much could be said about the dislike that a great part of the Russian élite felt for plastic beauty, beauty expressed in forms. What is often called bad taste or lack of taste among

Russians springs basically from this instinctive distrust of over-beautiful external forms which, in the eyes of the more sensitive constitute what amounts to an insult towards the misery of mankind. An abyss has always separated the way of life of Western people and that of the Russians ('poor and oppressed'). And the great writers are, first and foremost, the defenders of these people: Russian literature owes its greatness in the first place to its humanitarian sense, its incomparable human warmth. Aestheticism is directly opposed to this spirit of justice and charity; it appears superficial, egotistic and futile to those who are, all things considered, apostles. This was the view of the so-called 'populist' writers, of Tolstoy, and even of Chekhov, who admitted loving 'luxury and riches'. He certainly loved them, but it was luxury on the Chekhovian scale: modest, discreet, unostentatious and incapable of offending anyone. A luxury that is summed up in a gold watch, a well-cut suit, a bottle of good wine: the luxury of a 'proletarian', of a hard worker, always short of money.

The wealth and leisure of the people frequenting the Côte d'Azur drove him away from it. Paris, 'that seat of civilization', detained him for a few days. He visited the Exhibition, admired the Eiffel Tower and found the French people 'excellent', but he was bored because it was Easter, and, for the first time in his life, he was spending it away from his family. And, in addition, he had broken his pince-nez, which for a myopic was a catastrophe.

"I went to the salon and could not see more than half of the pictures because of my eyes," he to his sister, 21st April, 1891.

On the 21st April, Chekhov returned to Moscow. He was fed up with travelling: he wanted to work and could only do so properly at home in the Moscovite atmosphere.

Nevertheless, in September, 1894 he went back to Western Europe. He visited Abazzia, Lemberg, Vienna, Trieste, Fiume and Venice. In Milan, he saw an adaptation of Dostoevsky's *Crime and Punishment*, played in Italian, and went to the cir-

cus and had a look at the cemetery: "The Lombardy landscapes are extraordinary, probably unique." (Letter to N.
Lintvareva, 1st October, 1894.) He stopped at Genoa to visit
its famous cemetery, then moved on to the Hotel Beaurivage
at Nice. But despite Suvorin's presence, he was in a melancholy
mood. The sound of the sea depressed him and he "coughed,
coughed and coughed without end". (Letter to V. Goltsev, 6th
October, 1894.) After a few days in Paris, followed by a short
stay in Berlin, he was back again in Moscow on 14th October,
just a month after he had embarked on the trip.

In 1897 he had an acute lung haemorrhage and the doctors
prescribed a milder climate than that of Moscow or Melikhovo.
He left for France on 1st September and remained there for
eight months. On 4th September, he was in Paris, where he
bought a pullover, a stick and some ties and shirts at the Maga-
sins du Louvre. In the evening, he went to the Moulin Rouge
with Suvorin to see the belly-dancers. Paris was gay and attractive, but he had to leave the Suvorins – the weather was overcast
and humid and he was coughing again – and proceed south.
From 8th September, he spent a fortnight at the Hotel Victoria
in Biarritz before moving on to the Pension Russe, 9 rue Gounod
in Nice. Here he spent the rest of the winter.[4] The brilliant and
attractive Maxim Masimovich Kovalevski, a professor of socio-
logy and legal history who had been expelled from Moscow
University in 1887 for his liberal opinions, used to welcome all
the interesting Russians visiting the Côte d'Azur at his Villa
Batavia in Beaulieu-sur-Mer. Chekhov struck up a friendship
with this intelligent man who was brimming over with a zest
for life. Maxim Masimovich had a handsome, tanned face, magnificent blue eyes, the physique of an athlete, a ringing voice
and a catching laugh. The famous mathematician, Sofia
Kovalevskaya,[5] his name-sake, had loved him passionately. A
Professor at Stockholm University, and consequently separated
from him for most of the year, she had died in 1891, her health
undermined by a sense of despair that her most brilliant professional successes had done nothing to alleviate.

Chekhov used to see Maxim Masimovich almost every day. He admired his vitality, gaiety, wit and excellent appetite.

"We dined with Kovalevski the day before yesterday and laughed till our sides split. I ate lots of oysters," he wrote to Suvorin 1st October, 1897. He found everything in Nice very agreeable; the sun, the balmy air, the sound of the waves on the Promenade des Anglais, and French civility.

It is worth while living abroad if only to discover politeness and refinement in everyday behaviour. The chamber-maid is always smiling; she smiles like a stage-duchess yet one can see by her face, how tired she really is. When you get into a train, you must bow to the other passengers; you must not enter a shop without saying good-morning; even when speaking to beggars you must add 'monsieur' or 'madame'. (To his brother Ivan, 2nd October, 1897.)

He was enchanted by itinerant singers. In his opinion, the "least of the street-tenors" had more talent and elegance than the Russian opera singers.

"I'm not exaggerating," he wrote in a letter to his sister twelve days later, "every day I become increasingly convinced that Russians are not cut out to sing opera arias. Russians can only be good basses, but their real métier is to trade, write and work on the land, not to go to Milan to study singing!"

His health still left much to be desired, he spat blood for two or three weeks, but was gay and happy, and "'gambolled like a calf, which has not yet been forced into marriage: I gambol and do nothing else. Oh, what a blessing it is not to be married yet! What a comfort!" (Letter to E. Chavrova, 29th October, 1897.)

This radiant mood, however, was succeeded by fits of discouragement and depression.

"My last haemorrhage, which still continues, began three weeks ago. Because of it, I have to suffer various privations," he complained to Suvorin's wife on 10th November. "I do not go out later than three o'clock in the afternoon, do not drink, eat nothing hot, force myself to walk slowly; in short, I am vegetating, not living."

Nature in the south neither moved him nor brought him any solace, and struck him as alien and remote. But he liked the balmy air and "the culture that manifests itself here in every shop-window, in the smallest object; every dog here stinks of civilization."

Where work was concerned, he wrote little that pleased him, because the setting of his room and the writing desk were both unfamiliar. He felt uncomfortable, "as though I were suspended upside down by one foot." This condition was aggravated by the food, which was too rich and too plentiful. "One seems to be eating the whole time, whereas if one wants to write one must above all avoid repletion," he complained to his sister. And on 25th November he described for her benefit his daily routine:

> I get up at seven in the morning at half-past seven I eat two eggs, two croissants and drink a large cup of coffee. At midday, lunch: an omelette, beefsteak with some sauce or other, cheese and fruit. At half-past two, a large bowl of chocolate, which I have got into the habit of drinking. At half-past six, dinner: soup or borsch, fish, cutlets, chicken and vegetables (cauliflower, usually) fruit. In the evening, every now and then, tea with biscuits, which I take with friends.

The Dreyfus Case perturbed him and aroused his interest. Suvorin and his newspaper sided against Dreyfus. Chekhov was indignant with the attitude adopted by the *Novoye Vremya*. He wrote to Suvorin: "Zola is a noble spirit and I, who belong to the Syndicate and have already pocketed a hundred roubles from the Jews!, am full of admiration for his outburst. France is a wonderful country and her writers are wonderful, too."[6] (4th–17th January, 1898.)

A month later he attacked his friend's anti-Dreyfus convictions more violently : "Even if Dreyfus is guilty—what does it matter? Zola is right, anyway, for a writer's duty is not to accuse or persecute, but to defend even the guilty, as soon as they are sentenced and undergoing punishment. People will ask me : what about public policy and reasons of State? The answer is that great writers and artists should only become involved in politics in so far as they may be called on to protect themselves against them. There are already quite sufficient public prosecutors, lawyers and policemen about without them. And whatever the verdict may be, Zola will experience a keen satisfaction after the trial, his old age will be happy and he will die with a clear conscience."

For his part, Chekhov always refrained from judging and condemning. This attitude was deeply rooted in his nature, but it was reinforced by his long meditations on the danger of an artist becoming 'involved'. To allow oneself to be associated with a small section of opinion, enrolled in some côterie or other? Feel the weight, particularly heavy in Russia of official disapproval on the one side, or, on the other, the spiritual constraint of the liberal parties, of those who insist that a writer shall take sides, that an artist shall defend and support ideas only too often opposed to the demands of his art? No. Chekhov would always remain fiercely independent, remote from all politics.[7] And it was solely as a free man and free writer, convinced that his role in society was that of defender and not accuser, of advocate and not prosecutor, that he rose to defend both Zola and Dreyfus, "even if he is guilty."

The newspapers, the Dreyfus Case, the wonderful sunny weather, the blue sky, the sparkling sea and the trees in full blossom all combined to interest and divert him :

I have become as lazy as an Arab. I do nothing, absolutely nothing. Looking at myself and the other Russians around me, I am more and more convinced that a Russian can only work and be himself when the weather is bad. (To Suvorin, 13th March, 1898.)

Towards the beginning of April he moved to Paris, where he stayed at the Hôtel de Dijon in the rue Caumartin. His sister wrote to him that it was cold in Russia and that the snow had not yet melted in Moscow; she advised him to postpone his return. Consequently, Chekhov remained for three weeks in Paris (12th April–2nd May). He visited exhibitions, entered into negotiations with the sculptor, Mark Antokolski, about a statue of Peter the Great intended for the town of Taganrog and, in the end, enjoyed his stay immensely. He took a great liking to Paris: "What a town it is, my God, what an admirable town!" (Letter to Sumbatov-Juzhin 6th May, 1898.)

For the library of his native town, Chekhov had bought and dispatched from Nice to Taganrog three hundred and nineteen volumes by seventy-one classic French authors. He, himself, took advantage of this purchase to re-read Voltaire.

On 11th December, 1900, Chekhov left again for Nice. His health had once more deteriorated. And there was now a great secret in his life, sweet and tormenting at one and the same time: his 'affaire' with Olga Knipper. Sweet because he was seriously, deeply in love; tormenting because his illness compelled him to live far from Moscow, far from the Art Theatre, of which Olga was one of the stars. His letters from Nice (where he stayed from 14th December, 1900 to 26th January, 1901) from Pisa, Florence and Rome, where he went with Maxim Kovalevski, leaving on 9th February to return to Yalta, were almost all addressed to the woman he loved, the woman for whom he had written *The Three Sisters*, the rehearsals for which were proceeding in Moscow. These letters were full of gaiety, melancholy, tenderness and irony according to the mood of the moment, but spoke of little but the pain of separation or the play that was being rehearsed without him, of which the smallest detail preoccupied its hypersensitive and conscientious author.

Naturally, Chekhov from time to time compared Nice with the Crimean town to which he had moved in 1898: "Anyone who has spent a long time in Yalta feels as though he were in paradise here," he wrote to his sister, 17th December, 1900. "Life is quite different at home. The French are devilishly rich and healthy: they remain young and never stop smiling." (To Suvorin, two days later.)

Italy enthralled him for the fourth (and last) time ... "What a wonderful country this Italy is! An astonishing country! There is not a single corner here, a single patch of ground which is not highly instructive," he wrote from Rome to Olga, 2nd February, 1901.

His last journey abroad in June and July, 1904, took him to Berlin, then on to Badenweiler in the Black Forest, where he was to die. When he left Moscow, he knew that he would never see Russia again. He said to one of his friends, the writer Tikhonov: "I'm going abroad to peg out."

There are very few traces of Chekhov's numerous visits to Europe in his works. It could not be otherwise with someone so fundamentally rooted in his native soil, so attached to particular landscapes, so imbued with that particular tonality, typical of Russian life, grey, melancholy and slumbering, the same tonality that constitutes the background to all his plays. He had stated, in December, 1897 in a letter to F. Batiushkov, that he never painted from nature, always from memory: "important and typical memories" that deposited themselves at the bottom of his mind as at the bottom of a filter. The evidence would therefore seem to point to the conclusion that the West left Chekhov with few important and typical memories, capable of serving as material for his work. To be precise, one finds a few pages on Venice and Nice in *The Story of an Unknown Man* (1893); on Abazzia and Italy in *Ariadne* (1895); and just a few lines in that masterpiece of lyricism, *The Bishop* (1902).

In *The Story of an Unknown Man*, the hero is in Venice:

It smells of the sea. Somewhere in the distance one can hear a guitar and two voices singing to it. How beautiful it is! ... It makes one want to

1. Taganrog at the time that Chekhov was a student

2. The Gymnasium in which Chekhov was a student from 1868–1879

3. THE CHEKHOV FAMILY:
Seated l. to r.: Michael and Maria (brother and sister of A. P. Chekhov), Pavel Jegorovich (his father), Evgenia Jacolevna (his mother), Ludmilla Pavlovna (his aunt) with her son George

Standing l. to r.: Ivan (his brother), Anton, himself (the earliest photograph of the writer available), Nicholas and Alexander (his brothers), Mitrofan Jegorovich (his uncle)

4. Chekhov (*second from left*)
and his university friends in Moscow

5. Moscow University in 1880

6. The Chekhov family in the garden of the Moscow house
which he called the Commode

7. Chikinskaya Hospital, not far from Moscow,
where Chekhov served as an intern in 1884

8. The town of Melikhovo where Chekhov lived from 1892–1899

9. Chekhov can be seen seated to the left at his country home

10. Yalta, 1899

11. Chekhov in his Yalta study

12. The Moscow Art Theatre Company in a summer outing. Gorki can be seen in the third row, on the left, with dark hat, white shirt. Stanislavski in the centre in the pale hat

13. Chekhov and his wife Olga Knipper

live! Live – and nothing more! Some men are singing, seated in a gondola decorated with coloured lanterns, which are reflected in the water. The sounds of guitars, violins, mandolins and male and female voices emerge from the darkness ... With, now and then, a passionate cry: "Yam-mo! Yam-mo!"

In *The Bishop*, Monseigneur Peter, seriously ill, remembers his stay abroad, "the nostalgia he felt for his country, the blind beggar who sang love songs every day under his window, accompanying himself on the guitar; and how, listening to him, he always thought of the past. Eight years go by, he is recalled to Russia and now he is a bishop, with all that past vanished into the mist like a distant dream ..."

The blind beggar who sang for the Bishop is the same one to whom Chekhov listened in Nice, leaning out of the window of his bedroom in the rue Gounod. "Sometimes in the evenings, I used to sit by the open window, alone, so alone; I could hear music coming from somewhere, and such a nostalgia for my country came over me that I would have given anything to return, and see you again," the Bishop says to his mother, the Bishop behind whom the author conceals himself. In this short story, written two years before his death, Chekhov abandoned his reticence and for once bared his heart. He described his own tragedy in it, the tragedy of a man superior to his surroundings, misunderstood and condemned to utter solitude. A man who cries out with every fibre of his being for a beautiful and noble life, unattainable on this earth, and who, surrounded by respect, adulation and hypocrisy, dies as much alone as he lived. Even his mother, overwhelmed by his eminence is afraid of him and, though she loves him, keeps her distance. All of this high-minded man's life, all the joys, suffering and dreams that have filled it, will be cast into oblivion, forgotten by everyone immediately after his death.

And, it is characteristic that, from his long absence abroad, the Bishop had retained only this one memory so dear to

Chekhov – the songs and the guitar-playing of the itinerant musicians. The memory, on which he had already dwelt in *The Story of an Unknown Man*, in which the hero is moved to tears by the music floating over the Venetian canals; enchanted by the beauty of the Bay of Angels outside Nice; and intoxicated, as Chekhov had been, by the clouds of almond-trees in flower, the softness of the air and the blue of the Mediterranean Sea.

These details, deposited at the bottom of 'the filter of his memory', were almost the only ones that he felt worth weaving into his work. But who can say whether, by some process of the subconscious, the experiences through which he lived, the landscapes and the human beings whom he admired or merely caught a glimpse of, did not contribute to the development of that subtle composition, which is the basis of Chekhov's practical art?

NOTES

1. Merezhkovski 1866–1941, well-known novelist, critic and essayist.
2. Suvorin's *Memoirs of Chekhov*, 1904.
3. Words of Tolstoy, reported by P. Loewenfeld.
4. At the end of the 19th century, Nice was a veritable 'Russian' enclave. Many Russians had villas in the neighbourhood. In Nice, itself, there were two Russian libraries, one, in the rue Longchamp and the other, that of Alexander Herzen, the celebrated exile who was buried in the Château cemetery; there was also Rozanov's, a Russian bookshop, which stocked Russian reviews and books imported from Russia or published abroad. In Menton there was a Russian sanatorium and in Villefranche-sur-Mer, a Russian zoological research station.
5. Sofia Kovalevskaya née Korvin-Krukovski (1851–1891). Born in Moscow, the daughter of a general and sister of Anna Korvin-Krukovski to whom Dostoevsky proposed. Anna refused him and, six months later Dostoevsky married Anna Snitkina. But the young Sofia, then only thirteen, was secretly in love with the great writer. She, herself, relates this episode in her *Childhood's Memories*. Sofia Kovalevskaya was not only a famous mathematician, a pupil of Weirstrasser and a friend of Henri Poincaré, Hermite, Picard, and the greatest mathematician of her time, but also a very gifted writer of letters.

6. On the 13th January, 1898, Zola's famous letter to the President of the Republic, entitled *J'Accuse* appeared in the *Aurore*.

7. This was clearly manifested by his friendship with Suvorin, the fervent reactionary, which so perplexed his liberal friends. (Translator's note).

PART THREE

Melikhovo

1892–1898

[1]

The Background

CHEKHOV found it no longer possible to live in Moscow. His fame was growing and friends, admirers and sightseers besieged his home and made demands on his time with typically Slavonic lack of constraint. Since his return from Sakhalin, he had had no rest, and he felt exhausted. He dreamed of "becoming a little old man as soon as possible, sitting peacefully at a large writing-desk" (to Suvorin, 30th August, 1891) and being allowed to go on sitting there, musing and writing.

For, since his return he had not been able to throw off a severe 'cold'. He coughed, lost weight and began to "look like a drowned man." (To Schekhtel, 14th December, 1891.) His exhaustion finally made him decide to leave Moscow and live for nine months of the year in the country and for the remaining three in an hotel in Moscow or St Petersburg.

"Alas, this year, if I do not get away to the country and manage to buy myself a property there, I shall be committing a crime against my health. I feel as rickety as an old wardrobe . . . It is *imperative* for me to leave Moscow." (To A. Smaghin, 16th December, 1891.) In February, 1892, a property was at last found and on 5th March Chekhov and his family (his parents, sister and youngest brother, Michael), left Moscow to settle in Melikhovo.[1]

Though the park and the fields were still covered in snow,

and he suffered some unpleasant surprises on arrival, Chekhov was happy:

> We have bought a large, cumbersome estate of which the owner, had it been in Germany, would have been given the title of a duke. Two hundred-and-thirty-two hectares of which over a hundred are a forest that will really look like a forest in twenty years' time, but at the moment only has the appearance of dense undergrowth ... We have an orchard, a park, large trees and long avenues of limes, the whole property is separated from the outside world by a wooden fence, a sort of palisade. The courtyard, orchard, garden and barns are also separated from each other by fences. The house is both good and bad. Good, because it's more spacious than the one in Moscow, light, warm, roofed with zinc and well situated. It has a terrace that looks out on the garden, Italian windows, etc. But bad in the sense that it is not high enough or new enough, that from the outside it has a silly, naïve appearance and inside abounds in bugs and cockroaches, which only a fire could exterminate. Nothing else has the slightest effect on them! In addition, there is a pond, full of carp and tench only a few paces away from the house which makes it possible to fish them straight out of one's window. (To Kiseliov, 7th March, 1892.)

His delight in his country estate bubbles out of the letter he wrote to his brother Alexander, a fortnight later:

> We are living on our estate! Like a modern Cincinnatus, I toil and eat my bread steeped in the sweat of my brow! Our mamma fasted all today and went to church in her own carriage: our papa fell out of the sleigh, so precipitate was the trot of the noble pair of horses. The pond is twenty paces away from the house. It is six archins deep. What a pleasure it is to fill it with snow and to anticipate the moment when the fish

will leap out of the water! What bliss to get up at 5 o'clock in the morning, knowing that you do not have to go anywhere and that nobody will come to see you! What bliss to hear the larks, starlings and tits singing! What bliss to get piles of newspapers and reviews from another world!

It was the first spring that Chekhov had spent out of Moscow. It had always been his favourite season. The gradual awakening of nature, the new delights, and miracles produced by the rising sap, each bud that burst, each flower that opened, every bird that launched its joyful cry towards the heaven, all enchanted Chekhov to such a degree that he used quite uncustomary superlatives in his letters. On 17th March he wrote to Suvorin:

Something quite amazing and overwhelming is occurring in nature, which is making up for all the inconveniences of life in the country by its poetry and novelty. Every day brings surprises, each one more beautiful than the one before. The starlings have arrived, water murmurs on all sides; in the spots where the snow has thawed the grass is beginning to grow green. The day stretches out like eternity. One feels as though one were living in Australia, at the other end of the world; one's mood is calm, meditative and sensual, in that one does not regret the past and does not look to the morrow. From here, mankind appears very good, which is quite natural, for when we go to live in the country, it is not from mankind that we are escaping, but our self-esteem which, in town close to one's fellow creatures, is often unjustified and inordinate. As I look at spring, I begin to hope fervently that there may be a paradise in the next world!

Chekhov wanted to share all these discoveries with his best friend. But would Suvorin, so rich and hard-to-please, appreciate the poetic qualities of this "silly, naïve house"?

You will not like Melikhovo [he wrote a fortnight later], anyway not to start with. Everything is small here; a small avenue of lime-trees; a pond no bigger than an aquarium, a small garden, small park and small trees. But when you have walked round it several times and looked attentively at your surroundings, the impression of smallness disappears. It is very spacious, in spite of being so close to the village. Lots of forestland. A multitude of starlings.

Yes, it is lovely now in the country. Not only lovely, but even astonishing. It is the true spring; the trees are in blossom and it is hot. The nightingales are singing and the frogs are croaking their heads off. I have not a kopeck to my name, but this is how I look at things; the rich man is not the one who has lots of money but the one who has the means to live at this moment in the splendour of the coming spring. Yesterday I went to Moscow and almost died of boredom and every kind of bother . . . (To Lydia Avilova, 29th April, 1892.)

Melikhovo entranced him so much that he forgave it for all its deficiencies, even one as great, for a passionate fisherman, as the lack of a river:

You are right, it is very annoying not to have a river. But what can be done about it? One is forced to console oneself by thinking of Voltaire's declaration that, in Russia, winter lasts for nine months, and for the remaining three, the weather is bad: in winter, the river is invisible, anyway, under the snow, and in bad weather, its absence is rather an asset! (To Kiseliov, 11th May, 1892.)

When summer came, friends flocked to him. Levitan installed himself in the guest-room and joined Chekhov in fishing and hunting. He loved Melikhovo, which inspired him to paint

[162]

many of his nostalgic landscapes. Friends of Maria Chekhova, such as the young poetess Tatiana Shchepkina-Kupernik, spent days and even weeks in the hospitable house, which exuded the good smell of Evgenia Jacovlevna's incomparable cordon-bleu cooking and the incense that the pious Pavel Jegorovich burnt in his bedroom. In the back of the house, his bass voice could be heard reading and chanting Holy Writ, while the birds twittered in the lime trees.

The Melikhovo house had soon become a typical Chekhovian home. Low, and lacking any style, it soon acquired a characteristic charm. The room that served as Chekhov's study was large, with wide bay-windows looking out on to the garden, a tambour to keep out the cold, a fireplace and an enormous low couch. In the winter, the snow lay piled half-way up the windows, and hares would sometimes climb to these drifts, stand on their hind paws and seem to be peering through the panes. The young people gathered in the 'Pushkin room', so called because of the large portrait of the poet hanging above a broad, comfortable sofa.

In spring, the apple trees in blossom raised their white branches right up against the windows. Chekhov was particularly fond of the blossoming of the apple and cherry trees. In his play *The Cherry Orchard*, it was the title he specially liked. When he watched the white and pink apple trees, his eyes became "bright and tender".[2]

Chekhov had a passion for gardening. Like another great artist, Tchaikovsky, Chekhov used to say that on the day he could no longer devote himself to his art, he would become a gardener. At Melikhovo, he hoed, dug, weeded and planted and transplanted trees and flowers. When he handled plants, he did so with surprisingly gentle, tender, almost caressing gestures. Few men loved flowers so much.

Spring was just starting and the real, luxurious beauty of the flowers was still concealed in greenhouses. But everything that flowered along the paths and on some clumps of shrubs already sufficed to transport you to a country of soft colours, especially at that hour, very early in the morning, when a drop of dew shines on every petal. (*The Black Monk*, 1894.)

His friends knew of his passion for flowers and often gave them to him. To a woman-friend, who brought him a bunch of mauve hyacinths and lemon-coloured tulips, he sent his *Plays*, with the dedication: "To the tulip of my soul, to the hyacinth of my heart". And the heroine of *The Seagull* speaks of her feelings as being like tender and delicate flowers.

Closeness to nature was a vital necessity for Chekhov. He was very susceptible to changes of seasons and the smallest variations in temperature. He constantly speaks in his letters about the weather, the colour of the sky and the balminess of the air, just as he employs impassioned expressions, quite rare with him, to describe a landscape, a tree or a flower.

The immediate surroundings of Melikhovo were neither beautiful nor picturesque. But there was a typically Russian charm in the vastness of the fields, the blue line of the forest and the red sunset on the haystacks and the black furrows. "When we sat on his favourite bench, outside the entrance to the estate, facing the fields and ploughed land, Anton's eyes lost their usual sadness and became clear and serene," wrote Tatiana Shchepkina-Kupernik.

But, very soon, the calm, idyllic life at Melikhovo became clouded over by the influx of relations, friends and friends of friends and patients. This situation, which recalled too closely the one which had caused him to flee from Moscow, compelled him to build a tiny wooden pavilion at the bottom of the orchard, where he could work in seclusion. It was here that he wrote *Ward No. 6*, *The Muzhiks*, *The Story of an Unknown Man*, *The Black Monk*, *Three Years*, *Ariadne*, and, finally, *The Seagull*. Stealing out of the big house, noisy with music, laughter and singing, he would walk past the rows of apple and cherry trees and shut himself up in the 'oven', as he called his little retreat in the fields.

But, apart from the guests, there were patients. The news

soon spread among the peasants in the neighbourhood that Chekhov was a doctor. At dawn, when he woke up he liked to go round the garden, which was growing more beautiful each day as a result of the care and attention he lavished on it. He was followed by his two dachshunds, Quinine and Bromide. It was a moment of relaxation, of total peace. Only the birds broke the silence: the humans were still asleep. Chekhov would remain there for a while, without moving, his eyes caressing the flowers covered in dew, the trees he had recently planted and the pond, over which a light veil of mist still hovered.

But, at seven o'clock, the family woke up, the samovar appeared on the table on the terrace and, a few yards away, a queue of women and children would wait patiently for Dr Chekhov.

NOTES

1. A village in the Moscow district, 9 kilometres from the Lapasnia railway station.
2. T. Shchepkina-Kupernik.

[2]

The Muzhiks

I believe that closeness to nature and
leisure are the two elements indispensable
for happiness – without them, happiness
is impossible.
(Letter to Suvorin, 9th May, 1894.)

AFTER the great ordeal of
Sakhalin and his first contact with the West, Chekhov re-
installed in the greyness and restlessness of Moscow, had been
subject to deep depression. It was this discouragement, this
mental lassitude, as much as his increasingly precarious state
of health, that had driven him to escape from the town and
his fellow-men and seek solitude and peace. If there was one
thing that Chekhov liked above all else, it was being close to
nature, to the serenity that emanates from the vegetable and
mineral kingdom, domestic animals, the unchanging alternation
of the seasons and the very indifference of natural phenomena
towards human agitation. Nature had the power to calm him
and even make him happy again. Spring, the first buds, the
flowering cherry, the balminess of the air, all these brought him
moments of perfect bliss, the only moments of unalloyed happiness that he had known.

To this happy relaxation, there was added something else:
inspiration. Nowhere else did he write so easily and so well as in

his tiny pavilion in Melikhovo, hidden among the apple trees.

"Nature is an excellent sedative. It pacifies, that is, renders man indifferent. Only those who are indifferent are capable of seeing things clearly, capable of being just and of working. Of course, this only applies to noble and intelligent men: egotistic and frivolous men are quite indifferent enough, anyway," he wrote to Suvorin, 4th May, 1889. But obviously, a man as complex and interested in everything as Chekhov could never be satisfied with a life of vegetating and indifference, nor even with the brief instants of peace and 'happiness'. During that spring of 1892, when he was challenged by so many pressing activities, his heart was heavy, as he told his best friend in a letter of 8th April:

I am well over thirty (he was thirty-two) and already feel the approach of the forties. I have aged not only physically, but mentally. I have become stupidly indifferent to everything, and, I do not know why, but the beginning of this state of indifference coincided with my journey abroad. I get up and go to bed with the feeling that my interest in life has dried up. This is either the illness that newspapers call brain-fag, or else an interior process, indiscernible to the mind, which, in novels, is called a 'moral crisis'. If it is the latter, then everything's for the best!

In a later letter, in June, he tried to explain the nature of this 'crisis':

My soul aspires to what is worthwhile and noble, but, willy-nilly, I am compelled to lead a paltry life, wholly directed towards earning those filthy roubles and kopecks. There is nothing more vulgar than a lower middle-class life, with its trivial earnings, victuals, stupid conversations and conventional virtues that no one needs. I am weighed down by the feeling that I only work for money and that money lies at the centre of

[167]

my activities. This wounding thought makes my work as a writer seem despicable to me, I have no respect for what I write, I am apathetic and a nuisance to myself and am happy to have medicine to fall back on, which, at least, I practise without any mercenary interest. I ought to take a dip in sulphuric acid and burn off my skin and then grow a new fleece!

Where not these aspirations towards a life of nobility and liberty, this discontent with himself and others and this desperate need for solitude, the natural reaction of the artist against the hectic, harassing life of the doctor?

Today I walked in the fields, in the snow. Not a soul around, and I felt as though I were walking on the moon. For men who have a lot of self-respect and neurasthenics, there is no life more comfortable than life in the desert. There's nobody there to affront your self-respect, and there is no need to throw yourself body and soul into things that are not worth it. (To Suvorin, 18th October, 1892.)

At the same time, he jotted down in his Notebook: "My motto: 'I need nothing'." And in his Diary: "To save his soul, the Muslim digs a well. It would be a good thing if each of us left behind him a school, a well or something else, so that one's life should not pass and be lost in eternity without leaving a trace of its passage on this earth."

By a logical exertion of willpower, Chekhov was gradually to emerge from this 'moral' depression. If personal happiness were a puerile notion, if even the hope of an improved humanity were a snare and a delusion, there still remained an outlet for the upright man: to work, overcome life and compel it to 'progress'. (*Notebooks.*) And, above all, with Chekhov, there was an all-powerful incentive: that "imperious need of the soul", which drove him "to serve the common good". (*Notebooks.*)

This need to "serve the common good" was the basis of

Chekhov's extraordinary efficacy in the social field, the basis of that faculty, particularly admirable in a great artist, of being able to forget himself and disregard his own feelings, illnesses and personal troubles.

Chekhov had always realized the prime importance of education for the mass of illiterate peasants. In his opinion, ignorance was the main cause of all the troubles from which Russia suffered, and here, too, he was in agreement with Tolstoy, whose pedagogic activities have remained justly famous. Now, living among peasants, treating them, entering their izbas, and observing from close quarters the village way of life, Chekhov constantly came up against superstition, misery, brutality, and utter despair at this inhuman life.

So, with his usual energy, Chekhov set out to battle against ignorance. On 19th November, 1894, the Moscow government's educational committee appointed him administrator of the primary schools at Talezh, a village situated five versts from Melikhovo. The school was in a miserable condition: its teacher lived in an old izba. Two years later, in 1896, at his own expense Chekhov built a new school and a clean, well-lit lodging for the teacher.

In October of the same year, 1896, *The Seagull* had opened in St Petersburg and proved a disastrous failure. The shock of this new 'battle of Hernani' had serious repercussions on the author's health. He was racked by coughing and a high temperature and he no longer attempted to disguise, as he had before, the real nature of his illness. But his activity did not diminish.

In January, 1897, the first general census of the Russian population took place. Chekhov was put in charge of the census for the Melikhov district. "We are taking a census again," he wrote to Suvorin. "Each of us has been provided with a hideous ink-stand, a hideous, vulgar badge that resembles a label from a beer factory, and a briefcase too small to hold the census papers. (This briefcase in beige cloth, bearing the inscription 'Census 1897', can still be seen in the Chekhov Museum in Melikhovo.) One has the impression of a sword that will not enter its sheath. It is disgraceful! From morning on, I visit the izbas and, being out of practice, hit my head against the lintels, whereon, as though conspiring to annoy me, my head proceeds to hurt me appallingly: I have migraine and influenza." It was obviously not influenza, but a more acute stage of his illness, which he wanted to ignore and overcome, despite the long nights of insomnia during which he was racked by coughing and bathed in perspiration.

During that same cruelly cold January, a delegation of peasants came to ask for Chekhov's help: it concerned the building of a school in the neighbouring village of Novoselki. Though exhausted by his illness and work on the census, Chekhov could not bring himself to refuse. "The zemstvo[1] have provided a thousand roubles," he wrote to Suvorin the next month, "the peasants have collected three hundred, and that's all. The school will cost at least three thousand roubles, which means that all through the summer I shall have to think about money and save it here and there." He, himself, drew up the plans for the new school, chose its site, dealt with the carpenters and hired vehicles to transport the material. He took charge of everything to ensure that the building would be ready in time for the next school term.

And, while carrying out these harassing tasks, he was also writing one of his most important works, *The Muzhiks*.[2] His daily association with the peasants gave him the opportunity to observe and analyse the misery of their lives with all the objectivity of a doctor and man of science. This objective insight was sublimated by art and elaborated by his incomparable 'talent for humanity'. The story made a sensation as soon as it was published. The life of a poor peasant family is seen through the eyes of a townswoman, Olga, who has married one of the sons, Nicholas, a waiter in a Moscow restaurant. Seriously ill, Nicholas returns to die in his parents' home in the village of Zhukovo. Chekhov describes the poverty, the continual undernourishment; the mixture of ignorance, superstition and deep, naïve religious beliefs; the passive attitude towards fate and catastrophes (such as the fire); the apathy and a desire for oblivion, the oblivion and euphoria provided by demon vodka:

How beautiful that morning was! And how beautiful life could be in this world, were there no misery, that misery from which there is no escape, nowhere to hide ... *The Fire.* The peasants stood there, grouped together quite close, but doing nothing, just watching the fire. Nobody knew where to start, nobody knew what to do, though all around stood stacks of corn, hay, wooden sheds, and piles of dead wood ... *Religion.* Maria and Fekla[3] crossed themselves and fasted each year, but knew nothing whatever of religion. Children were not taught prayers, nobody spoke to them of God, they were not given any rules to follow, they were only forbidden to eat meat during Lent. And it was just the same in other families: few people were believers, few people had any understanding about it. But, at the same time, they all loved the Gospels, loved them dearly and piously, but had no books and no one to read or explain them ... *Vodka.* Everything that went on in the village filled Olga with disgust and grieved her.

Everyone drank, did nothing but drink on holidays, on Assumption Day, on the day of the Exaltation of the Cross. On the day of the Virgin's Intercession, there was a parochial feast in the village and on that occasion the peasants drank for three days on end ... They drank fifty roubles'-worth belonging to the commune and then went hunting through every izba in the hopes of finding some more. Kiriak[4] was terribly drunk for three days, he drank all he possessed, even his cap and shoes, and he beat his wife so hard that she had to be doused with water to revive her. Afterwards, everybody was ashamed and nauseated ... *The only refuge.* There was, however, a real religious ceremony in Zhukovo. It was in August, when the ikon of the Virgin-life-giver was carried from village to village throughout the whole district ... It came to Zhukovo in the evening, with a procession, singing and full peals of bells from the other side of the river. Everybody stretched out their hands towards the ikon, gazed on it hungrily and repeated tearfully: 'Our comforter, our Mother, our protectress!' Everybody seemed to have understood that between the earth and the heavens there was not just a void, that the rich and powerful had not yet got their hands on everything, that there still existed a refuge, a safeguard against sin, against heavy, unendurable misery, against the perils of vodka ... *Misery*! Oh, what a hard, insurmountable winter! Since Christmas we had run out of our own bread and been compelled to buy flour ... From the stable, night and day, came the lowing of the hungry cow, that tore at Grandmother's and Maria's hearts. And, as though deliberately, the cold was intense, the snow piled up in huge drifts and the winter showed no signs of ending....

After her husband's death, Olga, accompanied by her daughter, returns to Moscow. She is sad, as she leaves the miserable village, and pities its wretched, defenceless menfolk:

During the summer and winter, there had been moments, whole days even, when it had seemed to her that those men lived worse than the beasts and that it was frightening to be living among them. They were coarse, dishonest, filthy, rarely sober, got on badly together, and were constantly quarrelling because they had no respect for each other, only mutual fear and suspicion. Who opens a tavern and makes people drink? The muzhik who spends the money belonging to the commune, the school and the church on drink? The muzhik. Who steals from his neighbour, sets fire to his house and bears false witness against him before the judge, all for the price of a bottle of vodka? The muzhik. Who is first to abuse the peasants in the local government and other councils? The muzhik. Yes, it was frightening to live among them, but, just the same, they were men who suffered and wept like men, and there was nothing in their lives for which one could not find a justification. Exhausting toil, after which their bodies ached all night, cruel winters, poor harvests, cramped izbas and no relief, no help to be hoped for from anywhere ... Could anyone expect good examples from these mercenary, greedy, dissolute, lazy civil servants who only came to the village to insult, frighten and despoil? Olga remembered the miserable, humiliated expression on his old parent's faces when the Kiriak was dragged away to be flogged. She felt pity now for all these men, her heart was heavy and, as she walked, she kept turning round to get a last glimpse of the izbas ...

Chekhov regarded *The Muzhiks* as a summing-up of his experiences among the peasants, as a farewell to his life among them. He said so explicitly in a letter of 26th June to Suvorin:

"From a literary point of view, Melikhovo has run dry for me after *The Muzhiks* and lost all its value."

The moment had, in fact, come for him to leave for good the house that he had loved so much, and settle down in the Crimea.

From the beginning of 1897, the strain of the census, his medical and school activities and his writing such an important work as *The Muzhiks* had had a disastrous effect on his health. He had haemorrhages during the night of 21st March, but being very anxious to attend a theatrical reunion in Moscow, he caught a train on the morning of the 22nd, went to the reunion and that evening had supper with Suvorin in the Hermitage restaurant. There he had another strong haemorrhage. Suvorin took him to his hotel and, for the first time, Chekhov allowed himself to be examined by doctors (exactly twelve years and three months after first spitting blood). And he said to Suvorin: "My colleagues tell me, a doctor, that it's an intestinal haemorrhage. And I listen and don't contradict, although I know very well it's consumption."

Chekhov entered Dr Ostroumov's clinic where later Leo Tolstoy visited him. He was placed in room No. 16 ("And not No. 6," he joked, referring to his story *Ward No. 6*). Though continuing to spit blood, he nonetheless wrote to the headmaster of the Novosiolki school, Nicholas Zabavin, enquiring anxiously about his lodgings and promising him a stove ("You will get it before Easter."). All of Chekhov lies in this small fact: gravely ill, exhausted from loss of blood and an ice-bag on his chest, he still worries about the life, the comfort of someone else . . .

On 11th April, after having spent a fortnight in the clinic, Chekhov set off with his brother Ivan for Melikhovo. But he stopped on the way in Novoselki to inspect the progress made in the building of his school. Still very weak, he continued to busy himself all spring with school affairs in his district; took part in amateur theatricals for the benefit of the schools; closely supervised the construction-work on the Novoselki school; and set an examination for the pupils of the Talezh school, of which he was administrator.

The Novoselki school was opened on June 13th. The peasants presented Chekhov with an ikon and a wood plate, on which words of gratitude had been engraved.

A friend of Chekhov's, Ivan (or as Chekhov called him, Jean) Shcheglov came to spend a few days in Melikhovo. The change in Anton horrified him: "His face was yellow and drawn, he coughed a lot and wrapped himself up snugly in a rug, though the evening was exceptionally warm. 'Do you know, Jean, what I need now? A year's rest, a year of relaxation, after which I would start working again like a convict.' "

On 31st August, Chekhov left for Biarritz and Nice, where he spent the winter. On 5th May, 1898, he was back again in Melikhovo. His health was scarcely any better and he had not gained any weight, but, on the other hand, he had written a lot. Immediately upon his return, he was taken up with medical and scholastic problems in the district. He founded a new school in Melikhovo, temporarily lodged in an izba rented and furnished for that purpose, and immediately undertook the construction of another building: when his health compelled him to spend the autumn in Yalta, his sister supervised the work. But there was a desperate lack of money. The doctors insisted on his passing all his winters in Yalta, which would mean buying some land and building a house. But how could he meet all these expenses? He would have to borrow since all his theatre royalties were pledged to the construction of the Melikhovo school, as he mentions in a letter to K. S. Barantsevich written on 2nd January, 1898.

So, unable to allow himself a year of relaxation, lacking the means either to take care of himself or build his house in the Crimea, Chekhov, his health mortally impaired, spent almost ten thousand roubles on the construction of the three schools at Talezh, Novoselki and Melikhovo.

In a field closely linked with that of schools – the field of libraries – Chekhov showed himself equally efficacious. As soon as he returned from Sakhalin he sent large quantities of books to the island's schools, and he continued to take an interest in Sakhalin's libraries during the whole period of his life in Melikhovo.

The library of his native town, Taganrog, was an object of his constant care. He bestowed on it an inscribed copy of Tolstoy's *The Power of Darkness*, a work of which he was particularly fond. In 1894–1895 the library received a large number of books from him, and in 1896–1897 he sent it eight big consignments, studied its catalogues closely, corrected them in his own hand and organized a museum adjoining the library, to which he sent among other things an inscribed portrait of Tolstoy.

In March 1898, as mentioned previously, Chekhov sent to Taganrog from Nice three hundred and nineteen volumes by French classic authors. ("I have no money – he wrote to his sister – but I could not restrain myself. And it cost me a packet.")

When he finally left Melikhovo for Yalta, Chekhov only kept one hundred and sixty volumes of his personal library and sent all the rest to Taganrog. During the last years of his life, between 1900 and 1904, he dispatched fourteen more large parcels of books to Taganrog. The last of them, selected by him only a few days before his death, were sent posthumously.

In addition to the Taganrog library, Chekhov supplied books to that of Serpukhovo, close to Melikhovo, and those of Armaviz, Perm and other towns. Few people knew (for Chekhov never spoke of it) that Nicholas II granted him a "hereditary nobility" and decorated him as a reward for his "exemplary zeal and exertions directed towards the education of the people." Chekhov never mentioned his entitlement to a "hereditary nobility" either in his *Diary* or his *Notebooks*.

On the other hand, he wrote to Suvorin with justifiable pride:
"I have built three schools and they are considered to be model ones. They are constructed with the best materials. The classrooms are five archins high and equipped with Dutch stoves. The teacher has a fireplace and an apartment, by no

means small, of three or four rooms. Two of the schools cost me 3,000 roubles each, the third, a smaller one, about 2,000." (26th June, 1899.)

In 1900, Chekhov was elected to the Academy (belles-lettres section). In 1902, he renounced his title of academician as a protest against Maxim Gorki's expulsion from the Academy.

NOTES

1. Local government.
2. Finished 1st March, 1897.
3. Olga's sisters-in-law.
4. Nicholas's brother.

[3]

Welfare Activities

The desire to serve the common goal must,
at any price, be a necessity of the soul, a
condition of personal happiness; if it does
not spring from there, but from theoretical
or other considerations then it is not what
it ought to be.

CHEKHOV (*Notebooks*)

A FEW months before establishing himself in the country, Chekhov had written to Suvorin:

> Ah, my friend, how bored I am! If I am to be a doctor, I must live in the country among the people and not in Moscow, in Malaia Dmitrovka Street, in the company of a mangosteen.[1] I must have at least a small, a very small morsel of social and political life, whereas the life I lead within four walls, without nature, without my fellowmen, without my native land, without health or appetite, is not a life at all, but a veritable ...
> (19th October, 1891)

Now he had them: nature, his fellowmen and "the morsel of social life", which he had craved and for which he had felt so nostalgic.

He was put to work as soon as he settled down in Melikhovo.

[177]

During the year 1891–1892, Russia suffered a terrible famine, followed by another calamity, cholera. From the end of 1891, Chekhov, with his usual commonsense, was busy setting-up an extremely useful operation. The peasants, exhausted from lack of food, had been selling their horses for a few kopecks. Chekhov organized the repurchase of these horses, which would have to be fed during the winter and then given back to their owners in the following spring. Thus, the peasants would be free to till their fields, and the next year's harvest would be assured. To realize this plan, Chekhov needed money and he took up a collection among his friends. ("I proved to be a very efficient beggar.") He wrote to Suvorin saying that the project was going well and asking him to be responsible for a soup-kitchen in one of the villages worst hit by the famine. The energy displayed by Tolstoy at the present moment filled him with enthusiasm:[2]

"Tolstoy is not a man, but a superman, a Jupiter," he wrote in a letter, 11th December, 1891. Though very ill himself, Chekhov made numerous tours of the worst affected areas and saw, close-to, the desperate situation of the peasants. Two months earlier, indignant at articles in the St Petersburg press, accusing the famine victims of laziness and negligence, he wrote to Suvorin:

> To talk now of laziness, drunkeness etc. is just as odd and devoid of tact as advocating prudence to a man who is vomiting or struck down by typhus. Satiety, as all other excesses, always contains a certain dose of impudence, and this impudence reveals itself principally in the fact that a replete man dares to teach lessons to one who is hungry. If, at a moment of great grief, one can be hurt by all attempts at consolation, what is to be said for this sort of admonition, and how stupid and wounding such a scolding can be!

He did not accuse anyone or attempt to lecture anyone. He was quite satisfied with helping and exerting himself without thought of the cost in his typically efficient, practical, silent, modest way.

But then cholera spread through the villages undermined by the famine. Chekhov was appointed doctor of the Sorpukhovo district, which comprised, in addition to Melikhovo, twenty-six other neighbourhood villages, a number of factories and a monastery. Now literature had to be put on one side and medical activities given first place.

I have no time whatever even to give a thought to any literary work. In 1848, there was a severe cholera epidemic in my district and we think this one will be just as bad. We have no proper accommodation; real tragedies will occur either in the izbas or in the open air. We have no help ... The roads are bad and my horses worse still. As for my health, I am tired already by midday and want to go to sleep. And that is before cholera has got here: what will things be like when it is at our doors! He wrote to Nicholas Leikin, 13th July, 1892.

It is interesting to note a declaration of faith that Chekhov made to the opportunistic Suvorin in August, which remains infinitely topical. (For whom and against whom, would Chekhov have been today?)

If our socialists try to exploit cholera for their own ends, I shall begin to despise them. Disgusting means used to achieve excellent ends make the ends, themselves, odious ... Were I a political man, I should never be able to bring myself to dishonour the present with a view to the future, even if, for a gramme of despicable lies, I were promised a hundred kilograms of future bliss.

While Chekhov worked without sparing himself, Suvorin escaped from Russia and the cholera and took refuge in Biarritz. Chekhov wrote to him in the middle of the month:

[179]

What is most irritating of all is that, after the whole series of letters I sent you, in which I set out our difficulties in dealing with the epidemic, you write to me from your gay, turquoise-coloured Biarritz, telling me that you envy me my leisure. May Allah forgive you! I am alive and in good health. The summer has been magnificent, dry, hot and rich in every kind of fruit, but since July, all its charm has been completely spoilt by the news of the epidemic. At the very moment when you were inviting me in your letters to join you in Vienna or Abbazia, I had already been appointed district doctor for Sorpukhovo, and was catching cholera by the tail and hastily organizing my district, which comprises twenty-six villages, four factories and a monastery. In the morning I receive patients, then I pay visits, go on my rounds and give advice and treatment. I lose my temper and, since the local government has not given me a kopeck for fitting out ambulances, I beg for this or that from the rich. I have proved myself a first-rate beggar: thanks to my eloquence, my district now possesses two excellent, well-equipped hospital buildings and five less good ones – actually, rather bad ones ... But I am tired, mentally. I am bored. Bored with not being my own master, of thinking of nothing but diarrhoea, jumping up in the night when the dogs bark or someone knocks on the door, trailing down unknown roads in an unspeakable vehicle, reading nothing but cholera and expecting nothing but cholera. All that, when I am not at all interested in the illness nor in the people to whom I am of service ....

Was he really as indifferent as he tried to make out? Or merely very tired and tormented by an urgent desire to write when he was unable to do so? "When you read in the papers that the epidemic is over, you will know that I am writing again. But while I remain in government service, you must no longer regard me as a man of letters," he wrote to Suvorin in the same letter. "One cannot pursue two hares at the same time."

Medical practice tired him and snatched him from his true vocation, but nonetheless, it gave him keen satisfaction. The compulsion to be useful, to serve and to succour was, in Chekhov's case, a "necessity of the soul". And when it was finally satisfied, he felt strangely at peace with himself :

> Life was hard this summer, but now it seems to me that I have never spent one so well. In spite of the anxiety created by the cholera and the lack of money that worried me till the autumn, I found pleasure in being alive and wanted to go on living. And what a lot of trees I have planted ! Melikhovo is unrecognizable and appears to me now astonishingly comfortable and beautiful ! (To Suvorin, 10th October, 1892.)

As always, he was ashamed of living in such comfort. He meditated sadly on his surroundings, on the wretched conditions of the illiterate masses, and on the villages he passed through while making his innumerable rounds. He wrote to Suvorin eight days later: "A high mortality rate is a serious drawback : we are poor and our land is uncultivated in Russia because we have so much land and so few men."

The intense activity of the summer had had at least one positive advantage. It had enabled Chekhov to emerge from the state of mental lassitude and torpor which had succeeded his return from Sakhalin, his first contact with the West and then his resumption of life in Moscow. His extreme physical exhaustion had been largely responsible for it. But, in addition, there had been the frustration due to his mental solitude, to the obligation to write and write ceaselessly in order to support himself and his family and, above all, to the absence of a *Weltanschauung*, "a well-defined conception of the world, without which a conscious life is not a life, but a burden and a nightmare," as he wrote to Suvorin as early as November, 1888.

And at this period Chekhov was still dominated by the Tolstoy doctrines; not yet free from what he later called the Tolstoyan "hypnosis".

NOTES

1. Chekhov had brought two mangosteen plants back with him from his trip to the Far East. His family had moved to Malaia Dmitrovka Street in 1890.

2. With an energy and equally remarkable practical sense, Tolstoy had organized canteens and the distribution of food and other articles of necessity. In 1891–2 he achieved a resounding success by assuring the daily upkeep of about 9,000 people and collecting more than 140,000 roubles in contributions.

[4]

Tolstoyan Interlude

For several years, roughly from 1882–1888, Chekhov had been under the ascendancy of the Tolstoyan "philosophy". The personality of the owner of Jasnaia Poliana played no part in it, for he and Chekhov only met for the first time much later, on 8th August, 1895. (Their last meeting was in the Crimea on 31st March, 1902.) It was solely Tolstoy's writings, the magnetism of his words (fiery as lava and not yet extinguished), that for a time subjugated the serene Chekhov. Genius is always seductive. One has the impression that Chekhov was glad to abandon himself to the power, the fire and the utter conviction ("I have found truth," said Tolstoy) of a man, whom he venerated in other respects as a great artist. He asserted on many occasions that Tolstoy was and would always remain in his eyes the apex of Russian art.

The Tolstoyan doctrine brought him what he had never found elsewhere: a well-defined conception of the world.[1] Chekhov's mind was far removed from the philosophical and the abstract. On the contrary, he possessed an eminently concrete intellect; he was an intuitive observer; his turn of mind was that of a naturalist and a poet. To observe reality and note the apparently insignificant details; to group these details and minute facts and perceive the innumerable ways in which they could be developed, this was the mental approach of a scientist, made even more effective in Chekhov's case by his exceptional intuitive powers. Now, a lucid and practical mind could not long be duped by the Tolstoyan mirage. Despite his desire to believe and admire, Chekhov could not fail to realize the Utopian, retrograde side of the almost mediaeval ideal preached by Tolstoy. Chekhov believed in science and in progress. Tolstoy ridiculed and damned them both. Chekhov liked culture, comfort, luxury and the arts. Tolstoy did not care a fig for them and rejected them in the name of puritanism and asceticism totally alien to Chekhov's nature. Tolstoy made assertions and laid down the law, sure of *his* truth, which to him was *the* truth. Chekhov was hesitant when confronted by the great problems, refusing to solve them on an intellectual and abstract plane, always bringing them down to a human, everyday level and suggesting for each of them not one but a thousand possible solutions; not just one wide, straight road but innumerable, barely perceptible paths.

Chekhov became estranged from Tolstoy in his capacity as moralist, instructor on life and prophet towards the end of the eighties, but up till his death he loved and passionately admired Tolstoy as an incomparable artist, a unique character.

In a letter to Suvorin on 27th March, 1894, Chekhov drew up a balance sheet of his Tolstoyan infatuation:

Tolstoyan morality has ceased to touch me profoundly. I no longer even feel the slightest affinity with it, which is no doubt unfair. But it is because the blood that flows in my veins is peasant's blood and you cannot astound me with peasant's virtues. From my childhood, I learnt to believe in progress ... I like intelligent people, sensitivity, politeness and wit. I am as indifferent to men scratching the corns on their toes or wearing stinking leggings as I am to the fact that young women put their hair in curlers! But the Tolstoyan philosophy affected me deeply, I was dominated by it for six or seven years, though it was not its fundamental precepts that attracted me ... but the way in which Tolstoy expressed himself, his immense commonsense and, no doubt, too, a sort of hypnosis. But now something inside me challenges it. Logic and a sense of justice tell me that there is more neighbourly love in electricity and steam than there is in chastity and abstention from eating meat. War is evil, men's justice is evil, but it does not follow from this that I feel obliged to wear laptis[2] and sleep on the stove next to a workman and his wife, etc. But that is not the real point. The fact is that, for various reasons, Tolstoy's ideas are a long way from mine and his philosophy is no longer an essential part of me.

Yes, the fact was that the Tolstoyan 'hypnosis' had worn off as a result of direct contact with reality, in particular the reality that Chekhov had observed on Sakhalin. From 1889 onwards, he published works that were clearly anti-Tolstoyan, such as *A Dismal Story* (1889), *Ward No. 6* (1892), *My Life* (1896) and *Gooseberries* (1898).

It is interesting to note how weak and substandard the stories were that were written while he was directly influenced by the Tolstoyan philosophy: *Good People*, *The Beggar*, *The Meeting*, *The Cossack*, *The Letter*. One feels that the influence of the wise man from Jasnaia Poliana remained superficial and never really penetrated to the deepest strata of Chekhov's creative genius. Yet, on the other hand, the great stories, in which Chekhov rejected and repudiated Tolstoyan doctrines, stand out in their originality, the depth of their conception and their inherent bitter truth. Like Nicholas Stepanovich, the hero of *A Dismal Story*, Chekhov believed that "science is the most important, beautiful and essential thing in human life; that it always has been and always will be the highest manifestation of love, and that it is through it that man will come to conquer both material things and himself."

But what was Tolstoy's view? "Experimental science is only engaged in satisfying simple intellectual curiosity or seeking improvements of a technical kind ... Whereas science should devote itself to solving religious, moral and social problems. While these problems remain unsolved, all our knowledge of nature will remain detrimental and futile."³

Chekhov wrote in a letter to Suvorin, 8th September, 1891 :

Diogenes spat in people's faces, knowing that he ran no risk in doing so. Tolstoy describes all doctors as scoundrels and displays his arrogance towards the great problems, for he, too is a Diogenes, whom one cannot take to the police station or attack in the newspapers. Devil take the philosophy of the great ones of this world! The whole of it is not worth a single one of the mares in *Kholstomer*.⁴

Chekhov had already become indignant, the year before, with the attitude adopted by Tolstoy, after reading his *Kreutzer Sonata* :

There is one thing for which one does not readily forgive him: the impudence with which he writes about things of which he has no knowledge and, from sheer obstinacy, refuses to acquire any.⁵ Thus, the judgements he lays down on syphilis, on houses of correction, on woman's horror of the sexual act, etc., not only can be disputed, but also reveal an ignorant man who during his long life, has not taken the trouble to read two or three works written by experts. (To Pleshcheev, 15th February, 1890.)

It was this 'obscurantist', anti-social, Utopian side of Tolstoy that Chekhov violently attacked in one of his most important works, *Ward No. 6* (1892). One of the story's heroes, the gentle, sensitive Dr Raghin is a disciple of Tolstoy. A man who would not hurt a fly, he has fabricated a philosophy for himself that allows him to tolerate and accept the inhuman conditions in which the hospital patients of whom he is in charge – in particular, those in Ward 6 — exist. What does Dr Raghin have to say?

I am serving a noxious, ill-fated purpose and am paid by people whom I cheat; therefore I am dishonest. But I, myself am only a particle of an inevitable social evil; all the civil servants in this district are noxious and draw their salaries for doing nothing. Therefore it is not I who am responsible for my dishonesty, but the epoch in which I live.

And of what use is medicine in general?

Why prevent people from dying, when death is everyone's normal and legitimate end?[6] What purpose does it serve to prolong a shopkeeper's or civil servant's life by ten or twenty years? And if one regards the justification of medicine to lie in the fact that its remedies relieve suffering, involuntarily the question springs to mind: what good does it do to relieve them? Firstly, suffering is supposed to lead mankind towards perfection; and, secondly, if humanity learns to relieve suffering with pills and drops, it will inevitably cast aside both religion and philosophy, in which up till now, it has found not only consolation for all ills, but happiness as well. Pushkin suffered agony before dying; poor Heine remained paralyzed for several years. Why, then should some X or Z not be ill, too, they, whose lives are so mediocre that, deviod of suffering, they would to totally empty and resemble those of amoebae?[7]

One only has to think of Chekhov's medical practice, his ceaseless exertions directed towards relicving suffering and his high conception of social duty and human solidarity (what he called 'human talent', the faculty of caring deeply about someone else's grief and making it one's own) to realize the profound incompatibility between his nature and that of Tolstoy.

Tolstoy's arrogant attitude ("I have found truth") is the exact opposite of Chekhov's. Tolstoy lays down the law, judges, condemns and absolves. Chekhov neither lays down the law nor judges. ("We shall not try to play the quack but will admit frankly that we cannot understand anything in this world. Only imbeciles and quacks understand and know everything," he wrote to Shcheglov in June, 1888.) And Chekhov's mouthpiece, Professor Nicholas Stepanovich in *A Dismal Story*, deplores his own lack of what Tolstoy possessed in the highest degree – a conception of the world, a well-defined, guiding idea:

In my longings, my passion for science, and my desire to live, in all my thoughts, aspirations and conceptions, there is a lack of that common denominator that would serve as a link between them. Every feeling and every thought dwells within me in isolation and, among them all, the most subtle analyst would be unable to find anything approaching a general idea or a living God.

It is not in Chekhov's nature to *lead somewhere*, to teach, or to guide ("the intelligent man likes to learn, the imbecile to teach"). He admits that he "does not understand anything"; he said so in his letter to Shcheglov in 1888 and repeated it three months before his death: "You ask me: what is life? It is as though you asked me: what is a carrot? A carrot is a carrot and no one knows anything beyond that." (To his wife, April, 1904.) But if he refused to make any pronouncement on the ultimate problems of life or death, it is certain that he gained some kind of moral support from two convictions. The first of these is that "the only aim of artistic literature is absolute, genuine truth. Man will only grow better when he has been shown to himself as he is." (*Notebooks.*)

The second certainty that helped him to live and write was his faith in progress. "In two or three hundred years, perhaps in a thousand, there will be a new and happy life. We shall not share in it, of course, but it is with this in view that we live, work and suffer. It is we who are shaping it and in it lies the *sole aim of our existence* and, if you like, of our happiness," he makes Vershinin say in *The Three Sisters*. And, like an echo, Dr Astrov repeats it, in *Uncle Vanya*, "Those who will be living a hundred or two hundred years from now and will be despising us for having lived our lives in such a foolish, dull manner, will no doubt find a way of being happy."

This faith in progress co-existed in Chekhov with an incurable misanthropy and pessimism ... "One says: at the end of all things, truth will be triumphant. It is not true! For one intelligent man there are a thousand stupid ones, for one intelligent word, equally, a thousand stupid ones. The majority, the masses, will remain eternally stupid; therefore, let the intelligent man abandon any hope of educating and elevating them to his level: *let him remain satisfied with constructing railways, telegraphs and telephones and in this way conquer life and make it progress.*" (*Notebooks.*)

In Tolstoy's case, on the contrary, the dream of a golden age, the faith in a mankind "living in amicable understanding with his neighbours, amidst fertile fields, gardens and forests, surrounded by friendly, tame and well-fed domestic animals" were closely linked with condemnation of the civilization and progress so dear to Chekhov: "Western civilization attempts to prove that all those recent inventions such as battleships, the telegraph, nitroglycerine-bombs, cameras, electric railways and the other stupid, harmful inventions that besot the people, are not only good and necessary, but also sacred, predetermined by higher and immutable laws; and that this deprivation, which is called civilization, is an essential condition of human life and has, inevitably, to be assimilated by mankind as a whole."[9]

Could any two men be more different? Can one envisage minds and temperaments more basically opposed? Nevertheless, Tolstoy loved and admired Chekhov deeply. "What intellect! What an incomparable artist! He has created new artforms, literary forms the like of which I have never come across elsewhere,"[10] he said to a journalist, who came to interview him after Chekhov's death.

As for Chekhov, he revered Tolstoy's artistic genius (the apex of Russian art) and declared that he had never loved any other man as much. (Letter to M. Menchikov, 28th January, 1900.)

The first meeting between the two writers took place in Jasnaia Poliana, Tolstoy's country house on 8th August, 1895. Chekhov arrived in the morning, just as Tolstoy was going to bathe in the river that ran across his property. The two men

[189]

had their first serious conversation naked, up to their necks in the water. The humorous side of the situation delighted Chekhov who, later, used to enjoy describing this first contact with Tolstoy "that vast man, that Jupiter." He once said, with an enthusiasm that was very rare in him: "When you talk to Tolstoy, you feel entirely in his power. I have never met a more attractive human being, one more harmoniously conceived, so to speak. He is almost a perfect man."

Tolstoy, on his part, deplored Chekhov's lack of religious feeling and lack of a general idea, which is a superficial judgement and far too sweeping. But he admired the artist (that "Pushkin in prose") and warmly appreciated Chekhov the man: subtle "charming, modest and as silent as a young girl."[11]

This first meeting at Jasnaia Poliana was followed by several others. In February 1896, Chekhov went to see Tolstoy in Moscow at his house in the Khamovniki district. Tolstoy spoke with displeasure of the 'decadents', as he called the men who had published three booklets in 1894, entitled *Russian Symbolists*, and of the leader of their clique, Valerij Briussov. Chekhov shared this aversion. He had no confidence in these grandiloquent aesthetes, who, in his opinion, spouted empty words and were wholly lacking in modesty and intellectual honesty. He said, laughingly: "You call them decadents! What nonsense! They're nothing but sturdy muzhiks, who ought to be sent to disciplinarian battalions. You mustn't believe a word they say! And, you know, they haven't got *pale legs* at all, just hairy ones like yours and mine!"[12]

Their third meeting took place a year later, on the 28th March, 1897, at Dr Ostroumov's clinic, where Tolstoy came to visit Chekhov.

After that serious lung haemorrhage, Chekhov had to give up Moscow, Melikhovo and any active life. The last six years of his life were largely spent in the Crimea. Tolstoy was his neighbour during the winter of 1901–1902. Gravely ill himself, Tolstoy was staying at Gaspra, an estate ten kilometres from Yalta, placed at his disposal by Countess Sophia Panina. It was there that Chekhov visited him, often accompanied by his new friend, Maxim Gorki.

The last meeting of the two writers took place on the 31st March, 1902. Tolstoy was in bed. Chekhov noted sadly his "look of extreme old age" and admired for the last time, the mind which had remained so marvellously alert and "his astonishingly intelligent eyes". (To Kondakov, 1902.)

Chekhov died two years later: Tolstoy survived him by six years.

It is clear that Chekhov had not only admired and loved Tolstoy, but had also been able to understand and analyse with great subtlety the grandeur and the weaknesses of this exceptional man. Tolstoy's verbal genius, his inexhaustible strength, his authority, his originality, his intellectual sallies and his pride had all combined to attract and subjugate Chekhov. He had been drawn to this 'vast man' and had studied the Russian Rousseau with great curiosity. On a literary plane, the impact produced by the Tolstoyan doctrines had penetrated deeply. The positive thought waves emanating from this impact were weak: they gave birth to nothing but mediocre works. But the negative ones, those of protest and revolt against the arrogant, old-fashioned doctrines led to works of the highest order.

NOTES

1. "I live in fear of Tolstoy's death. If he died, he would leave a great vacuum in my life ... I have never loved any man as much as him; I am not a believer, but of all the beliefs it is certainly his that I consider closest to me and the one with which I am most in agreement." (To Menchikov, 28th January, 1900.)

2. Peasants' shoes of woven birch-bark.

3. *What Is Art?* Tolstoy (1898).

4. A short story of Tolstoy's.

5. Chekhov himself, wrote in his *Notebooks*, "God preserve me from judging anyone or talking about things I do not know or understand."

6. When Countess Tolstoy, dangerously ill, had required a surgical operation, Tolstoy had violently opposed it and only gave in at the last minute under pressure from his children.

7. *Ward No. 6.*

8. *On the Meaning of the Russian Revolution* (1906).

9. As above.

10. A. Zenger. Memories of a *Visit to Tolstoy* (in the newspaper *Russ*, July, 1904).

11. Maxim Gorki : *Three Russians*, 1935.

12. An allusion to a poem by Briussov, which consisted of this single line : "Hide, oh, hide, your pale legs!"

[5]

Chekhov and Women

By his own choice, love played little part in Chekhov's life. He was attracted by pretty women: "in women, I like beauty most of all" (to Suvorin, 30th August, 1891) and was fond of their company, provided they were gay, witty and lively. But he repulsed their demands on him, and defended himself doggedly and deliberately from the possessiveness that a woman can exercise on a man in love with her. Under no circumstances was he prepared to let himself be 'devoured', engrossed or diverted from his essential task. That a man of talent should sacrifice everything to his talent, was young Chekhov's firm conviction. A desire to protect his independence and concentrate on the aims that he had set for himself, was the basic reason for Chekhov's extremely cautious attitude towards the pretty young women who surrounded him in his youth, some of whom loved him deeply.

There were occasions, however, when he yielded to temptation. There was, for instance, his brief engagement to the young Jewess, Dunia Efros.[1] At the beginning of 1886, when he was twenty-six he wrote to a friend:

> Yesterday, as I was taking a young girl home, I asked her to marry me. Give me your blessing ... my marriage will no doubt fall through! She is a Jewess. Will she have the courage to adopt the ortho-

dox religion, with all the consequences that that will en-
tail? If not, it can't be helped! Actually, we have already
had a quarrel. Tomorrow, we shall make it up, but we
shall quarrel again in a week's time. Furious about religion being an obstacle, she goes and breaks the pencils
and destroys the photographs on my writing desk, which
is typical of her: she is a real bitch. It is quite clear that
I shall divorce her after a year or two of marriage . . .
nothing is yet settled about my marriage. I am not married
yet. I have definitely broken with my fiancée, or, rather,
she has broken with me. But I have not bought a revolver
and I have not started keeping an intimate diary. Everything in the world is inconstant, provoking, approximate
and relative. (Letters to V. Bilibin, 18th January, 11th and
14th February, 1886.)

A month later, however, he wrote again about Miss Efros:

I have broken with my fiancée
ne plus ultra. I saw her again yesterday . . . I complained of
my poverty . . . Enough. I shall not mention her to you any
more. (To Bilibin, 11th March, 1886.)

He did not, in fact, mention her again, but he remained her
friend, as his dedication to his collection of short stories *At
Twilight*, ten years later, testifies.

In September and October, 1887, Chekhov wrote his play
Ivanov.[2] It contained some personal reminiscences. Ivanov is
married to a Jewess, Sarah Abramson, who has become a convert and is now called Anna. He pays her this tribute: "She
is a remarkable, extraordinary woman. She gave up her religion
for me, left her father and mother, renounced her fortune and
had I demanded hundreds of other sacrifices, she would have
agreed without a murmur. Yet there is nothing remarkable
about me and I have not sacrificed anything." But, immediately
afterwards, comes the famous profession of faith: "Don't marry
a Jewess or a blue-stocking; choose someone mediocre, dull,

colourless, without any unnecessary qualities. Build your life after the most current pattern. Don't tilt at windmills; don't batter your head against walls."

Chekhov himself, that wise and cautious man, had avoided the traps in which his hero was caught.

After Dunia Efros, there had, of course, been other temptations. There was Olga Kundasova, a university friend of Maria Chekhova's. She was beautiful, with a rather heavy, almost virile beauty, did not give a fig for fashion, refused to wear bustles and always appeared in a black dress with a small white collar and a broad leather belt round the waist. Olga Kundrassova was extremely gifted, with a strong predilection for science, particularly astronomy, and Chekhov always called her the 'astronomer'. Enthusiastic, sincere and passionate, she was very congenial to Chekhov, and loved him dearly. When he embarked for Sakhalin in 1890, he was surprised to find the impetuous astronomer aboard the boat sailing up the Volga; she had been unable to resist her yearning to pass a few days of the journey in the company of the man she loved humbly and secretly.

Chekhov painted a fond portrait of the 'astronomer' in *Three Years* (1895), in which she appears as Pauline Rassudina:

She had beautiful dark eyes and an intelligent, kind, sincere expression, but her movements were angular and jerky. It was no easy matter to talk to her, since she was incapable of listening or answering calmly ... She liked to dress-up but did not know how to, did not want to spend money, and her clothes were ugly and untidy. She took long, rapid strides when she went out walking and could easily have been taken for a young nun.

Chekhov remained a loyal friend of Olga's, and she continued to love him in silence, though she admired and associated with other 'great men', notably the painter Korovin and Feodor Chaliapin. At all the first nights, and all the private views, one could see the ungainly, gesticulating figure and hear the loud voice and strident laughter of that 'restless soul', the 'astronomer'.

Another friend of Maria Chekhova's was to play a far greater part in Chekhov's life and work. The very beautiful Lydia Misinova was an assistant teacher in Rajevski school, where Maria Chekhova taught geography and history. From September 1889, the two young girls became close friends and Lydia, or Lika as the young Chekhovs called her, appeared for the first time in the 'chest of drawers' in Sadovaia-Kudrinskaia Street. By then, Chekhov was already the well-known author of *The Steppe* and *Ivanov* and had been awarded the Pushkin Prize. There was, therefore, nothing surprising in the fact that the beautiful Lika should fall in love with this famous and attractive man, who, for his part, seemed very susceptible to her blonde, luxurious and very Russian beauty and her magnificent grey eyes with their 'sable' eyebrows. At that time, Chekhov was twenty-nine, with thick, chestnut hair, and an open frank face, with regular features and a piercing, bright, slightly ironic expression. He was handsome and attractive. They saw a lot of each other in the winter of 1889–1890 and Lika was captivated. Some years later, in 1898, she sent Chekhov her picture from Paris, where she was living. On the back of it, she wrote a verse by Apukhtin to a Tchaikovsky song:

> *Whether the days be bright or sad,*
> *Whether I die young, having made nothing of my life,*
> *My thoughts, my pain, my songs and all my strength,*
> *Shall be for him alone.*

And she added: "May this inscription compromise you. I should be delighted. I could have written it eight years ago, I write it now and could write it again in ten years' time. Paris, 11th October, 1898."

On the 21st April, 1890 Chekhov left for Sakhalin. The day before, he had given Lika his photograph with the inscription: "To the excellent creature who has caused me to flee to Sakhalin." This ironic tone, which he adopts once and for all towards Lika, conceals a profound truth: his desire to break an *amitié amoureuse*, which might tie him down and lead to marriage. "I don't want to get married and have no one to marry," he wrote to Suvorin on the 18th October, 1892. "It would bore me to have to take care of a woman. But it would not be bad to fall in love. I languish without a great love."

Chekhov obviously did not experience that great love for Lika: he did not like her indolence, her lack of willpower or her bohemian habits. His feelings towards her were complex. He was certainly attracted, but his commonsense and his desire to safeguard his independence, to protect his talent against the baleful influence of a woman appear to have got the upperhand easily enough. Chekhov's letters to Lika are public property.[3] They reveal the mixture of attraction and repulsion that she exerted over him.

He wrote to his mother from Siberia: "I must be in love with 'Never'[4] because I dreamt of her yesterday." (7th June, 1890.) But he never wrote a word to Lika during his whole stay on Sakhalin. As soon as he returned, the teasing started again. "Greetings to Lydia Yegarovna Mizinkova. Tell her not to eat pastry and to keep away from Levitan.[5] She will not find a more faithful admirer than me anywhere." (To his sister, 14th January, 1891.)

"My Lika in gold, mother of pearl and lisle! When you go to the Alhambra with Trofim,[6] I hope you accidentally puncture his eye with a fork . . ."

"Dear Lydia! I love you passionately, like a tiger, and offer you my hand . . . Give me your reply in mime, as you are blind in one eye . . ." (Letters to Misinova 17th May and June–July, 1891.)

Great 'poet in prose' though Chekhov was, he avoided lyricism in his correspondence, particularly in letters addressed to women. Later, when he was really in love and the one to suffer, he still continued to hide his feelings, and it was only at the very end of his life that he allowed a genuinely heart-rending note to pierce his customary irony. But in the present case, a benevolent and affectionate irony served to conceal a basic indifference. This ironic, cold attitude of a man towards a woman's love and despair is often reflected in Chekhov's work. In *The Story of an Unknown Man* (1893, the heroine, Zinaida, cries out to her lover: "You respond with irony and coldness to my foolish love." In *The Lady with the Dog* (1899), the hero, Gurov, calmly eats a slice of water-melon while the heroine Anna, in a state of hysterics, weeps over her 'downfall'.

Chekhov, the moralist condemned this attitude of coarse indifference so often displayed by men of low breeding. But, in his own life, coldness and indifference were the means of defence, which he frequently employed to discourage women's demands on him. He used this weapon against Lika and it was only very rarely that his letters contained here and there brief sentences that came straight from the heart: "Alas, I have already become an old young man," he wrote to Lika on 27th March, 1892. "My love is not a sun that creates spring either for myself or for the bird I love." This was quite true. In their relationship, there was neither sun, nor spring, nor happiness. On the one side, there was a beautiful girl full of charm; on the other, a man of letters, absorbed in his work and fleeing from life's dangerous ambushes and seductions:

> Noble and good Lika! Now that you have written to me that my letters do not commit me in any way, I can breathe freely, and here I am writing you a long epistle, without fearing that some aunt or other, seeing these lines, will force me to marry the monster that you are. On my part, I hasten to assure you that, in my eyes, your letters are only sweet-smelling flowers and not legal documents ... A great, big crocodile lives inside you, Lika, and I am right to listen to the dictates of my common-sense and not to my heart, that you have bitten. Well, *au revoir*, my soul's ear of maize! I envy your old shoes, which see you every day. (28th June, 1892.)

Weak, unhappy and at a loss what to do, Lika embarked on an increasingly dissolute life. She wrote to him the following October: I am burning the candle at both ends, come and help me burn it as quickly as possible, for the sooner it burns out, the better it will be.

Chekhov, however, disapproved strongly of this state of mind and wrote to her at the end of December:

> You wrote to me that you had stopped drinking and smoking, but you are still doing so. Lika is deceiving me. That is good. Good in the sense that I can now tell my friends, when dining with them, that I am being deceived by a beautiful blonde.

Lika replied:

> There is only one man in the whole world who could have still held me back from this deliberate self-destruction, but that man takes no interest in me whatever. In any case, it is too late ... I have not seen you for three months, and for me, it is such an event when I do ... write to me, I beg of you and do not forget the one you have abandoned. Your L. Misinova.

The situation was exacerbated in the autumn of 1893, when the seductive, disturbing face of the young actress, Lydia Javorskaya, came into Chekhov's life. Her beauty, wit, feline figure and hoarse, fascinating voice immediately aroused his interest. Lydia's snakelike gracefulness, her flirtatiousness and her impudent sallies attracted and held Chekhov for a short time. During her stay in Rome, in March 1894, the actress wrote him letters that leave no doubt as to the nature of their relationship. She signs herself: "Yours in my heart and thought, Lydia ... I miss you and love you. Your Lydia."[7]

From November 1893, Lika Misinova was aware that she had a dangerous rival. She wrote to Chekhov:

> Madame Javorskaya spent the evening with us. She told us that Chekhov was charming and that she wanted to marry him at all costs ... She asked me to help her and I promised to do all in my power for your mutual happiness ... Write a few lines to say

whether you are in love with Lydia Javorskaya – write them to me, of course, not to her! *Au revoir*, executioner of my soul, write, I beg you!

Chekhov replied in his jocular style, calling Lika his 'dear procuress'.

But Lika lost all hope and plunged headlong into a romantic adventure from which she emerged deeply hurt: her 'affaire' with the popular novelist Potapenko, a prolific writer and a friend of the Chekhov family.[8] A handsome, physically attractive man, Potapenko often met Lika at Melikhovo: she accompanied him on the piano. He had a warm baritone voice and Chekhov liked to hear him sing Tchaikovsky's and Glinka's songs. Lika and Potapenko's 'affaire' started at Melikhovo and ended in Paris, where they both went in March, 1894. But Potapenko was married and had two children and his wife had no intention of divorcing him. Poor Lika, alone and separated from everyone she cared for, buried herself in Switzerland.

From 14th September to 14th October, 1894, Chekhov was abroad (Vienna, Venice, Genoa, Nice, Paris and Berlin). Lika begged him to come and see her, but he did not respond to her appeals: he refused to make a detour by way of Switzerland. On 8th November, 1894, Lika returned to Paris, where she gave birth to a girl, Christine.[9] Shortly after came a complete break with Potapenko; he did not have the strength to endure domestic complications; his weak, pliable character was not of a kind to cope with such dramas. Lika remained alone and soon returned to Russia with her daughter.

The attraction that Chekhov had felt towards Lika did not last long; only from 1891–1892. Very soon, the first strong impulse grew weaker, faded, lost all its romantic flavour and transformed itself into a calm and staunch friendship. The beautiful girl 'with golden hair', original, daring and witty, had interested him and caught his fancy, but he was afraid of responsibilities, the weight of conjugal ties. He only accepted them later, much later, towards the end of his life, when death was very near and his mental outlook changed under a tragic feeling of loneliness, isolation and increasing physical weakness.

Nevertheless, he immortalized this love that he had not shared and which had, on the whole meant very little in his emotional life, in one of his most popular works.

In *The Seagull* (1896), of which the central theme is the tragedy of an innovator with advanced ideas, who is scorned and mocked – ("how difficult life is for those who have the courage to be the first to venture down an unknown road! Everything always goes badly for members of the *avant-garde*" he wrote to Suvorin some years earlier in May 1889) – Chekhov introduces two feminine characters, directly inspired by the real life personalities of Lydia Javorskaya and Lika Misinova. Javorskaya appears in the play as Arkadina, a brilliant actress, spoilt by success, greedy for further triumphs and eaten up with vanity. Modest, timid, deeply in love with the successful author, Trigorin,[10] Nina Zarechnaia, on stage, endures experiences very similar to those of Lika. If Nina's profoundly serious character and her destiny represent the type of modern actress dear to Chekhov, and one which was to find its finest incarnation in Vera Kommisarzhevskaia, the Russian Duse, the play's romantic plot follows very closely the real facts of Lika's and Potapenko's 'affaire'. And Lika, herself, recognized this to be so. Whenever she saw a performance of *The Seagull*, she wept and recalled the past. She had been one of life's victims: her love for a man and her love for the stage had both come to nothing. But on the stage, Nina (Lika) is able to surmount her unhappy love affair: she rises above the cruel side of love. She becomes a real, a great actress, she feels her 'power growing day by day', she understands that the 'most important thing is not glory, not success, not what one has hoped for, but the ability to endure, to carry one's cross and to have faith'. She carries that cross, she feels like a bird flying on the wings of inspiration, her love of art saves her, she 'dreams of her vocation and is no longer afraid of life'. (*The Seagull.*)

At the same time as Lika's drama was pursuing its course, there was another woman in Chekhov's life, a beautiful, charming, woman full of talent and very much in love with him: the young novelist Lydia Avilova. They met for the first time in St Petersburg on 24th January, 1889. Chekhov was twenty-nine and Lydia Avilova, twenty-five. She was the sister-in-law of the editor of the *St Petersburg Gazette*, Serge Khudekov. After an unhappy love affair, she had married on the rebound a dull, commonplace bad-tempered civil servant, Michael Avilov, and had three children by him. When she met Chekhov, she already had a child of nine months but she could have been taken for a young girl, with her slenderness, freshness and her blonde hair worn in two thick plaits. The 'young Flora' immediately felt an overwhelming attraction for the writer, whom she had admired for a long time. But she only saw him again three years later on 1st January, 1892, since he lived in Moscow and she in St Petersburg. This time he seemed to seek her out particularly, and spoke to her as to an old friend. Then he left and three more years elapsed without anything apparently occurring between them. Admittedly they corresponded, but Chekhov's letters, which have all come down to us, were cold and only touched upon literary subjects. During the carnival of 1895, Chekhov was again in St Petersburg and met her twice at a friend's house. At last, on 14th February, he saw her alone in her own home: her husband was away on official business in the Caucasus. According to Lydia Avilova's memoirs, it was during this visit that Chekhov spoke to her for the first and last time of love, and then only in the past:

"Do you know that I really lost my heart to you? I loved you. I felt as though there were no other woman in the world whom I could love like that. You were beautiful and touching. I loved you and thought of no one else ... but I knew that you were not like many of the women whom I had left or who had left me, that one could only love you in a pure, holy way, for life ... I was afraid to touch you for fear of hurting you. Did you know that?" Having made this confession, he left her abruptly, 'looking angry'. Next day he sent her his latest book with a short inscription: "To L. Avilova from the author", and a very dry letter, full of literary advice and criticism. The letter is dated 15th February. He left for Moscow the following day without seeing Lydia again. She was thrown into a highly emotional state, tormented by regrets, doubts, hope. Finally she made up her mind: she sent Chekhov a watch-charm in the shape of a book. On the one side, she had had engraved: *Stories and Tales by A. Chekhov*; on the other: *Page 267, lines 6 and 7*. It was a reference to a sentence in *The Neighbours*: "If ever you want my life, come and take it."

Chekhov did not reply. Did he sense, grasp from whom the anonymous gift had come? Lydia did not see him till a year later (27th January, 1896) at a masked ball. Shielded by a black domino, it was she, this time, who spoke to him of his life. Did he recognize her? Had he received her present? She only got a reply on 17th October, when *The Seagull* had its first performance. Chekhov had introduced the episode of the charm into the third act of the play: Trigorin receives a medallion from Nina, on which she had had engraved the title of one of his books and the following directions: *Page 121, lines 11 and 12*. Trigorin opens the book and reads: "If ever you want my life, come and take it." Thus, from the stage, Chekhov told Lydia that he had received her present and had understood! At the same time, using Trigorin as his spokesman, he gave his reply: "See such-and-such page, such-and-such lines." As soon as she got home, Lydia rushed to Chekhov's latest book and feverishly turned to the page indicated. It was not the right one! The lines made no sense! Then, suddenly, light dawned: it was in *her own* latest book that she must look. And what she read there was: "It is not becoming for young ladies to attend masked balls!"

Chekhov was living in Melikhovo. But learning that Lydia had to go to Moscow in March (1897), he promised to meet her there. A rendezvous was in fact arranged for 23rd March, but Chekhov did not keep it: his acute haemorrhage had led to his being taken to Professor Ostroumov's clinic. Lydia visited him there twice, on 25th and 26th March, and brought him a bunch or roses and lilies-of-the-valley, his favourite flowers.

Then Chekhov returned to Melikhovo and, shortly afterwards, went abroad. Life separated them more and more, though they kept up a friendly correspondence. They met again, for one last time, on 1st May, 1899 at a Moscow railway station, where Lydia had to spend an hour between two trains. Her children were with her. Chekhov gave them some caramels, wrapped in paper decorated with portraits of Turgenev, Tolstoy and Dostoevsky. He asked Lydia to stay in Moscow just till the following day so that she could attend a private performance of *The Seagull*, which the Art Theatre was giving that evening specially for him. But Lydia could not stay : there were children, their nurses, her sister who was expecting her in the country and her husband who would have to be informed of the change of plans . . . So they said goodbye and Chekhov left her there.

That was the end of their 'romance'. Lydia recounts : "What follows remains a torturing enigma to me. I wrote to him. He did not reply. I wrote to him a second time. But this second letter also remained unanswered. Later, when I learnt that he was in the Crimea, I wrote to him at Yalta . . . Chekhov did not reply to that letter either and I then understood that there was no misunderstanding between us, but a complete break."[11] This break had an explanation which, at that time, Lydia knew nothing about. It was Chekhov's love for Olga Leonardovna Knipper, his future wife.

On 20th July, 1904, eleven days after Chekhov's funeral, Lydia wrote a long letter to his sister, whom she did not know personally, pouring out her grief :

I do not want to insinuate in any way that I knew your brother well, or that I meant anything at all to him. No, I undoubtedly knew him very little, but he had a great influence on my life, I owe him so much . . . With his death, something so beautiful, valuable and luminous has disappeared from my life. And I have no one, no one apart from you, to whom I can say how terrible the loss is, how difficult it is to grasp and, once one has grasped it, how sad and dull it is to go on living . . . I have many letters from him. But I do not know at all what his feelings were towards me, and I find this very painful. . . .[12]

What part had Lydia played in Chekhov's life? It is difficult to say with any precision. The young woman's personality, her sincerity, lively mind, subtlety and talent all tend to support what she claims in her memoirs. But what exactly does she claim? That Chekhov was interested in her and admired her is certainly true. That he had any deep feeling for her is much less so. It is only necessary to read his letters to her and bear in mind the dates between which their platonic 'romance' occurred.

Their friendship covered a period of ten years from 1889 to 1899. During those ten years, there were so many events in Chekhov's life, so much travelling, so much work, so many varied activities and, finally, so many other women (those whom he only mentions casually such as Lika Misinova, Lydia Javorskaia and, after 1898, Olga Knipper), that it would be wrong to speak of 'a great love' as Bunin and others do. Chekhov had deliberately deprived himself of any 'great love', any deep attachment while he was still himself, before illness, weakness and the fear of approaching death overcame his resolution. He was unquestionably attracted by Lika and – in another way – by Lydia Javorskaia and, in yet another way, by Lydia Avilova. Attracted, because he was a man of flesh and blood, a man who enjoyed life and, what is more, an artist profoundly susceptible to beauty. But he was always on his guard and his intrinsic attitude was a defensive one, aimed at preserving his liberty as a man and an artist. One should never forget what he wrote to his brother Nicolas on the duties of a man of talent, who must be prepared to sacrifice everything to it: rest, pleasure, and women. Equally, one should not forget that he was a misogynist, to whom women appeared as beasts of prey, devouring youth and the lives of such men as were weak enough to submit to their capricious demands.

"Oh, vulgar women, how I hate you! . . . Women do not love art; only the excitement and fuss by which art is surrounded . . . The intellectual woman is only remarkable for her duplicity . . . If you fear solitude, do not marry!" Chekhov declares in his *Notebooks*. And he wrote to Suvorin (three years after meeting Lydia Avilova):

"Your opinion of women is extremely true, women are repugnant largely because of their injustice and the fact that justice appears to be a feeling that is organically alien to them." (Letter of 6–7 March, 1892.) And three years later he wrote to the same Suvorin: "Women grab men's youth, but not mine!" (21st January, 1895.)

He did not allow himself to love, yet love, nevertheless took its revenge: Chekhov's last years were darkened by the lucid, desperate love of a dying man for a woman brimming over with life and, though married to him, distant and unattainable.

NOTES

1. Evdosia Efros (1861–1943) friend of Maria Chekhova, lived in Paris after the Revolution and, during World War II was deported to Germany, where she died in February, 1943.

2. The first performance of *Ivanov* took place on 19th November, 1887 in Moscow.

3. Ninety-eight letters from Lika to Chekhov have not yet been published and are kept in the manuscript department of the Lenin Library in Moscow.

4. Chekhov kept inventing nicknames for Lika: 'Never', 'Ter-Misinova', or 'Misiukova', 'Melon', etc.

5. Levitan was courting Lika.

6. An imaginary person, supposedly in love with Lika.

7. Her letters are kept in Lenin's library in Moscow.

8. He left some interesting memoirs on Chekhov.

9. The child, Lika and Potapenko's daughter, died in November, 1896 at the age of two. Lika made several attempts to join the Paris Opera Company and to make a stage career, but met with no success; her gauche manner and her shyness prevented her from even playing walk-on parts at the Moscow Art Theatre. In 1902 she married a stage director, Alexander Sanin, and lived with him in Paris, where she died in hospital in 1937.

10. Trigorin, who presents many of Potapenko's characteristics.

11. Avilova : *Chekhov In My Life*.

12. This letter was first published in 1960 by Chekhov's sister in Maria Chekhova's book *From a Distant Past*. I. Bunin who had stressed in his book on Chekhov, published posthumously by his wife in 1955, the important part played by Lydia in Chekhov's sentimental life, had had no knowledge either of Maria Chekhova's memoirs, or of the above letter, or of Lydia's own non-expurgated memoirs. In the first edition of these memoirs many passages were omitted and the complete text was only published in 1960, seven years after Bunin's death.

PART FOUR

Yalta

1898–1904

[1]

Last Residence –
Last Friendships

"If you knew how tired I am!"
(Letter to Suvorin, 8th December, 1893)

I HAVE no intention of getting married. All I want is to be a small, bald old man behind a large writing desk, in a comfortable study ... Ah, if I only could become a little old man sitting peacefully behind a writing desk as soon as possible!" This, as we know, was Chekhov's cry from the heart as early as 1891.

But the years passed by and this dream of renunciation and peace always remained unrealizable. Then came the haemorrhage in March, 1897 and the doctors pronounced their verdict: he must leave Moscow and spend three-quarters of the year in a warm climate, either in the South of France or the Crimea.

It meant giving up Melikhovo, which he found empty and gloomy after the death of his father, that faithful, if naïf chronicler of everyday life, on 12th October, 1898:

"My father is dead ... my mood is far from cheerful. We shall probably sell Melikhovo and settle down in the Crimea, where we shall live until the bacilli leave me," Chekhov wrote to Suvorin five days later.

Chekhov decided to build a house on a stony, barren piece of land on the outskirts of Yalta. He entrusted its construction to the young architect Lev Shapovalov, who was advised by Chekhov's great friend, Isaac Sinani, owner of a tobacco and newspaper shop, The Little Russian Izba, which stood on the quayside and served as a club and meeting-place for authors, artists and writers staying in Yalta. The good, devoted Sinani spared no effort, and the architect and the contractor, Babakai Kalfa excelled themselves: on 9th September, 1899, Chekhov, his mother, his sister and their old cook, Mariushka, were able to take possession of the new house. Alexander Kuprin described it in his memoirs.[1]

Chekhov's villa was situated on the outskirts of the town, set well back from the white, dusty Aiutka Road ...

White, clean, light, attractively asymmetric, built in no particular style, all in unexpected protrusions, flanked by a sort of turret, with a glass veranda on the ground floor and an open terrace on the first, well provided with windows, some big and broad, some small and narrow, it could have looked like any modern-style building if one had not clearly divined the presence of original and careful thought, of unerring personal taste behind its general conception. Close to the garden wall lay an ancient Tartar cemetery, always green, silent and empty, with the pathetic stones of the abandoned graves ... Through the window of Chekhov's study one looked out on the slopes descending to the sea and then the sea itself, bordered by houses, built in tiers. To the left, to the right and behind the house, the mountains reared up.

Chekhov tried to turn his garden into an oasis of greenery, shade and peace. He remarked to Kuprin:

You see – it is I who planted every tree here, so naturally they are dear to me. But that is of no importance; what matters is that, before I came here, there was nothing here but waste ground and arid gullies, full of stones and thistles. Then I came and transformed this lost corner into a place of civilization and beauty. Do you realize, in three or four hundred years, the whole earth will be transformed into a luxuriant garden, and life will be unbelievably light-hearted and easy.

This hope is the predominating theme of his last works, as though this ailing, lonely man, knowing himself to be doomed, were unconsciously seeking consolation in the vision of a pacified mankind wholly directed towards goodness and beauty.

"It seems to me that everything on this earth must be gradually transformed, that everything is already altering before our eyes. In two or three hundred years, or it may be a thousand, there will be a new and happy life," are sentences that are constantly repeated in his stories and plays. Life, however, brought him constant disappointments.

In 1899, the year that Chekhov established himself in his Crimean house, famine broke out in the lower and central regions of the Volga. Despite the increasingly precarious state of his health, Chekhov was active in raising money, writing appeals and contributing articles to newspapers. Yet, he had already shouldered another heavy burden: that of help to the tubercular. On 25th November, 1899, he wrote to Gorki, telling him that he had decided to build a sanatorium for 'the needy suffering from consumption'. But first the money had to be found. Chekhov wrote an appeal, which was published in various newspapers in St Petersburg, Moscow and the provinces. With the funds so raised, a small but sadly inadequate nursing home, 'Yanslar', was opened, capable of housing twenty patients. The sick continued to pour in and knock at Chekhov's door. Frequently, he put them up in his own house until he found lodgings for them elsewhere, paying for their board out of his own pocket.

In January, 1899, Chekhov had sold the rights of everything he had published before 1899 to the publisher A. Marx for the sum of 75,000 roubles.[2] This very disadvantageous contract exasperated his friends. But Chekhov would never go back on his word.

At the end of 1902, Chekhov wrote another appeal for public charity: "It is not we, a small group of Yalta residents, who can satisfy the many needs of the sick, who come to us from every corner of Russia. Yet it is urgent, it is vital to build hospitals for them. People who are seriously ill come to us. They come to Yalta as though it were a court of final appeal, where the question of their life or death will be decided. They arrive pitiable, lonely and exhausted." Chekhov went on to appeal for help, from "all those who can appreciate the horror of the loneliness and sense of abandonment experienced by the gravely ill in a strange town".[3]

This appeal went all over Russia and brought in 40,000 roubles. Chekhov added another 5,000 and bought a house on the outskirts of Yalta, which was visible from the windows of his own home and later became the Chekhov Sanatorium.

One of Chekhov's characters declares: "I suffered cruelly, unceasingly." (*The Story of an Unknown Man*.) Chekhov, too, suffered cruelly,[4] but his suffering never prevented him from taking action, from shouldering the burden of other people's sufferings. Though gravely ill himself, he took care of others; built schools when he did not have enough money to build his own house; gave money away generously when he was almost penniless: as, for instance, the five hundred roubles he gave in 1901 to a teacher who came to tell him that his school would have to be closed from lack of funds.

In spite of all his various activities, Chekhov felt that life was slipping away from him. He was very ill, an exile in a part of the country he did not like, far from the landscapes dear to his heart, far from the woman he loved, far from literary life. He was, of course, surrounded by a crowd of admirers, visitors and 'friends', but his solitude remained complete. Unable to adapt himself to the local people, to this unfriendly nature and the vegetation 'cut out of cardboard', he was irremediably alone. "Just as I shall lie alone in my grave, so, all my life, I have lived alone." (*Notebooks*.)

And yet, he was famous, admired, loved and revered by a number of young men, of whom the most notable were the companions of his last years: Gorki, Kuprin and Bunin.[5]

Maxim Gorki had known dazzling success from the very outset of his career as a writer. In October, 1898, he sent Chekhov
a letter and two volumes of his *Stories*, and the two authors
met for the first time in Yalta on 19th March, 1899. Gorki
literally fell in love with Chekhov, who, on his part, showed a
great fondness for the younger man. Gorki's passionate friendship was one of Chekhov's last joys, as was the attachment of
two other young and brilliant writers, Kuprin and Bunin.

The correspondence between Chekhov and Gorki is infinitely
interesting and reveals the two writers' very different natures:
the sober restraint, the delicate wisdom of the one and the over-
flowing spontaneity, the violent idealism, the brutal frankness
of the other.

No less interesting and colourful are Gorki's memoirs of
Chekhov, written in 1905:

I have never known a man feel the importance of work as a foundation of civilization as profoundly and completely as Anton Chekhov.
It was apparent in the smallest details of his everyday life, in his
choice of themes, and in that noble love of things which, free from
any desire to acquire them, never tires of admiring in them the
creations of the human mind. He loved to build, to plant gardens, to
embellish the world: he felt the poetry of work. With what touching solicitude he watched the growth of the fruit trees and ornamen-
tal shrubs that he had planted! While his house in Yalta was being
built, he used to say: 'If everyone, on his little patch of ground, did
what he might, how beautiful our land would be!'

When it comes to Chekhov as a man, it is Bunin's memoirs
that present the best picture of him. Bunin was a first-rate
painter and, when he condescended to be attentive and impartial, a wonderful observer and a man of rare psychological
insight. It was almost impossible to deceive Bunin. He was only
mistaken, himself — and then completely — when his vanity,
his opinions and his prejudices, sometimes violent and unjust,
were involved, or, more simply still, when he was annoyed and
was determined to play the *enfant terrible*.

Some of the literary portraits which he has left us are blemished by partiality and insincerity. But when Bunin was fond of someone, his intuition and the sharpness of vision were unsurpassed. He loved Chekhov and Tolstoy dearly and, in consequence, wrote about them penetratingly, practically and warmly, with transparent truth.

Chekhov appreciated the wit, epigrams, shrewdness and unfailing good taste of this slender young man, with his elegant ways, easy manners and a piercing look. If Gorki was an admirable story-teller ("You talk better than you write," Tolstoy told him) Bunin possessed exceptional talent as mimic and actor,[6] and was better than anyone else at amusing Chekhov and making him laugh. During the last three years of his life, Chekhov saw a lot of Bunin, who had swiftly become a regular guest in the house in Yalta. And in his memoirs and an unfinished manuscript published after his death, Bunin has left us many intimate glimpses of Chekhov.

I remember a spring night. It was late. The telephone rang and I heard Chekhov's hushed voice: "My dear fellow, choose a good cab and come and fetch me. We'll go for a drive." "A drive? At night?" I said, astonished. "What, what has happened, Anton Pavlovich?" "I'm in love." "That's all very well, but it's almost 10 o'clock and you might catch cold." "Young man, no arguments!" Ten minutes later, I was in Aiutka.[7] Darkness and dead silence reigned over the house where Chekhov lived alone with his mother. Just a faint glimmer of light came from beneath the door of Evgenia Jacovlevna's bedroom and Chekhov's study was dimly lit by two small candles. As usual, I was moved by the sight of that peaceful study, where Chekhov had spent so many lonely evenings, no doubt filled with bitter thoughts on the destiny that had given him so much and, at the same time, treated him so harshly.

"What a night!" he said to me with a gentleness, unusual even for him, as he welcomed me with a sort of melancholy pleasure on the threshold of his study. "Let's go to Oreanda. If I catch cold, it can't be helped!"

The night was mild and silent, with a bright moon and light, white clouds. The carriage bowled down the white road and we kept quiet as we watched the sparkling surface of the sea. Then we reached the forest, and the faint patterns of its shadows, followed by the darkness of the cypresses, with their tops rising to the stars. We got out of the carriage and, as we walked under the cypresses, beside the ruins of the Palace, pale and bluish in the moonlight, he suddenly stopped and said: "Do you know for how many years people will go on reading me? Seven." "Why seven?" I asked. "Well, let's say seven and a half." "No, poetry lives for a long time, and more and more intensely. You're sad today, Anton Pavlovich," I said gazing at his guileless, handsome, kind face, which seemed so pale under the moon.

He was looking down and absentmindedly poking the gravel on the road with the end of his stick. When I told him that he was sad, he looked at me with a teasing glance: "It's you who are sad, because you've spent so much money on the cab." And then he added, serious again: "But it's true, you know. They'll only go on reading me for seven years and I've got even less time than that to live – six years at the most." There he was wrong: he had much less time to live.[8]

Bunin refers to the days he spent with Chekhov as being "one of the best memories of my life".

The white Aiutka dacha under a southern sun and a blue sky; the little garden, tended with such care by Chekhov, who was in love with every flower, tree and animal; his study, with two or three canvases by Levitan as its sole ornaments and an immense round bay-window, looking out on the valley of the river Uchan-Su, swamped in greenery, and on the blue triangle of the sea.[9] The hours, the days, sometimes months even, that I spent in this villa, impressed by my intimacy with a man who fascinated me, not only by his intelligence and talent, but also by his stern voice and his charmingly childlike smile.

All these details were recalled by Bunin a short while before his death. He wrote with admiration of Chekhov's stoicism, of the magnificent courage of this doctor, who was aware he was dying and never complained.

Even on the days when he suffered most, no one was allowed to suspect the pain he was in. "Aren't you feeling well, Antosha?" his mother or his sister would ask, seeing him sitting in his armchair with his eyes closed. "Me? Oh, no, it's nothing, just a slight head-ache," he would reply placidly, opening those eyes that were so bright and gentle when you saw them without the usual pince-nez.

And Bunin added: "If that profound and complex soul is to be properly appreciated, someone very great, with deep insight, must write of the life and work of that *incomparable* (Tolstoy's expression) artist."

Bunin laid particular stress on Chekhov's spiritual strength, his patience and his serenity. The exceptional spiritual strength which enabled him to bear the long expectation of death, which was the substance of his life during his last years; the solitude and silence in an isolated house, occupied by a sick man and two old women; the interminable evenings in that peaceful study, from which he looked out on the lights of Yalta, the lighthouse on the jetty, the stars in the vast black sky. When, in the past, he had told Suvorin that he would like to be a little old man sitting quietly behind a large writing-desk, he had not yet learnt how appressive the calm of an empty house could be nor what solitude could really mean. Bunin recalls:

A winter's day in the Crimea, grey and cold. Heavy clouds slumbering on the mountains. In Chekhov's house, everything is silent. All one hears is the regular ticking of an alarm clock in Evgenia Jacovlevna's bedroom. Chekhov, without his pince-nez, is sitting at his desk, unhurriedly, methodically jotting something down on paper. Then he gets up, puts on his overcoat, hat, and galoshes, and goes to a corner to where a mousetrap has been set. He comes back holding a mouse, still alive, by the tail, goes out on the porch, crosses the garden and reaches the wall, behind which on a rocky hillock, lies the Tartar cemetery. He gently throws the mouse over the wall and closely inspects the young trees in the garden on his way back. A tame stork and two dogs follow behind him. Chekhov sits down on a bench in the middle of the garden and teases one of the dogs with the end of his cane, as it lies on its back at his feet. He smiles; fleas hop along its pink stomach ... Then he leans back in his chair and gazes into the distance, his head raised, turning something over in his mind: he remains like this for an hour or an hour-and-a-half ...

I can remember his silences, his cough, his closed eyes, and the thought, serene, sad, almost solemn, that I could read in the expression on his face.

There are many first-hand accounts of Chekhov's life in Yalta, but who could ever see into the mind of that reticent man, who was loath to give any outward manifestation of his feelings, particularly when they were concerned with his own inner life? As it approached its close, that inner life was undoubtedly taken up with three matters: his illness, his love for his wife and his urge to emerge from his solitude by speaking to his contemporaries through the most direct mouthpiece of all the arts — the theatre.

The illness was undeniably there, exercising complete domination over a body scarcely able to offer any further resistance: it became steadily worse and his suffering increased, as can be seen from his short, infinitely pathetic letters to his wife.

Love was there, too, deep, tender and despairing as it had to be if one was Chekhov, hypersensitive, clearsighted and in love with a brilliant, famous, flirtatious and remote woman.

The dialogue with the public, equally remote, was carried on because it was the last outlet, the only means of expressing, pouring out and communicating all he felt, thought and had learnt during these long months face to face with the supreme interlocutor — death.

NOTES

1. Moscow, 1960.
Chekhov's house is now a museum. From 1919 until her death on 15th January, 1957, the writer's sister was curator of this museum, which became a place of pilgrimage.
2. "I have become a Marxist," he said jokingly.
3. This appeal was headed *Help the Dying* and can be seen in the Chekhov Museum in Yalta.
4. At the end of his life, his pulmonary tuberculosis was complicated by intestinal tuberculosis. In his letters, he referred to it as 'catarrh'. He suffered agonies from it.

5. Maxim Gorki – the pseudonym of Alexei Peshkov (1868–1936); Alexander Kuprin (1870–1938); Ivan Bunin (1870–1953) – won the Nobel Prize in 1933.

6. Stanislavski was enthusiastic, and in 1901 suggested that he join the Moscow Art Theatre.

7. The suburb of Yalta, where Chekhov's house was situated.

8. The walk took place in April, 1903. Chekhov died fifteen months later, in July, 1904. Bunin: *On Chekhov*, unfinished manuscript, New York, 1955. (Bunin's posthumous work.)

9. It was in this study that Chekhov wrote such masterpieces as *In the Ravine*, *The Lady with the Dog*, *The Bishop* and *The Three Sisters* and *The Cherry Orchard*.

[2]

Chekhov's Marriage

It was only now, when his head had become white, that he was really in love, for the first time in his life.
Lady with the Dog, 1899

C HEKHOV saw Olga Knipper for the first time on 9th September, 1898, in Moscow.

On a dimly lit stage, a company of young actors was rehearsing *The Seagull*. (The Art Theatre itself, did not actually exist as yet; it was only to open its doors on 10th October of the same year.) From the back of the dark, empty auditorium, the author was watching the actors' performances and was displeased with everything he saw: with his play, with the cast, with the cold, gloomy auditorium. So displeased in fact that he scarcely paid any attention to the dark-haired woman who was playing Arkadina. But a few weeks later, 7th October, in the yet unfinished auditorium of the Hermitage, equally gloomy and cold, the same young company was rehearsing Alexei Tolstoy's *Tsar Feodor*. It was raining outside. Chekhov, ill, shivering and wrapped up in his overcoat, listened to Olga Knipper playing the Tsarina, Irina. "What a voice, what dignity, what feeling," he wrote next day to Suvorin. "If I were staying on in Moscow, I should certainly fall in love with that Irina." But his illness compelled him to return to the Crimea, that 'Southern Siberia', where he felt himself to be in exile. He was unable to attend the first night of *The Seagull* on 17th December, 1898, when the play proved to be one of the Art Theatre's biggest successes, but, in that splendid spring of 1899, the newly established Theatre performed it specially for him during Lent, when the public performances were suspended. He had finally managed to escape from Yalta. In Moscow's public gardens and suburbs the syringa and lilac were in full bloom. He saw a lot of Olga Knipper, who, during the winter, had become close friends with his sister, Masha.

Chekhov found her gay, witty, attractive and versatile; she could sing Tchaikovsky's and Glinka's songs, mime theatrical anecdotes, discuss literary subjects and talk about her dresses and favourite food. Miraculously, despite her immense popularity, she had been able to preserve what the sick and despondent man appreciated most of all: her naturalness, spontaneity, health and exhilaration. When the holidays came and Olga went off to stay with her brother, near Mtskhet, the ancient capital of Georgia, Chekhov missed her very badly and felt an urgent desire to see her again.

On 16th June he wrote to her, in the jocular style that constituted his usual means of defence: "Where are you? We are beginning to think you have forgotten us and may already have married someone in the Caucasus? If you really have, at least tell us who he is? . . . So the writer is forgotten! How awful, how cruel, how perfidious!"

Olga Leonardovna replied, suggesting that he meet her on the boat that was to take him the following month from Taganrog to Yalta, where he had just bought the piece of ground on which he was to build his house.

They met at Novorossijsk on 18th July and sailed together for Yalta.

By then Chekhov's house was in the process of being constructed and he spent a large part of his time on the building site. Far too often he ate nothing but bread and cheese, and Olga, staying comfortably in Yalta with friends, the Sredins, tried her best to lure him to the hospitable home of her hosts. He rarely accepted the invitation, preferring to take her to a small Tartar restaurant in the harbour, where they served shellfish and a dry local wine.

In August, rehearsals at the Art Theatre called her back to Moscow, and Chekhov went with her.

He only stayed in Moscow for a few days. From 3rd September, an almost daily correspondence started between the young actress and the writer. It was several months before they met again. At the end of March, 1900, Olga arrived in Yalta, a few days ahead of the rest of the company, which was coming to the Crimea to give performances of *The Seagull* and *Uncle Vanya*. She wrote in her memoirs:

> I arrived during Holy Week and everything was so warm and comfortable in the house which, only the previous summer, had not even been built. The acacia-walk had grown with extraordinary rapidity; long and pliant, their pensive branches bowed at the smallest breath of wind, bent forward and stretched out in movements that were somehow weird, disturbing and nostalgic. Anton Pavlovich would constantly watch them through the large bay-window in his study. Holy Week, a week of rest, passed only too quickly, and I had to leave for Sebastopol and join the Art Theatre company, which had just arrived from Moscow. I can remember the acute feeling of loneliness which seized me when, for the first time in my life, I found myself all on my own in an hotel room. Alone on Easter night! And this after the comfort and warmth of the Chekhovs' home.[1]

But very soon afterwards she found herself caught up in a whirl of performances, festivities and receptions. First Sebastopol, then Yalta, acclaimed Stanislavski's young company and their favourite author. The actors came over to Chekhov's house daily, dined there, strolled round the garden and invaded his pleasant study, much to his delight; he loved this animated, tumultuous life. Young writers mingled with the actors: Maxim

Gorki, Ivan Bunin, Alexander Kuprin. But everything has to come to an end – even this spring, so rich in laughter, excitement and vivid flowers. The Art Theatre and Olga Knipper with it, went back to Moscow. Presently Chekhov joined them, but fell ill and was compelled to return to Yalta within a few days:

Dear, adorable actress, good day to you! I felt very ill on the journey and when I reached Moscow, I had a terrible headache and temperature, I hid it from you, I admit. I feel better now . . . Keep well and be happy. Your A. Chekhov (20th May, 1900).

From the end of June to 5th August, Olga Knipper was again in Yalta, staying with the Chekhovs. These six weeks proved to be the turning point. It was during this visit that the 'affaire' between the writer and actress came into being.

In the evenings, when everybody else was asleep and the house silent at last, they remained alone together. Olga would put on the white dress, which was Chekhov's favourite. With her black, wavy hair falling over her shoulders, she would softly sing Glinka's song: "Don't tempt me in vain . . ." Or else, abandoning all romanticism, she would show herself to be a perfect Hausfrau and prepare exquisite coffee and delicious sandwiches, which they devoured, joking and chaffing each other like schoolchildren. But happiness does not last, as Chekhov had always known. On 5th August, Olga left Yalta. Chekhov wrote to her on the 9th:

Dear Olga, my joy . . . The whole time, I feel the door will open and you[2] will come back. But you won't come back . . . You are far from Yalta and me . . . Goodbye, may the heavenly powers and the guardian angels protect you. Goodbye, my good little girl.

He was desperately bored. Very susceptible to the changes in the weather, the lack of sun and the depressing aridity of this sultry August, almost grey under the haze of heat and humidity he wrote:

> Dear, nice, splendid actress, I am alive and well; I think of you, dream of you and am bored because you are far away. Yesterday and the day before I was at Gursuf and now I'm back again in Yalta, my prison. A violent wind is blowing; the steamer is not running; there is a heavy swell; people are getting drowned; and, in addition to all that, there is not a drop of rain, everything is dry, everything is drooping. In short, since you left, everything here has gone wrong. Without you, I'd hang myself.

And, as always, he sought consolation in his work. He wrote a play, in which everything revolves round a beautiful, passionate young woman (Masha), who is unhappily married and in love with a weary, middle-aged man, burdened with a family to which he sacrifices himself (Vershinin). This play, *The Three Sisters*, was conceived, written and accomplished to the greater glory of Olga Leonardovna Knipper.

He lays bare his heart in this tragedy, far more than in his letters, which are usually brief and often dry and curiously impersonal.

On 14th August, Olga Leonardovna wrote to him:

> Saturday, after rehearsal, I went into the country . . . I breathed the wonderful scent of the forests with wild enthusiasm and walked and rejoiced at the sight of every birch tree, every autumn flower. I scratched up the moss and sniffed the earth. I even found a mushroom though there are scarcely any about this year. In the morning there was dew on the grass. The trees are hardly beginning to turn yellow yet, one cannot believe it is already autumn. It rained very hard today, but before that it was unbearably hot. Anton, my darling, would you like us to spend next summer somewhere hereabouts in the country? I kept thinking, all the time, how much you belong to this Russian nature, this vastness, these fields, these meadows, these valleys, these shady streams . . . .

[225]

And he, at the same time, put these words into Vershinin's mouth: "The forest, the stream, the birch trees, over there! Dear, humble birches, I like them better than any other trees."

The marvellous July interlude was far away. She, in Moscow, was caught up in a whirl of rehearsals, receptions, parties and successes. He, alone again for several months, was sitting at his writing desk, on which the pages of *The Three Sisters* were beginning to pile up. And, using Vershinin again as his spokesman, he bluntly expressed a bitter conviction: "We are not happy, happiness does not exist, we can only long for it . . . Life is hard to bear."

But the fundamental equilibrium of the great artist in him made him moderate this gloomy judgement:

"What today seems to us important, weighty and fraught with consequences – well, the time will come when it will all be forgotten, when it will all cease to have any importance."

Chekhov's own realism did not allow him to hope for any other conclusion to his love and the illness, which was sapping his strength, than loneliness and death. He transposed the cold, the clear-sighted despair, that possessed him into *The Three Sisters*. No poet has ever depicted so effectively the different forms of separation that lie in wait for lovers.

His own life had consisted of little else than separations, illness and loneliness.

I'm afraid of disappointing you. My hair is falling out to such an extent that, in a week's time – who knows – I may well look like a bald old man . . . I'm terribly bored. Do you understand? Terribly! I'm living on nothing but soup. In the evenings, it is cold and I remain alone . . . I have less and less money. My beard is white. (8th September, 1900.)

The letters he received from Moscow seemed to come from another world entirely:

The day before yesterday, Gorki came to dinner and charmed everybody. He told us how, this summer, he read your story *In the Ravine* to the peasants and what an impression it made on them. Gorki suddenly leapt to his feet and he had tears in his eyes, as he recalled the memory of it. He said that the peasants had gazed at your portrait with great curiosity and love; they were moved to tears as he read to them. It all took place on the banks of the Psiol, in the forest. Isn't it lovely? (4th September, 1900.) Our expedition to the Sparrow Hills was most successful. The weather was warm and pleasant, and the air so light. Everything around us was smiling, pensive and touching. I longed to lie down and 'listen to the silence'. We took a tram to the Novodevichi monastery and then walked about two versts through the kitchengardens. They smelt of cabbage and parsley. We crossed the Moskva and reached the Hills. Luckily there wasn't a soul there, just an extraordinary silence. There was not a breath of wind, so nothing moved, and I wanted to be alone, quite alone, or sitting beside you in that autumnal mellowness without speaking, just drinking in the nature around me. You would have understood how I felt ... In the forest one can already see russet maples, birches and red aspens; the oaks are still green. The soil is dank and smells of mushrooms; one comes across late flowers, the ones I like best; spiders' webs float in the air and, in short, everything is so beautiful that it is difficult to tear oneself away. The sun is caressing and contemplative and, in the sky, the same sweetness is reflected in the outline of the clouds ... We had tea on a terrace, joking, laughing and playing ... Then at 10 o'clock I went home and we sang and laughed till two in the morning. I can't remember ever having laughed so much in my life. (10th September, 1900.)

Chekhov replied:

My darling, my dear Olga, my remarkable little actress, your last letter, in which you describe your expedition to the Sparrow Hills, touched me;

it is just as adorable as yourself. As for me, I haven't been out now for six or seven days because I'm ill, with a temperature, cough and a cold in the head ... Write me another interesting letter ... although doubtless, you have other things to do than write to me ... Firstly, a lot of work; secondly, you are beginning to forget me. Is that true? You are infernally cold, as, in fact, an actress should be. Don't be cross. (15th September, 1900.)

And he observed in his *Notebooks*:

Love is either the aftermath of something in the process of degenerating that was formerly boundless, or else part of something that will become boundless in the future. But in the present, it cannot satisfy, it brings much less than one expects of it.

He finished the play. In it he painted an intimate and very Chekhovian portrait of Olga. This work absorbed him to such an extent that for the time being, he did not want, actually, to go to Moscow and see the real-life Olga Knipper. She urged him to leave Yalta and complained about their separation and the levity and scarcity of his letters. He writes back:

I have no desire to write and, anyway, write what? Tell you about my life here? I don't want to write to you, I want to talk to you or even just be with you without talking. But what would I do if I came to Moscow? What? See you and then leave again? How interesting that would be! To come, catch a glimpse of the theatrical crowd and go away again. (22nd September, 1900.)

Hurt, she accused him of coldness, hardness and deceitfulness. He replied on 27th:

The poor trees, particularly those on this slope of the mountain, have not had a single drop of rain all through the summer and are standing there now, quite yellow; in the same way, it sometimes happens that men do not receive a single drop of happiness all through their lives. No doubt, it has to be so. You write: "You have a loving, tender heart, why do you want to harden it?" Exactly how have I displayed this hardness? My heart has always loved you, and been tender towards you, and I have never kept it secret from you, never, never. To judge by your letter, you want and expect an explanation, a long conversation, with serious faces and serious consequences. But, I, I don't know what to tell you, except what I shall no doubt tell you for a long time to come: namely, that I love you, and that is all. If we are not together just now it is not my fault, nor yours, but that of the devil, who has inflicted me with bacilli and you with a love for art.

But as always, he gave in. *The Three Sisters* was finished by the middle of October and he took a train to Moscow at the end of the month. There, for six weeks, Olga and he saw each other every day. He stayed in the Dresden Hotel: between rehearsals, she would rush up the four flights of stairs, introducing the cold and animation of the outside world into the peaceful room, kept in that slightly monastic state of tidiness which Chekhov always established around him wherever he went. She would bring sweets; a pot of laurel; scent, of which this innately chaste man loved the sensual smell. Or amusing knick-knacks, such as a crystal sow, followed by three little piglets. The samovar would be brought in and Olga Leonardovna would serve tea, with the thin slices of bread-and-butter, honey and cream prescribed by the doctors.

It would be snowing outside, but the heavy velvet curtains isolated them from the dark street, the cold and the indifferent crowd passing by. They loved each other. Every passing hour brought them closer together, formed a stronger bond between them, created an intimacy that was so delectable and yet so precarious, so threatened.

Very soon, the hard Moscow winter compelled Chekhov to

escape to the south. He left Moscow on 10th December, 1900, and went to stay in Nice, at the Pension Russe in the rue Gounod. An almost daily correspondence ensued. It has often been said that in every love affair there is one who loves and one who lets himself be loved. During that winter of 1900–1901, it seems as though it were Olga who loved and suffered. Chekhov responded with his habitual reserve and even a shade of dryness. It was because he had not yet surrendered, as he was to do at the very end of his life under the increasing impact of his illness, his independence as a man and an artist, that imperative need for complete liberty, which he had always regarded as the prerogative of any man worthy of the name.

At the moment, though separated from her, he felt almost happy. The balminess of the air, the sun, the sea, the elegance of clothes and manners ("the humblest French chambermaid has the manners of a queen"), all enchanted him: "The rose bushes are in bloom. There are other flowers, too. I can't believe my eyes! In front of my window a monkey-puzzle tree, like yours but the size of a pine tree, is growing straight up out of the ground . . ." (14th December, 1900.) "I feel as though I were on the moon. It is hot, the sun is shining,[3] the windows of my room are wide open, so are those of my soul . . . I'm making a fair copy of my play (*The Three Sisters*) and am surprised at having written one like it." (15th December, 1900.)

But Olga was far from happy. She wrote to him on the day after he left:

I can't resign myself to this separation. Why did you go away, when you ought to be beside me? Yesterday, when the train was moving away and you were moving away with it, it was the first time that I really felt we were parting. I walked after the train for a long time, as though I didn't yet believe it, then I began to cry, to cry as I haven't cried for years. I remained motionless at the end of the platform for a long while, waiting for all the people who had come to see you off, to go away; I couldn't bear to see them, they disgusted me so much; it was a relief to cry, my tears were so warm, so abundant. When I got to Masha's, I sat down in a corner and went on crying softly. Masha sat beside me, without speaking ... I sat there, with my head buried in the cushions, and, in my thoughts, I was there with you, in your compartment, listening to the regular sound of the wheels, breathing that special train smell, and trying to guess what you were thinking, what was in your mind and – will you believe me? – I guessed it all, absolutely all ... You know, Anton, I'm afraid of dreaming or, rather, of expressing my dreams in words, but I feel that something beautiful and strong will emerge from our love. When I begin to believe that, I want to live and to work, and the paltry things in life no longer affect me, I no longer wonder why I am alive.

Chekhov replied:

I haven't had a letter from you for a long time, [he wrote her on 3rd January, 1901] apart from the one of 11th December which came today in which you describe your tears on the day I left. What a wonderful letter by the way! It can't have been you who wrote it, but, no doubt, someone else at your request. An astonishing letter ... Tell me about at least one rehearsal of *The Three Sisters*. Are you acting well, my darling? Above all, never look sad. Discontented yes, but never sad. Those who have been secretly enduring a sorrow for a long time and have been accustomed to enduring it, only whistle under their breath and frequently look pensive. You, too, frequently become pensive while others are talking. Do you understand? Of course you do, because you are intelligent ... I wish you a lot of happiness, tranquillity and love that will last as long as possible! Fifteen years, for instance. Do you believe such a love can exist? With me – yes, with you – no ...

And, with his usual melancholy :

> I love you, but the truth is that you don't understand it. You want a husband or, rather, a consort, with side whiskers and a civil servant's rosette. And I – what am I ? Nothing very much.

Nice, which had enchanted him at the beginning of his stay, very soon struck him as appallingly dreary. He escaped to Italy, spent three days in Florence, a week in Rome and then, tired, as always, of being abroad, returned to Yalta "to write and write".

It was during this March of 1901 that he wrote *The Bishop*, one of his finest and most poetical short stories. It contained the reminiscences of Nice that we have mentioned before : the sound of the sea and the blind beggar who sang under his window in the rue Gounod, the nostalgic songs that made him dream of the past. He felt increasingly 'ill and lonely', but he never complained in his letters. It was not in his correspondence, where he felt himself too exposed, but only in his writings, sheltered by his characters, protected by fiction, that he sometimes murmured his precious confidences. The life, the tragedy and the death of the Bishop are like a summary, a prefiguration of his own life, his own tragedy. During this time, Olga Knipper was playing Elena Andreevna in *Uncle Vanya* and Masha in *The Three Sisters*. Following Moscow, St Petersburg was enchanted by Chekhov's plays and its interpreters :

"Yesterday, we were invited by the Writers' Union. There were flowers and gold medallions in the shape of lyres on our places at table. I sat in the place of honour . . . in a black velvet dress, with a little lace collar, and my hair well waved by a hairdresser. But do these details interest you?" (5th March, 1901.)

Next day, there was another reception, another banquet; the day after that, an excursion to Finland, to the Imatra waterfall. The actors went ski-ing, took boat trips, threw snowballs, joked and had a thoroughly good time before returning to St Petersburg, tanned, tired, happy.

By the end of March, Olga was in Yalta. She stayed there for a fortnight and left at the same time as Chekhov's sister. Chekhov did not try to detain her: the situation was artificial and embarrassing for everyone. And, in any case, it had been agreed that he should join her in Moscow in a few weeks' time.

A few days after she left, he wrote to her:

> If you give me your word that not a soul in Moscow will hear anything about our marriage until the moment it takes place, I will marry you, if you like, on the very day I arrive. I don't know why, but I have a horror of marriage ceremonies and conventional congratulations and the glass of champagne that one has to hold in one's hand, with a vague smile on one's face ... Here, at home, all is well, except for one small detail: my health. (18th April, 1901.)

Ah, if only I didn't have to drag myself along, if only I could be well! My cough saps all my energy, I think of the future with apathy and write without any zest. Think about it, take the reins and advise me; I'll do whatever you tell me; otherwise, instead of living, we shall have to be content with swallowing life at the rate of a spoonful an hour ... (22nd April, 1901.)

I sit in my study without ever leaving it and for lack of any other occupation, do nothing but think and cough. We'll do anything you want. I'm in your hands. (2nd May, 1901.)

In the middle of May, he went to Moscow. The doctors found that his condition had seriously deteriorated. He would have to leave town as soon as possible and enter a government sanatorium in the Ufa district: the doctors prescribed a mare's-milk (kumiss) cure, a treatment very much in vogue at that time.

The marriage took place in Moscow, in the greatest secrecy.

Olga Leonardovna records in her memoirs:

We were married on 25th May and went by steamer down the Volga, the Kama and the Bielaia to Ufa. From there we took the train to a sanatorium situated near the Aksenovo spa. On the way, we visited Maxim Gorki in Nizhni-Novgorod, where he was living under police supervision. At the small port of Piani bor, on the Kama, we spent the night in an izba, a few versts from the landing-stage. We slept on the floor. No one knew at what time the boat for Ufa would arrive. We had to go outside several times during the night and at dawn to see if the boat was coming. That night, so remote from the civilized world, a grandiose, silent night, full of a serene and slightly frightening beauty, followed by such a tranquil poetical dawn, made a great impression on Anton Pavlovich. He admired nature in Aksionovo, the elongated shadows on the steppe at sunset, the neighing of wild horses, the flora and the river Dioma, described by Aksakov,[4] where we went fishing one day.

But the lack of comfort, the solitude and their dislike for mare's milk drove the newly-weds away and, less than six weeks after their arrival, they sailed down the Volga to Tsaritsin and returned to Yalta by way of Novorossijsk.

Olga remained in Yalta until 20th August, when rehearsals at the Art Theatre started again. Less than three months after their marriage, the couple were once more separated.

Six years earlier, in a letter to Suvorin, who had been urging him to marry, Chekhov had written:

I should never be able to stand happiness that continues from day to day, from one morning till the next. I promise to make an excellent husband, but give me a wife who, like the moon, would not appear day after day on my horizon.

This rash wish was fully granted by a malicious destiny. Olga records: "The separations and reunions began again, only the separations were more and more painful and, a few months after the first one, I seriously thought of giving up the stage. But immediately the question arose: did Anton Pavlovich want a wife deprived of all artistic activity? I felt him to be a recluse to whom a radical change in his life and mine might well be a burden. In addition, he prized the link that, through me, he retained with the theatre."

So Chekhov was to spend the thirty months of life still left him in Yalta, with a few brief visits to Moscow, from each of which he returned with his health further impaired.

His sufferings took place in solitude.

"I have had the armchair from your bedroom, dejected and brooding, moved into mine. Your room downstairs is silent and empty. Your mother's picture is on your table ... I love you very much, my dearest, I love you very much. May God protect you. I bless you. Write, write and write every day or you will be beaten. For, as you well know, I'm a very severe and harsh husband ... I'm so terribly bored without you." (23rd August, 1901.) "We are committing a dreadful sin in not living together!" (9th November, 1901.)

She felt twinges of remorse at deserting him. It was he, the seriously ill man, who reassured her, consoled her and found excuses for her:

"I'm not expecting you for the holidays, you mustn't come here, my dearest. Go about your own business; we'll still have plenty of time to live together. I bless you, my little girl ..." (11th December, 1901.) "My darling, don't be upset or angry or sad, everything will fall into place again, everything will be all right, exactly as we both want it to be, my incomparable wife. Be patient and wait ..." (12th December, 1901.) "Oh, my dearest, how I envy you, if you only knew! I envy your zest, your freshness, your health, your good humour; I envy you that nothing like blood-spitting or anything similar has overtaken you and prevented you from drinking and living." (13th December, 1901.) "You are silly, my darling. Not once since we married have I reproached you about your acting; on the contrary, I was delighted that you were occupied, that you had an aim in life, that you weren't dragging out a useless existence like your husband." (29th December, 1901.) "I want to be living

[235]

in Moscow, at your side, seeing and watching your life." (11th January, 1902.)

She reproached him for not having joined her in Moscow. Chekhov replied:

"You should be careful not to be unjust. You should be guiltless in this respect, completely guiltless, particularly when you are so kind, so very kind, and so understanding. Forgive me, darling, for these sermons, I won't preach any more of them, I dread them . . ." (27th August, 1902.) "My little crocodile, my remarkable wife, I didn't come to Moscow, in spite of my promise! And this is the reason why: I had only just arrived in Yalta when the barometer of my health began to fall. I began to cough terribly and completely lost my appetite. It became out of the question to write or to travel." (6th September, 1902.) "But when I come to Moscow I shall do nothing but eat, drink, caress my wife, go to the theatre and, in my spare time, sleep. I want to live like an epicure!" (24th September, 1902.) "My little crinoline, my nails have grown very long and there is no one here to cut them for me! I have broken one of my teeth. A button has come off . . . You and I have a fault in common: we married too late . . ." (15th December, 1902.) "You write that you envy my character. I must tell you that, innately, my character is hard and I am quick-tempered, etc., but I have acquired the habit of dominating it, because it ill-becomes a decent man to let such things slide. In days gone by, I allowed myself to do God knows what." (11th February, 1903.)

Many unkind things have been written about Chekhov's wife. Nevertheless, she undeniably loved him. But she had an impulsive, passionate nature, and was greedy for pleasure, ambitious and very conscious of her gifts.

Endowed with a powerful temperament, her talent lay mainly in giving expression to this inner exuberance with infinite charm, intelligence and tact. She was not a great actress in the sense that Eleonora Duse was. She never was the medium, the Proteus with a thousand faces that a really great actor succeeds in being. On the contrary, she belonged to that category of actors who always remain themselves, but whose personality is so engaging, their projection so arresting that they fill the stage, captivate the audience and suppress any tendency to criticize.

Her impetuous, demanding personality was incapable of exercising restraint and, even less so, of making sacrifices. It was the richness of her gifts, her bubbling-over with life and her extreme femininity that had attracted Chekhov. But, by a tragic piece of irony, it was just these qualities that were the cause of his solitude and desertion.

He became increasingly remote from the world outside, isolated by his illness and a sort of final detachment. She was tormented by all the invitations and temptations that lie in the path of a young woman, who is attractive and famous. Love existed on both sides, but it was a cruel, harassing, very Chekhovian love. For neither for the one nor the other could it result in happiness or peace of mind. He rightly jotted down in his *Notebooks*: "If you are afraid of solitude, don't marry."

She was constantly torn between the harrowing tenderness, which this man, whom she knew to be unique, inspired in her, and the intense excitement of *living*. She was constantly gnawed by remorse at deserting him, but her whole being recoiled from the prospect of isolation, solitude and self-sacrifice.

She suffered and was quite sincere when she wrote:

No letter today, a completely clouded day. How do you feel, my darling? Anton, I need you, I need your great mind, your thoughts, your originality, your love, your tenderness, your gentleness and your affection. I want to kneel down in front of you again, and have you looking into my eyes and gently stroking my hair. (9th January, 1902.)

But these same letters contain so many other things, the other things that made up her life: the "flame-coloured dress" that made her look like a serpent; the delicious dinner she had had the evening before: "Zakouski, a carp with sauce tartare, a woodcock, pirozhkis, good wine"; her successes: "Someone in the audience called out, 'Bravo, Chekhova!' Several men were crying and a woman in hysterics had to be taken out"; her parties: "After the performance we went to dine in the Hermitage and laughed a lot. I flirted with Konstantin Sergevich (Stanislavski). Do you mind? . . . Afterwards, oh horror! We went to a night-club and were received like royalty . . ." (11th January, 1902.) "I danced till half-past five in the morning in a golden dress, very décolletée"; her love of the theatre: "I know that you need me, need me very badly and that I ought to give up the theatre, yet I cling to it, fool that I am. Forgive me for bringing it up again, I know you don't like me to, and that it's nasty of me to mention it. Don't be cross with me!" (12th January, 1902.)

He needed her and he needed Moscow which, in his eyes, symbolized life, love, friendship and the human warmth of which he was deprived. He had written to her one day: "Suffer and keep quiet . . . Whatever people may say, whatever you may think, keep quiet, and go on keeping quiet." (3rd September, 1901.) So he kept quiet and only very rarely allowed a complaint to escape him, though he was well aware he was doomed.

Olga Knipper tells us: "The doctors allowed him to spend the winter of 1903–1904 in Moscow. How happy and moved he was, to see the snowy winter, as happy to attend rehearsals, happy as a child with his new fur coat and beaver hat! It seemed as though fate had decided to spoil him this last time, grant him during this last year of his life, all the pleasures that he appreciated most: Moscow, the snow, the first night of *The Cherry Orchard*, the friends to whom he was so very devoted . . ."

Bunin records that he spent all his evenings with Chekhov during that last winter: "Every evening, I used to go and see Chekhov and stay with him till three or four in the morning, that is to say, until Olga Leonardovna came home. She usually went to the theatre; occasionally, to a charity concert. Nemirovich-Danchenko would come to fetch her, in white tie and tails, smelling of cigars and eau-de-Cologne. She, in evening dress, beautiful, young and scented, would say to her husband: 'Don't get bored without me, darling. Anyway, you're always perfectly happy when Bouguichon[5] is with you.' I would kiss her hand and they would leave. Chekhov never let me go before her return . . . Towards four o'clock — sometimes it was close to dawn — Olga Leonardovna would come back. She smelt of wine and scent. 'Not asleep, darling? It's not good for you. Are you still here, Bouguichon? He's certainly never bored when you're with him.' I would then jump up and go."

On 2nd June, now acutely ill, Chekhov left with his wife for a sanatorium at Badenweiler in the Black Forest. Bunin writes:

"The question that always torments me is: why did they take him abroad in the condition he was in? He, himself, said to me before he left: 'I'm going away to peg out.' So he knew just how ill he was. Sometimes I think it was so that his family should not be present at his death, to spare them such a painful scene . . ."

During the night of 4th July, 1904, after three extremely sultry and uncomfortable days, Chekhov asked for a doctor. "Champagne was brought to stimulate his failing heart," Olga Knipper relates:

"He sat up and said very loudly in German (he knew very little German): 'Ich sterbe.' Then he picked up his glass, turned to me, smiled his wonderful smile and said: 'It's a long time since I drank champagne,' quietly emptied his glass, settled down gently on his left side and was silent for ever."

[   ]

Everything I have written will be forgotten
in a few years. But the paths I have traced
will remain intact and secure, and there
lies my only merit.
CHEKHOV

NOTES

1. Olga Knipper on Chekhov, Moscow, 1934.
2. Chekhov here uses the Russian equivalent of the intimate French 'tu'.
3. In Moscow at the same time there was 27° of frost. (Letter from Olga, 16th December, 1900.)
4. Aksakov, 1791–1859, author of *Family Chronicles* (1856), etc.
5. Chekhov's nickname for Bunin.

[Index]